BUS
STO

ACPL ITE ☑ Y0-BSM-404

3 1833 02208 3254

DISCARDED

616.
Quin
When self-help fails

V

**DO NOT REMOVE
CARDS FROM POCKET**

ALLEN COUNTY PUBLIC LIBRARY

FORT WAYNE, INDIANA 46802

You may return this book to any agency, branch,
or bookmobile of the Allen County Public Library.

DEMCO

Paul G. Quinnett

When Self-Help Fails

A Guide to Counseling Services

New Expanded Edition of
The Troubled People Book

CONTINUUM • NEW YORK

Allen County Public Library
900 Webster Street
PO Box 2270
Fort Wayne, IN 46801-2270

1991

The Continuum Publishing Company
370 Lexington Avenue
New York, NY 10017

Copyright © 1982 by Paul G. Quinnett
New material Copyright © 1991 by Paul G. Quinnett

All rights reserved. No part of this book may be reproduced,
stored in a retrieval system, or transmitted, in any form
or by any means, electronic, mechanical, photocopying,
recording or otherwise, without the written permission
of The Continuum Publishing Company.

Printed in the United States of America

Library of Congress Cataloging-in-Publication Data

Quinnett, Paul G., 1939–
When self-help fails : a guide to counseling
services / Paul G. Quinnett.
p.   cm.
"New expanded edition of The troubled people book."
Includes bibliographical references.
ISBN 0-8264-0495-2 (pbk.)
1. Psychotherapy.   2. Counseling.   3. Consumer education.
I. Quinnett, Paul G., 1939– Troubled people book.   II. Title.
RC480.5.Q56   1991
616.89'14—dc20   90–44824
                                       CIP

Contents

Introduction

This book was written to answer questions about mental health services. It was also written to spur the reader to ask questions that will lead to finding the right kind of help from the right kind of person.

I can think of no quicker way to become informed about therapy than to ask appropriate questions. Getting answers to our questions not only expands our knowledge, but makes the uneasy feelings about seeking help less uneasy. It is tough enough to have a psychological or emotional problem without the additional stress of feeling ignorant about how to find competent help, how much it costs, and how it works.

What follows is a sampling of the kinds of questions people ask when they begin their search for help. If you know the answers to all or most of these questions, you probably don't need this book.

Getting Started Questions:
1. How do I know if help is warranted?
2. How bad do I have to feel before I ask for help?
3. Isn't it better to "tough out" emotional problems?
4. How do I pick a psychotherapist?
5. Do I need a psychotherapist or can someone else help? What's the difference in the kind of care I will get from a psychiatrist, psychologist, social worker, psychiatric nurse, para- or nonprofessional? Who's qualified to do what?
6. Does the kind of therapy make a difference? How would I choose an appropriate therapy for me—on what basis would I make the choice?

Without answers to "getting started" questions, many people never take the first step. Their problems may eventually go away or they may not. Sometimes the problems that don't go away are costly—lost jobs, broken marriages, unhappy relationships, and persistent feelings of self-doubt, depression, insecurity, and fear. Sometimes things get so bad that someone suggests we get help or even tells us we must.

None of us likes to admit we have a personal problem that can't be handled alone. But if we finally admit we aren't getting straight A's in managing our lives, we still have to get past our pride to reach out for help. We have to get past fear as well. Most of us are afraid of what we don't understand, and this book is written to allay those fears by making this whole business of seeking professional help understandable.

Once You're in the Office Questions:
1. What will happen on my first visit?
2. Are there things I should ask to get off to a good start?
3. Is it okay to get a second opinion?
4. How will I know what I want to get out of therapy? (Setting Goals)
5. How should I feel about the therapist? Should I like him or her and what if I don't?
6. What should I do if I'm disappointed?

Since I can't know exactly what you might experience on a first visit to a therapist, I can't, with any degree of certainty, predict what you will think or feel about that first appointment. But I do know how most therapists are supposed to work, how they can be expected to behave toward you and what, in my judgment, constitutes a good first session. I know that the more you understand about what to expect, the more comfortable you feel in asking these and other questions, the more likely it is that a positive working relationship can be established. You may not feel much confidence in yourself at this particular time in life but, to get off to a good start in therapy, you must at least have some confidence in the person you've chosen to help you. Answers to these questions should help boost that confidence.

Questions of Ethics:
1. Are there any risks to therapy? What are they?
2. What should I do if the therapist breaks a promise to me?
3. What is ethical for therapists to do? Unethical?
4. Is my privacy protected?
5. If I had a complaint who would listen to me?
6. How should I ask for information?

These questions may never come up—I hope they don't. Still, we read and hear enough about the unhappy experiences of others who have sought professional help to cause many of us to fear our problems may be made worse in the hands of an unprofessional or unethical therapist. These are delicate, awkward questions. I have tried to answer some of these for you, reasoning that if you know the rules of fair play, the ethical standards that govern the practice of professionals, you will be better able to protect yourself or someone you love against the few therapists who violate these rules.

Helping Someone Else:
1. How can we help them? Should we try to help?
2. What should we look for in someone who seems to have a problem he can't handle on his own?
3. Where should we go to find out how to be helpful?

Besides the problems we face personally, there are those faced by our friends, spouses, loved ones and family members. If we're not anxious, depressed, irritable, dissatisfied, or demoralized, we know someone who is. We want to help them but don't know how, or even where to begin. These questions of how to help someone else are asked by concerned people every day; many of the answers are in this book.

Because professional helpers are such an interesting lot, and because people often ask me what it's like to work with human problems day in and day out, there is a chapter devoted to the private life of the therapist. A therapist's private life is a curiosity to many people and this chapter might help the reader to see therapists as they are rather than as we might want them to be.

Again and throughout this book, I encourage the reader to ask questions. People, especially troubled people, need to know what they're paying for, and they can't know what they're supposed to be getting unless they ask questions. In psychotherapy, counseling, or any of the available therapies, the doctor doesn't always know best. Any therapist who tells you otherwise is pulling your leg. The inquisitive consumer, the one who asks, "Hey, what are we doing this for?" might meet with some resistance from therapists who are accustomed to controlling the therapy situation. Many may be unsettled by questions they can't or would rather not answer. Ask them anyway. If the therapist gets too upset, maybe that's his or her problem.

While this book can't answer all the questions about mental health services, it can answer enough of them to help you decide to do something, something for yourself or someone else, something positive.

A Couple of Final Notes
The self-help movement is alive, vital, and changing the very scope and nature of how mental health services are and will be delivered in this

country. While some professionals fret about the implications of family members and consumers getting into the act, many more of us welcome the raising of the curtain around what has been, for too long, a group of professions whose power and influence has never been justified by its accomplishments.

With too little research on the effectiveness and measurable benefits of the services we render, the professions of psychiatry, psychology, and social work have enjoyed a kind of untouchable status with the general public. While there is some small comfort to be taken from this elitist status, it is not a good bargain—for us, or for you.

Being different from "real" doctors and nurses has helped make mental health care a secondary consideration in this country—both in terms of public funding and in health insurance coverage. The result has often been needy people seeking the wrong care from the wrong provider. Even as I write this, the majority of prescriptions for tranquilizers, antidepressants and mood-altering medications taken by the American consumer (generally for stress symptoms associated with quite ordinary problems of everyday living) are written by physicians with less training in counseling and psychotherapy than your average college senior psychology major. I know, I help train them.

In my own view we, the mental health professions, have been a part of the stigma problem associated with going to a professional for professional help. Unwittingly, we have discounted what are, in fact, not only worthwhile but life-saving methods of helping people with problems. And in our reluctance to step forward, we have not been forthcoming about sharing what we know with a public hungry for psychological knowledge. It has taken people like Phil Donahue, Oprah Winfrey, and Sally-Jesse Raphael to drag us professionals onto the stage to share what we know about human behavior with the American public.

But change is in the wind. A recent poll by the Robert Wood Johnson Foundation indicated that not only are Americans more aware of the apparent increase in mental illness over the past twenty years, but they would like to know more about these illnesses. Unhappily, some of the stigma associated with mental illness is still with us, although more and more people are beginning to believe in the effectiveness of treatment and understand that emotional problems are *everyone's* concern.

We professionals know a few things for certain about what it is we do, and the research confirms it: counseling works. People get better. Suicides can be prevented. Marriages can be saved. Sobriety and staying clean and sober is not a fantasy, but an achievable reality. Children can unlearn bad habits, and learn good new ones. Improved medications have made modern psychiatry truly modern. We now have scientific knowledge—about the brain and endocrine system and how people learn and act and think—that we didn't have even a few years ago. It's time we brought mental health services out of the dark and into the light; for only in the light of shared understanding can we bring an end to the stigma associated with helping ourselves. The sooner this happens, the better. I hope this book makes it sooner.

Self-Help

The self-help movement has been a wondrous thing; it has brought relief where there was suffering, relationship where there was loneliness, and acceptance where there was rejection. In the few years since I have observed and been a part of it, I have seen something special, unique, and wonderful: ordinary people helping heal other ordinary people. Whether it is a twelve-step program for drug addiction or a suicide survivor group, it is a plain and obvious fact that one human being can save another by the simple act of sharing and caring.

More now than when this book was first written, professional therapists are working closely with self-help groups and no longer view, for example, Alcoholics Anonymous as a threat to their fee or occupation. In my own mental health agency, space is provided free for consumer groups, family advocate groups, AA meetings, Narcotics Anonymous meetings, and parent-support groups for troubled children. We helped develop Alzheimer's caregiver and family-support groups throughout our community and provide clinical information, seminars, and the latest technical, medical, and psychological information to any self-help group that asks. This, in just ten years, is real progress toward a goal of finding common ground between the consumers and the professionals who are committed to serve them.

But sometimes a self-help group is not enough. Or it is too frightening a place to begin. Or the issue that needs to be worked on and through lies buried deep in the soul and, like a fresh wound, remains too painful to touch—especially in front of a group of strangers. I have worked with many women who, in a whole lifetime, had never told another person they had been victims of incest. And until they felt safe and secure with me—and for a period of several months—they would not accept a referral to a women's group especially designed to help victims of childhood sexual abuse.

Self-help books can be a comfort and a starting place, if only to help us gain knowledge from the lives of others and to help normalize in us what seems so abnormal. But it is through human contact that most psychological harm is done, and so it is through human contact that it must be undone. This other human can be a friend, a caring uncle, a kindly priest, a special teacher, a football coach, a tribal medicine woman, an AA sponsor, a hairdresser, or just about any thoughtful, sensitive, nonjudg-mental caring person who, once trust is established, will not exploit our vulnerabilities.

But sometimes we don't have such a person in our lives and/or the specter of a self-help group meeting seems overwhelming. Failing our best self-help efforts, it may be time to turn to a professional.

If the title of this book caught your attention, then it is my hope you will find something here that will help you decide to act, to change, and to take some step toward a better, healthier and more rewarding life.

A Word of Thanks

Let me finish by saying thank you to all my clients—past, present and future. For it is through their tolerance, help, and teaching that I have been able to do a couple of things I never dreamed possible: learn deeply about the human condition, and earn a living for my family.

Many clients do not realize they are the source of the counselor's true knowledge about people and that, in the course of this work, what one learns from one client is shared with the next—not in the form of con-fidential information, but in a broad and sweeping sense of how it is that we, as human beings, think and feel and experience this thing we call life.

As to the names, anecdotes, and examples used throughout this book to illustrate and share my personal experiences as a counselor and therapist, I have, in accordance with the ethical standards of my profession, carefully disguised all the players but me.

When Self-Help Fails

1

Personal Views

Some years ago a student therapist asked me what the ultimate goal of psychotherapy was. Almost without hesitation I replied, "termination." And now, having decided to outline some of my views on psychotherapy, I would only add the word "successful" to that reply.

Just what constitutes a successful termination of a therapy relationship remains a much-debated issue among professionals, but it seems fairly obvious to me that in most instances clients will ultimately decide if the help they received made a positive difference in their lives. The kind of therapy and therapist, the duration of treatment, and how the treatment worked is, perhaps, less important than the actual outcome; whatever was sought, was found, whatever needed to be changed was changed, and the bright hope a client had for gaining something better in life was not diminished in the process.

In this chapter I will outline some personal views and biases which should help the reader to frame and evaluate the remainder of the book and put what I have to say into some useful context.

At the outset I should state that early on in life I had no intention of becoming a psychologist—in fact, I doubt very much I could spell psychologist before I entered college and am sure I hadn't a clue as to what a psychologist did or was. And, like a lot of young people of my generation, I wasn't at all certain just what I was suited to do and therefore I didn't know what to study to become whatever it was I was destined to become. When I finally did decide on a psychology major, I did not know what I had gotten myself into.

I won't describe the circuitous route through which I eventually became a psychologist, except to say the journey was long and uneven—alternately punctuated by moments of panic and humor, accentuated by triumphs and failures, but always exciting.

I had what I think was good, solid training. My undergraduate and graduate psychology professors presented the world of ideas as though they were an assortment of chocolates—everything tasted different and everything tasted good. I learned much from my professors, more from my clinical supervisors in the hospitals and clinics where I interned and worked, and maybe most from the people I have tried to help.

If there was much to learn then, there is even more now. The field of psychology is expanding at a prodigious rate. And, now middle-aged, I'm quite sure I know less and less about more and more until I suppose one day, I will know nothing about everything.

While I cannot say with any great conviction that I now practice a particular kind of therapy, I am convinced that each brand of psychotherapy has something to offer, even if only a consistent interpretation of how the therapist construes the world of human behavior. Maybe what a therapist does to help a troubled person is nonspecific, intangible, yet to be measured (although efforts are under way to do exactly this). But I am sure that where research has demonstrated the superior effectiveness of one technique or method over another, competent therapists should be aware of this research and should bring the best methods to bear on their client's problems.

If cornered by the question, "What kind of therapy do you do?", I would try to hedge my answer. I was trained mostly by behaviorists (some more rabid than others), but admired Freud. I was enchanted by Jung, but loved the easy manner and respect for the other guy inherent in the client-centered work of Carl Rogers, especially the promise that people, given the right environment, could get better on their own. In the end, I wrote a major graduate school paper on the benefits of eclecticism—the use of any therapy that produced results. There is, to my way of thinking, some little piece of truth in all of these theories. What Einstein did for physics, some yet-to-come-along thinker needs to do for the science of human behavior.

But whatever one's therapeutic approach, I feel strongly that there is simply too much to know about people and their problems for any one therapist to be good at everything. Infants are special, teenagers, women, and men are special, older people are special and there is a ton of information about each of these broad groups—information the therapist must have before he or she can claim expert knowledge. And there are sets of problems each of these groups can have: fears and phobias, sexual problems, depressions, learning problems, developmental problems, common transitions and uncommon crises—all of which require depth of training, special sensitivities, and expertise.

In my view, the most important thing any therapist has to recognize is his or her limitations and, in knowing these, to know also where and how to use books, fellow therapists, or the services of others appropriately to bring the right talents to bear on the problem. Nothing is more discouraging to me than when I see a troubled person's problem misdiagnosed, misunderstood, or mismanaged.

In my role as a therapist, I see myself basically as a hired hand—a consultant who doesn't actually change anyone, but can be an agent for change. This is not to say I may not feel strongly about what should happen or that I won't try to influence a client's decision here and there. Rather, I think that in the process of helping people examine their lives or habits or relationships, I can ask questions, help them probe the whys and wherefores, the payoffs and punishments, and maybe even the meaning of what they do or don't do to themselves and others.

As best I can, I try to keep my values and opinions to myself, unless someone seeks my diagnostic opinion directly. In other matters I will, if asked, answer any fair question about my training, my philosophy, or my personal beliefs.

As a hired hand, I'm easy to fire. I must be able to prove my value to a client in his or her terms, or it doesn't much matter what wonderous art or science I think I practice. With new clients, I hope to arrange from five to six sessions (provided we've agreed to work together to gain an understanding of what might be accomplished), so that we have enough time to evaluate goals and how we might accomplish them. I also like to evaluate how we're doing from time to time. While I believe much can be done in a few hours of therapy, I have also worked with the same client for five years.

It has always been important for me to find something to like about the clients with whom I work. And for me it occasionally happens that (contrary to Will Rogers' statement that he never met a man he didn't like), I've met a few I didn't care for. When I'm sure I know I don't like someone, I find them another therapist. I don't know why or where these feelings come from, but they're real enough and when I can't get around them, deal with them, then it is not good for the client. After all, my problem with a client is *my* problem, and it would be unfair to use his or her time to study my own feelings and reactions.

I also figure I should learn something from everyone. And though that's my goal and not necessarily the client's, still there is more to therapy than solving problems for a fee. I am as much interested in the inconsequential but interesting facets of people's experiences, knowledge, and beliefs as I am about the "big problem."

I have dozens of pet peeves with the helping professions, many of which will become more or less clear in the text that follows. But despite these, it is difficult for me to find fault with a fellow traveler whose mission in life is the betterment of humankind, the relief of suffering, and the improvement in the welfare of other people. The broad goals, to be sure, are noble ones. To help a single troubled person find some small parcel of understanding, or contentment, or joy, or freedom they might otherwise not have found has, for me, been reward enough.

2

Got a Problem?

Over the years I have observed that if you gaze long enough at your own navel, you will discover you have a stiff neck. A similar result can be achieved if you stare long enough into your own psyche. To avoid giving you a psychological stiff neck, I'm going to avoid doing what most self-help writers do: offer the puzzled reader lists of symptoms, feelings, thoughts, or behaviors that if honestly answered in the usual format lead to a diagnosis that something is wrong. The reader of such self-administered questionnaires earns a critical score of some kind and, armed with this new bit of intelligence, he or she now is assumed to be a self-propelled patient.

I think this is mostly nonsense. These kinds of self-report devices, checklists, and questionnaires are a poor substitute for the standard diagnostic interview or formal psychological tests and assume the reader doesn't know enough to know something is wrong. Most people know when they have a problem (or why would they bother to read and answer such questions?), and the important question is once you decide you have a problem, what should you do and why don't you do something about it?

A Personal Bias

Human beings, like nuclear particles, are unstable masses. They are frequently moody and unpredictable, cry for insufficient cause, or refuse to cry when the cause is compelling. They fall in love with the wrong people and wrong the people who love them. They can be terrified of insects (over which they have a considerable weight advantage) and can be brave in the face of unmitigated disaster. The most successful may see themselves as failures and those whose lives are the envy of no one can appear blissfully happy. There are some too dumb to come in out of the rain and others so clever they don't know it's raining. There's no making any sense of this species except that it seems capable of all possible good and all possible evil and that, while it breathes, it experiences a constantly shifting variety of emotions: pleasure and pain, comfort and discomfort, love and hate, and a thousand adjectives to describe sensations that can never be nouns. For those who seek constancy in feelings, thoughts, or actions, the only solution short of death is to be transformed into a rock.

Despite the unstable nature of human emotions, there has been something of a national drive to achieve absolute "normal." "Doctor, is feeling this way normal?" "Isn't it abnormal to think such things?" "Do you think I'm emotionally normal or emotionally abnormal?" These questions and dozens like them are asked of therapists every day and every day therapists studiously avoid answering them. In fact, except for the extremes of human behavior represented by major mental illnesses, the questions can't be answered.

But, to be sure, there *are* extremes. What is clearly abnormal in our expectations of how human beings should act and think are those people who experience and exhibit the symptoms of serious mental illness. Those symptoms include an array of disturbances in thought, feeling, and behavior and go by many names: schizophrenia, manic-depressive illness, and various psychotic and nonpsychotic syndromes that are too varied and complicated to detail here. These are the symptoms and behaviors that most everyone agrees are irrational, illogical, and obviously not normal. Hallucinations, delusions, staggering and immobilizing depressions, uncontrollable rage and anger, repeated acts of violence directed at oneself or at others (often at the instance of terrifying impulses or commanding hallucinations), and other unusual and sometimes bizarre behaviors are those that constitute the obvious deviations from whatever normal emotional behavior is.

Even though the nature of mental illness is poorly understood by the average citizen (and sometimes not much better by the experts), most people know and recognize the obvious symptoms of grossly abnormal behavior—even if they may not be able to label it correctly. Most of us know that if a housewife in our neighborhood believes and behaves as if her tap water were being poisoned by the Communists, she is not thinking or behaving within the bounds of normality. We also know that if our friend is too depressed to eat, to leave the house for a traditional poker game, and talks about ending his life, he too is not like us.

But these signs of serious disturbance have never been the problem for the lay diagnostician. It is rather the subtle differences, the not-so-noticeable changes in the way we or others feel or think or act that present the difficulty, that raise the question: is something the matter?

But beyond these obvious symptoms "normal" is often in the eye of the beholder. Comments that "most people grieve when someone close to them dies," "a lot of people are anxious when meeting strangers," or "it's not unusual for married people to go through a period of readjustment in midlife," are all the kinds of psychotherapeutic balms therapists state to help people feel they're not odd or peculiar or different. Any authority figure willing to tell us we are functioning "within normal limits" has already made us feel better. But whatever else "normal" is, it is at best an abstract idea and at worst an invention of statisticians. I'm not at all sure it's anything people should try to be. My own bias is that people are wonderfully different and, unless they're miserable or making someone else miserable, they ought to enjoy being unique, even incomparable.

Point of View

Having a psychological problem is, to some extent, a matter of point of view and the one that usually matters most is yours. Whether you have a pimple on your psyche or emotional gangrene, you may think this is a decision for experts. In most cases, it isn't. If it hurts, it hurts and for once, the customer is always right. Whether you consider some problem a temporary inconvenience or a major tragedy depends on a couple of factors: what you're used to and what you expect from life.

For a time, I supervised a group of volunteers who answered telephone calls from people who felt they had a problem. Since the answering service was called a Crisis Service, anyone who called had, by their own definition, a crisis. One of the volunteers was an upper-class, blue-blooded lady married to a successful surgeon. She was a sensitive and understanding woman who felt constantly frustrated by the problems people called in about and often said it was "just simply awful" that so many people were so desperate and unhappy. From her perspective, the callers were all in dire psychological straits and nothing less than a ton of love and several thousand dollars could alleviate their problems.

Another volunteer in the same group was also frustrated. A young black man born and raised in Harlem and the product of a broken home, he had come West to stay one step ahead of an environment that had destroyed his brothers and sisters and done a pretty good job on his own sense of security and self-worth. As he listened to people's problems coming in over the phones, he was dismayed that so many of these people "thought" they had problems.

If there's a lesson here, it's that the only person whose definition of the problem mattered was the one who placed the call. And it is pretty much this way with most psychological problems.

Any Problem Will Do

I can almost guarantee that if you think you have a psychological problem, you can find several people who will agree with you and several who won't. Generally, your friends will minimize what you feel is a problem, your family will hedge, and most therapists will confirm your worst fears. If the therapist is in private practice and not guarding the waiting-list gate in an agency under siege by troubled people, whatever problem you present is in fact a problem and worthy of at least an initial visit and of course, an initial fee (this isn't as cynical as it might sound).

Therapists are trained helpers and their first response to someone calling for help is to listen, communicate that they want to understand, and be empathetic. If the customers say they have a problem, they have a problem. You would not, for example, feel very good about a therapist who, after you tried to explain a personal dilemma, replied: "It doesn't sound serious to me. Call me if things get worse." Again, the customer is always right.

Putting a Handle on a Problem

If we start with the premise, "if you think or feel you've got a problem then you have one," we have, at least, a beginning. If your sense of the situation, how serious it is, how unhappy or frustrating or bothersome things are, how dissatisfied you are with yourself or how you would like to be different, represents as legitimate an appraisal as anyone's, then what remains is doping out what can be done about it.

The size, scope, breadth, and depth of personal problems are never easy to define. To pinpoint causes and consequences is even more difficult and, if anything, what you can expect from a therapist is some assistance in putting a handle on what has been too slippery to grasp. Anyone who can analyze rationally a personal or emotional problem, evaluate circumstances, and decide on a course of corrective action that results in a better life adjustment is very likely sitting on the wrong side of the desk—although sitting in the therapist's chair doesn't mean you can put two and two together and come up with a healthy four for yourself.

Most therapists would fall out of their chairs in a dead faint if a client came to them and said: "I've been depressed for several months, not to the point of considering suicide, but sufficiently so that my housework is suffering, my relationship with my husband is deteriorating, and I'm losing interest in things I used to enjoy. I'm depressed because I recently turned forty, my last child started college in the fall, and I'm now alone at home feeling like a used mother. The career I once wanted seems out of reach, but probably isn't. Our family doctor agrees I'm not menopausal and so, what seems left to me is to set some personal and meaningful goals that will improve my sense of self-worth and self-esteem and get me started on a life of fulfilling and gratifying experiences. What do you think?"

Therapists may dream about such clients but that's as close to reality as it gets. What *is* reality is that clients typically present a tangled, confused, disconnected string of problems and concerns that lack both coherence and logic, that often defy simple description, let alone definition. Given the messes people find themselves in, this shouldn't be surprising.

Some years ago as an intern I had just interviewed a new client for the first time. I complained to my supervisor that the client's problems seemed vague, his presentation of complaints rambling and confused, and that I wasn't at all sure what the matter was. My seasoned and sometimes salty boss replied: "Good! Now that you and the client are in the same boat, maybe the two of you can figure out how to get to shore."

If therapists aren't good for anything else, they should be good at helping you define your problem. They should nod when they understand, ask questions when they don't, poke around in the closets where you keep your fears, take down some history, and in general help you unclutter the jumble of thoughts and feelings you have been stumbling around in. And while therapists are trained to define problems in all sorts of ways and use all sorts of fancy medical-psychological terms in thinking about people's problems, the end result of such a conversation is supposed to be some shared understanding of what's wrong. What to do about what's wrong is another matter, but feeling understood is essential. My best guess is that more clients quit their therapists because they feel misunderstood than for any other reason.

Self-Reliance and Other Obstacles

Once you've decided something in your life is pretty fouled up and now that you've been convinced that there is someone out there who will confirm your diagnosis, what's holding you back? If you're stuck for an answer, let me outline a few of the more popular kinds of resistance.

Reaching out for help is not the hardest decision troubled people make—but it's near the top of the list and usually right behind deciding to tough it out. Anyone who says it's easy to ask for psychological help probably hasn't had to, and those sophisticated folks who consider psychotherapy chic don't count. It is commonplace to think that asking for help amounts to an admission of personal failure and none of us finds that easy. But in my experience, it takes more courage to reach out for and accept help than it does to let a situation fester or let your friends and family continue to suffer along with you.

"I thought anyone who had to see a psychiatrist was just a weakling," a successful businessman once told me. He was speaking for a large majority of American males—tough-minded, self-healing, bullet-proof fellows who believe themselves immune to such petty indulgences as fear, sadness, insecurity, self-doubt. Big boys don't cry—or do they?

This reluctance to admit having difficulties is less of a problem for women (if you look at statistics of who willingly asks for mental health help these days), but the fairer sex is no less proud or less motivated to take care of things without assistance. This is probably as it should be, and I'm not advocating that everyone call a therapist and schedule an appointment—just that you examine whether the bullet you have bitten into is the best alternative to a bad situation.

Next to this natural reluctance to admit that you can't cope with a problem, there is the stigma of becoming a "psychiatric patient." Don't let anyone kid you, there *is* a stigma.

"Aren't people who see psychiatrists and psychologists crazy?" The answer is yes—some of them are. "And if I go see a psychiatrist, doesn't that make me mentally ill?" No, and I hope therapy won't make things worse, but you may have to convince your friends and family otherwise. There's no getting around it, in most of America, seeing a mental health professional doesn't put a shine on your reputation. If you do decide to see someone, you can keep it private and most people do.

A third reason people don't ask for help is that they feel so beat down they don't want to bother anyone with their problems. Or they think no help is available for *their* problem. These are precisely the people who should ask for help. Therapists are trained to be bothered, so bother them; make them feel useful.

3 1833 02208 2254

3

Before You Call
a Professional

It is the great irony of the therapy business that while you may spend hundreds or thousands of dollars for professional help, the therapist will usually tell you that if you changed for the better, you did it yourself. If that's true, that you made all the improvements yourself, then *why* therapy, and do you get a refund? Could you have accomplished whatever you set out to accomplish by yourself? Did you really need a therapist? The doubters will say you wasted your time, and the believers will say you could never have done it by yourself.

If there is anything remarkable about human beings, it's that they can correct a personal situation in mid-course and turn disasters into triumphs. The fact that they can also turn triumphs into disasters won't concern us for the moment. Though I can't think of a single scientific study to document the usefulness of self-help, there is little doubt that people are capable of grabbing their own bootstraps and lifting themselves up and out of problems. Exactly how they do this is the stuff of the human adventure, and it takes an abnormally large ego for a therapist (or anyone else) to make claims that only through them can an individual make lasting, positive changes.

We've all met people who stopped bad habits simply by stopping them, dropped friends who weren't good for them, or who gave up neurotic wishes when they realized it was nutty to want things that could never be. We've all made conscious decisions to change something about our lives and have been the better for it. Just what we did and the reasons why we did it may be good, bad, or indifferent, but the important thing is that we believed we could do something to improve our lot. We believed we could change.

This book isn't about self-help or how to achieve a perfect emotional life, but a couple of comments about helping yourself are needed.

In the first place, you may already have a very good idea about what is wrong and what needs doing to fix it. More than once, I have asked clients if they didn't already know what the trouble was and what they needed to do to stop hurting. Many of them did. The second thing is that I'm sure self-help works and that you ought to try it. If it works, not only will you save a lot of time and money, but you'll get all the credit.

Taking a long and critical look at oneself is the first step to bringing about any change, and if it didn't take a monumental amount of courage, we would all probably be better off taking such an inventory four or five times a year. Examining your job, your friends, relationships to loved ones (or hated ones), how you spend free time, and wrestling with the meaningfulness of your life is a tough assignment—but if you decide on professional help, you'll end up doing it anyway. Changing your life, the way you see things, do things, think and feel about yourself and other people is something you can undertake with as little effort as saying to yourself, "I want to be different."

Before I make this sound too easy, I should point out that while people have an enormous capacity for change and adaptation, they also have a great capacity for resistance to anything new, including and maybe especially making changes in themselves. So, if you're trying to help yourself (like most of us do every day), don't be discouraged by your own hardheadedness, backsliding, lack of concentration and drive—it comes with being a member of the species.

The Telephone—First Line of Assistance

If you've tried self-help and weren't too excited with the results, try the telephone. In most communities, it takes about ten seconds to dial a seven-digit number and find yourself talking to someone whose sole purpose in answering your call is to be of help. America is overcrowded with helpers; there are so many helpful people out there, they are literally bumping into each other, and must be regulated by laws and organizations to keep them from helping so much that the average client in need of help isn't torn to shreds.

The problem in getting such help—most of it free—is sorting out what will be useful. There are so many promising kinds of assistance available that the average person in emotional pain can be overwhelmed by the choices.

These sources should be considered carefully since they can be to the point, timely, helpful and less costly. On the other hand, depending on your abilities as a self-diagnostician, you could end up wasting time, becoming discouraged with the wrong help, and in the end, deciding help really isn't available. If the cause of your problems happens to be physical, you could end up very sick or dead. Still, a telephone call is a lot less expensive then a professional consultation.

A good place to start to get some low-cost help is by telephoning whatever your community calls its crisis intervention center. These crisis lines came into existence in the sixties out of a sense of obligation to drug-overdosing kids whose sense of timing was poor. The overdoses created crises around the clock, and so the crisis telephone systems were initiated with a twenty-four-hour response capacity. Also, there was (and is) a theory that immediate help to people in need makes for good service.

In your community, your crisis system could go by any of the following names: Crisis Services, Help Line, Hot Line, Suicide Prevention, Community Mental Health, Emergency Call Line, Information and Referral, and others. If you have trouble finding such a name in the white or yellow pages, try the operator. In a small town, she'll know who you should call and may also know why you're calling. You may have to call a neighboring city where the service may be less personal but more confidential.

In large cities, where there are hundreds of helpers and thousands of people who need help, dialing the right outfit the first time is a long shot. Your best bet is to start off with a call to an information-referral number or a community mental health center, and you might as well expect to call more than one place. You've got to keep in mind (to keep your spirits up) that humans have so specialized in creating problems for themselves, they now need highly specialized problem-solvers.

In the average American community of a hundred thousand or so, you'll find a crisis line, emergency medical line, poison control center, rape crisis line, a line for child abusers, suicide prevention number, alcohol information referral service, drug crisis line, and lines for divorced people, elderly people, runaways, cancer victims, heart patients, and, in the midst of this, a line that claims to be "the" line for all general information. The probability of getting a wrong number is fairly high.

Who answers all these phones? For the most part, volunteers. And for the most part, dedicated people whose sense of service to others in their communities prompts them to give freely of their time. The majority receive professional training and supervision, and so can be quite informed about what might be a reasonable course of action for you to take. Help- or crisis-line volunteer staff vary considerably in their levels of sophistication, and within any one group of volunteers, there are highly capable and talented therapists who do a first-rate job of informal counseling. Unfortunately, each group of volunteers also has a few nitwits who, while they intend no harm, are about as helpful as talking to a doorknob. They usually don't last as volunteers and will be asked to resign sooner or later, but you might find yourself carrying on a conversation with someone whom you doubt could find his or her way home from work. My advice is to try again—at twenty-five cents a call, you shouldn't expect miracles.

Help From Friends

They say a true friend will give you a hug and a kiss or a kick in the pants, depending on what they see as most therapeutic. The very least a true friend will do is listen carefully to your problem, and for lots of problems, talking them all the way through is all that's needed. There is nothing quite so useful or practical as laying out a problem on the kitchen table and, taking turns with a good friend, smashing it with a shovel.

The problem is that friends, true or not-so-true, want to stay friendly and often feel a sense of obligation to say or do something to make you feel immediately better. "Cheer up, that doesn't sound so bad" or "things could be worse" or—an old favorite of mine—"look on the bright side" are all fairly predictable responses friends make after you have spilled some problem in their lap. It's not that they don't want to be helpful, it's just that they may not have a clue about how to go about it.

It is not, in my opinion, a fair test of friendship to expect even your best friend to ask just the right question to elicit what you're afraid to state plainly, offer a diagnosis, a remedial course of action, and provide the confrontation, support, and understanding necessary for you to work out a serious problem. Even if your best friend is a professional therapist, he will not want to treat you as a client and, if he has his wits about him, he'll keep his professional hat off his head.

Even if friends may be marginal therapists, they are the greatest resource any of us has, and talking over our problems with them isn't bad advice. Studies show that people who have close friends, someone they can confide in, rap to, someone with whom they can share their miseries, tend to have fewer mental health problems. Life is tough enough without going it alone. Friends are so important to making it in life that one of the things a responsible therapist will do is to encourage you to make friends or deepen existing relationships so that you don't find yourself struggling alone with a burden whose weight can be shared with others.

Skill Training

A lot of people assume that when they graduate from school, they are prepared for life—competent to succeed in a job, make a marriage work, raise children, handle stress, relax, assert themselves to get what they need, and otherwise roll right through life with a B+ average. It is much more the case that most of us get through life successfully by signing up for a sixty-year course at the university of hard knocks.

I am not surprised that the same boy who can build an atomic bomb in his basement can't figure out what to say to a girl on his first date. Or that the girl who got straight A's in home economics is pregnant for the second time and isn't yet nineteen. And so as not to be accused of picking on young people, what happens to the forty-five-year-old wife whose husband leaves her and she's never learned how to balance a checkbook, fix a leaky faucet, or put together a résumé?

What these people need and a lot of us lack are skills in living. Our problems in making it in life may have less to do with our so-called emotional stability or lack of it than in not having "how to do it" information, and some practice in getting things done. If a person becomes anxious and depressed over the demands of modern life, it may mean he or she needs some specific skills, some sense of competence or mastery over a complex and often confusing environment, not a therapist. Much of what's needed is now available and the cost is reasonable.

Mental health centers, junior colleges, universities, training institutes, health maintenance organizations, and some private therapists now offer a wide variety of these educational courses for all kinds of human problems. Announcements of these programs appear in newspapers, on church bulletin boards, in class catalogs, clinic waiting rooms, and other places, and usually include the information necessary to find out more about the what, who, how, and where.

The great advantage of these psychoeducational offerings is their usually competent staffing, pointed focus on specific problems, and low cost. We're all accustomed to learning new things—even about ourselves—and so the stigma of becoming a client or patient simply isn't there. We are, rather, students who have a common interest and common goals.

Drawbacks of these kinds of courses include a lack of personal attention, the fact that a professional and individual assessment of your problem is unlikely and, for reasons which may be entirely your own, you may feel uncomfortable either being a student or mixing with other people. The degree of intervention by the group leader or teacher will also be less intense since you, as a student, are but one of several who are paying for the service.

A partial list of these kinds of educational, skill, or informational groups would include: parent effectiveness training, assertiveness training, relaxation training, stress management workshops, as well as inventive and creative offerings for people recently divorced, dealing with death in their families, or facing some human situation that can be shared with enough others to constitute a class or group.

As with anything else, the choice is yours. If you've been able to narrow down a problem to the point where you can see it has the same focus and source of pain as those experienced by other people (for example, you can't ask for a raise because you are too passive), then you may find something like an assertiveness training group to be just the answer. If you can find what you need in one of these educational groups, you may not need to make the much heavier investment in professional therapy.

People-to-People Groups

A young man referred to me a couple of years ago stated that his chief problems were that his marriage was headed for the rocks, his job was dull and boring and he was about to be fired, and, for all this, he was depressed and "tired of it all." After taking a history, it was fairly obvious to me (although not to him) that the ten to twelve cans of beer he had been drinking in the evenings for the past four years were making him dull company for his wife, lethargic on his job, and contributing mightily to his feelings of depression. Confronted with the notion that half a case of beer was an excessive after-dinner drink, he grudgingly admitted that his father had been alcoholic and that his wife had asked him on several occasions to "cut down."

The young man wanted therapy for his depression, and I explained that was fine with me except that I thought he could save himself a bundle of money if he'd first take a long look at his drinking and attend a few meetings at a local chapter of Alcoholics Anonymous. He didn't much like the idea, but agreed to go with the understanding that if drinking wasn't the problem, he could come back and see me. Six months later, he called to thank me for the referral. He was sober, his marriage was again running on all eight cylinders, and he had been promoted to foreman.

Alcoholics Anonymous, or AA, is one of the oldest people-to-people groups in America, and has been the forerunner of a movement that has been gaining momentum daily. There are literally hundreds of people-to-people groups organized locally, some nationally, but with the same basic rules for membership—an acknowledgement that the problem you have is a common one, and a belief that people who have "been there" can help eath other. Whether these groups have burgeoned into existence out of frustration over the lack of response or empathy from the professional community doesn't really matter so much as the fact that they are there, useful, inexpensive, and waiting to be helpful.

These organizations, sometimes called peer groups or self-help groups, are a testimony to the growing belief by the average person that the problems we face as individuals are not unique, need not be incapacitating, and can be coped with better in the context of compassionate and understanding others. Reassurance, expression of concern and support, giving hope where there was little or none, and being able to tap the knowledge of people who have experienced the same problem are immeasurable sources of strength to the troubled person. Just to see someone else make it back from whatever hell you may feel you're in is a kind of psychological reprieve.

Parents Without Partners, Gamblers Anonymous, Pills Anonymous, Narcotics Anonymous, National Association to Aid Fat Americans, Weight Watchers, are but a few such groups. Many of these can be found in your phone book. There may be a chapter in your local community and your information and referral or crisis line folks will know.

If you live in one of America's smaller communities, the group you need may not exist and you may have to drive to a larger city to find it. Or, if you're the organizational type, you might want to contact a national office of a people-to-people group and get the particulars about how to start a chapter in your own locale. After all, when two people talk to each other about a problem they both share and begin to feel better about having talked it over with someone who knows what it's like, a people-to-people group is already under way.

A couple of final comments are needed. Whatever you decide to do —call a crisis line, set about a study of yourself as a first step toward self-betterment, sign up for an assertiveness training course, or attend a people-to-people group—when you act, you begin to change. You're doing something you haven't done before and it's for you. Whatever happens, you won't be the same person you were before you started, and, while there are no guarantees your problem will vanish like a bad dream, there's nothing to say it won't get better either. At the very least, you can begin to like yourself for having taken the first steps and for grabbing hold of those old bootstraps.

As for seeking professional help, nothing you can do for yourself or derive from any of the groups or classes outlined here should present a handicap to therapy. In fact, many therapists will want you to become involved in these groups and will encourage your efforts at self-help.

Unfortunately, if you call a therapist first (before trying the help suggested here), he or she is unlikely to suggest you try these avenues before making an appointment. After all, there's money at stake. Besides, most therapists will assume you've tried at least a few things before you decided to call for an appointment with a professional. There are, of course, some therapists who believe that only psychotherapy (usually their particular brand) can bring about permanent changes in people. To these therapists, the idea that people can discover truths about themselves, analyze their own predicaments, and follow through on a series of self-curative actions is completely foreign. And since it's sometimes difficult to tell the good-guy therapists from the bad-guy therapists, it's probably best first to try the self-help route.

4

Choosing a Therapist

Deciding you need professional help is a major decision, not simply because you will be spending hundreds and possibly thousands of dollars, but because you'll be asking someone you don't even know to have a major influence in your life. A troubled mind is at least as important as a troubled heart, and while you wouldn't dream of picking a vascular surgeon from the phone book, people do just that when it comes to finding a therapist. Oftentimes, people take considerable care to select a barber or hairdresser to work on the outside of their head, but are hesitant to exercise the same degree of caution to find someone to work on the inside. There is an obvious reason for this—to ask someone (a friend, relative, minister, family doctor, or whomever) to refer you to a therapist, you have to admit you think you need one.

If, like a lot of people, admitting you've got a personal problem that is so serious that it needs professional attention is too big an obstacle, there are still ways you can improve your odds of finding a good therapist. What follows is some information, tips, and a few warnings that will help take the guesswork out of finding a competent professional. To find good help requires gaining some knowledge, and a little leg work, but the effort should be worth it, especially if you like to make informed decisions.

The first task is to be sure the therapist you are investigating is a professional. The generally recognized professionals capable of independent practice include psychologists, psychiatrists, social workers, and psychiatric nurses.

Psychologists

Psychologists are trained to do all sorts of things, many of them totally unrelated to helping people. The field of psychology is extremely broad and diverse, and just because someone has had psychological training or majored in psychology in a college or university does not make him or her a psychologist competent to help you. Clinical or counseling psychologists are typically the ones with the training and experience necessary to be recognized as mental health professionals.

In checking out a psychologist, you should look for the following credentials:

1. A doctorate in psychology, i.e., Ph.D. or Ed.D.
2. A license to practice. Call your state licensing board—they will tell you if the person holds a valid license. (Some individuals with masters degrees may hold licenses as they were grandfathered under the early licensing laws or have passed exams for specialty areas.)
3. Registered in the National Register of Health Services Providers. (Not all licensed practitioners are listed but many are.) To be listed, a psychologist must have a Ph.D., two years of supervised experience, and be licensed.

Membership in the American Psychological Association does not equal a credential as a professional helper since the American Psychological Association has several divisions and special interest groups, most of which are outside the definition of clinical or counseling psychology.

Clinical and counseling psychologists will have completed four years of graduate training after the bachelor's degree, specializing in various aspects of human learning, personality, normal and abnormal behavior, psychological testing, diagnosis and treatment, psychotherapy, and research. Beyond this, they will have had at least one year of supervised work with troubled people during their graduate school years, and usually an additional year of internship, during which they are observed and supervised in the delivery of clinical service.

Psychiatrists

A psychiatrist is a medical doctor who has chosen to specialize in the diagnosis and treatment of mental and emotional disorders. To become a psychiatrist, a physician must undertake a course of study (usually three years) called a residency, in which full-time attention is given to both academic learning and the practice of treating people with mental illnesses. This work is often completed in hospitals, university clinics, and other settings where people with problems seek help. All psychiatrists have training in psychotherapy, but as in psychology, there are specialty areas, and any given psychiatrist may have interests that focus less on psychotherapy than, say, on the prevention of mental illness, community psychiatry, research, or even administration. Many psychiatrists attend institutes in psychotherapy and this usually indicates the particular psychiatrist has a bias in favor of psychotherapy as opposed to the use of drugs, for instance, in the treatment of human problems.

One major difference between psychologists and psychiatrists is that the latter, by dint of being physicians, are qualified to prescribe drugs— not a small thing in a culture where pills are considered by many to be as essential to life as food and water.

Since it is possible for any physician to call himself a psychiatrist, it is essential to establish the psychiatrist's qualifications as follows:

1. Completed a residency in psychiatry.
2. Board certified. Many practicing psychiatrists are board eligible, but have not yet taken the national exams to be certified by a national examining board.
3. Full member in the American Psychiatric Association. (Membership in the American Medical Association is not an indication of competence as a psychiatrist.)
4. Graduate of a psychotherapy institute.

If you feel your problems are so severe that some kind of medication is going to be needed, you're better off to contact a psychiatrist first since, though he may not prescribe medications, he at least has the ability to evaluate your need of such help, and if you and he agree it is needed, he can solve that problem immediately.

Social Workers

As is true with the other professions mentioned here, social workers are a heterogeneous group of professionals within whose ranks you can find excellent help. All social workers are not therapists, but those who have specialized in psychotherapy as a helping art have read the same books, attended the same workshops, and received much of the same training and supervision as psychologists and psychiatrists.

Schools of social work vary in their course requirements, depending on the focus of a particular graduate department, but all graduating students earn a masters degree in social work (M.S.W.), considered the entry-level degree to this field.

An M.S.W. degree requires two years of graduate study with heavy emphasis on field placement (actual work in an agency or institution) where the student works daily with clients and applies what knowledge he or she has acquired in classes.

Not all social workers specialize in helping people with mental or emotional problems, but those who do will almost always have worked in some kind of mental health facility—outpatient clinic, mental health center, psychiatric hospital—prior to opening a private practice or joining a group of professional therapists.

While some states certify or license social workers for independent practice, many do not. If you've decided to consult a social worker, you can call your state licensing division to see if certification statutes are on the books, and if so, whether the social worker you are considering has this credential.

The Academy of Certified Social Workers, the accreditation sponsored by the National Association of Social Workers, also provides an avenue for advanced training and recognition for social workers who wish to improve their level of skill and qualifications. Certification by this organization requires two years of supervised work beyond the masters degree. This supervision must be conducted by a member of the academy, and the applicant also must pass successfully a national exam.

A further help in determining credentials is the *Register of Clinical Social Workers*, published by the National Association of Social Workers. This register lists all A.C.S.W. members whose past degree and supervised work was in providing professional help to people with problems and is, therefore, probably your best guide to qualified help from the profession of social workers.

As is particularly true of psychology, the profession of social work is plagued by many people who claim to be social workers because they majored in that field while in college, or have worked in an agency whose mission was largely social or dealing with social problems. These "field promotions" (usually self-proclaimed) do not a social worker make, and you should check carefully for the following credentials before assuming you are getting the genuine article:

1. A masters degree in social work
2. Certification or license in your state (if available)
3. Membership in the Academy of Certified Social Workers
4. Evidence of clinical training or specialized work in psychotherapy

Psychiatric Nurses

Psychiatric nurses are a relatively new group of professional help-givers. Since they are a new group, little in the way of specialty training or licensing exists in most states, although many nurses are every bit as competent to conduct psychotherapy as are psychologists, psychiatrists, or social workers.

To be a psychiatric nurse, one must first graduate from a nursing program that includes training in psychology or psychiatry as part of the curriculum, and pass a licensing exam at the state level. Successful state licensure leads to the designation of registered nurse (R.N.).

Oftentimes, a nurse who goes to work in a psychiatric setting, a mental health center or hospital "becomes" a psychiatric nurse by experience and, except in states where certification is available, this is the only way he or she may become recognized as having developed a specialty in this field.

A number of nursing schools now offer a masters degree (a few offer a Ph.D.) in psychiatric nursing and any nurse-therapist with this kind of background can be considered to have met minimum academic standards as a professional psychotherapist. In a few states, nurses have the qualifications and statutory authority to prescribe certain kinds of medications, including those used in psychiatry. This is always done under the close supervision of psychiatrists.

The following credentials are recommended if you choose to see a psychiatric nurse in private practice:

1. R.N. licensing in the state in which you live
2. Masters degree in psychiatric nursing from an accredited university. A masters degree in psychology and an R.N. is *not* a substitute.
3. Certification as a psychiatric nurse by the state nursing association if such certification is available. You can call the state licensing division to determine if certification is available.

Who Else Is Out There?
Not long ago, my fingers were walking through the yellow pages in search of a pet shop where I hoped to find a replacement for the family dog who died in a car accident. There, just above pet shops, I ran across an ad in the personal consultants section that read: "Psychological Assessments."

Curious, I dialed the number and the conversation went something like this:

"Psychological Assessments. Can I help you?"

"I saw your ad and am calling to find out what kind of services you provide."

"We offer complete psychological assessment, including testing, diagnosis of personality traits, and we can make recommendations about courses of action which would be best for people." The voice was quite businesslike.

"What kind of tests do you use?"

"Subjective tests."

"What are the names of these tests?"

There was a pause. "Could I ask you who you are?" I told her my name and that I was a psychologist.

"Oh, I see. Well . . . we use subjective tests . . . actually samples of handwriting."

I politely explained that state law prohibited the use of the words "psychologist," "psychological," or any other like term by anyone except a licensed psychologist, and that it was very likely their ad was illegal. The woman (who was the sole proprietor in her firm) assured me her attorney had checked this all out before incorporating the name, but agreed to review it with him. She called later to state there had been an error, and would promptly make the necessary correction.

I cite this as an example of the problem faced by a public in search of professional help. As in this case, such misrepresentation is often an act of ignorance, and not a conscious ploy to impersonate a professional. A listing in the yellow pages only means the person paid for the advertisement and that the check didn't bounce. The people who publish telephone directories are not interested in either credentials or scruples, so picking a name in the yellow pages is a risky business.

There's probably nothing wrong with graphoanalysis, astrology, tarot card interpretations, palm reading, or any other effort to understand the mysteries of the human personality, but none of these is a substitute for those professions requiring years of college, graduate school, supervision, and experience that lead to the kinds of credentials outlined in this chapter. The credentials in and of themselves do not mean the therapist is competent, only that he has completed a sometimes difficult and always expensive course of study, and that at least some of his peers think that he will not harm the public.

Being a member of a profession means the practitioner has at least read the ethical standards for that profession and *knows* the difference between what is proper professional conduct and what is improper. It's unfortunate that familiarity with what is good practice does not translate to good practice, or provide you a guarantee against the therapist being a scoundrel. But being a member in good standing with his profession does give you some assurance that the therapist is probably not an imposter, and probably has survived the rigors of earning his credentials without serious or flagrant violation of the rules of good therapeutic practice.

Seeking help from a professional provides some other, less visible guarantees of which the public is generally unaware. One of these is the fact that only professionals may buy malpractice insurance. The company providing liability insurance for the therapist does so because properly accredited therapists are good risks, i.e., they don't get sued for behaving badly, or at least not very often. And so, in a way, this is an insurance policy for you as well.

Also, professionals are accountable to each other. Their work is reviewed increasingly through peer review systems, and as a whole, the helping professions are becoming more and more aware of the need to inspect themselves, establish standards, and develop ways to police themselves—something that will never happen among those helpers who are not members of established professions.

Aware of the fact that the education one completed ten years ago is sadly out of date, most professional therapists are now required to produce evidence of continuing education in order to maintain their licenses. This requirement to keep learning is relatively new, but again underlines the conscientious nature of professionals, and also provides clients with the latest research findings in terms of trying to help solve their problems.

Are Good Therapists Available Outside the Professions?

The answer to this question is an equivocal yes. Certainly, there are many nonprofessionals or paraprofessional helpers who provide high-quality services to troubled clients, and they are often both readily available and charge a smaller fee. They go by many names: counselors, psychotherapists, personal advisors, or simply therapists. You can assume most of them have had some formal training, but they lack the education, experience, and supervision accorded certified members of the professions—otherwise, they would have earned this status and with it, higher fees.

Paraprofessionals may have college degrees; some will have attended college and a few will have only high school diplomas. The great majority of these helpers are employed at mental health centers, alcohol and drug treatment facilities, or nonprofit service agencies that provide therapy services. In most of these settings, paraprofessionals receive training and supervision by the high-priced staff—psychiatrists, psychologists, social workers, nurses—and you can count on their work to be of good quality. In such a setting, a paraprofessional is regulated by the professions, has access to consultation, and is insured through the agency's umbrella malpractice policy. In a word, if the paraprofessional fouls up, the doctors responsible for his work will get named in the same lawsuit. This keeps everyone on their toes. It's when a paraprofessional opens his or her own office that the risks to the consumer take a sharp increase.

There are several reasons you should be suspicious of a nonprofessional providing therapy service to the public. First, more than in any other service system designed to alleviate human pain and suffering, the field of psychotherapy attracts kooks and charlatans. There's a ton of money to be made from the miseries people experience, and a clever opportunist can literally open an office, hang up a shingle, phony up some credentials (you can purchase a Ph.D. by mail for around a hundred dollars), and start accepting clients. As long as the "therapist" never calls himself a psychologist, psychiatrist, nurse, or, in some states, a social worker, and breaks no laws, he is legally free to do just about anything. He may call himself a psychotherapist or a personal counselor, hypnotherapist, marriage and family counselor (except in states where marriage and family counselors are licensed), or whatever, and no one can challenge his right to join in the free enterprise system. Maybe that's the way it should be and since that's the way it is, it's doubly important that you, as a person in need, make a few inquiries before you put yourself in the hands of someone whose primary motivation may be to separate you from your cash.

Sex Therapists

One particular area in which extreme caution in picking a therapist is warranted is in finding someone to help with a sexual problem. Like the gold rush of '49, therapists of every persuasion and every degree of competence (or incompetence) have flocked to the aid of clients in need of sexual counseling and treatment, and more than a few of them are untrained, unethical, and unscrupulous.

The treatment of sexual disorders requires extensive training and supervision beyond whatever formal degree a professional has earned, and no reputable institute admits students who do not already possess established credentials from other helping professions. The simple fact that a therapist is a "doctor" of medicine or psychiatry or psychology does not qualify him or her as a sex therapist, although it's a fair bet that if a therapist with these credentials offers to help with a sex problem, he or she will have had at least some experience and will not abuse the client with some kind of unethical conduct, e.g., prescribe intercourse with the therapist.

To find a therapist competent to help with a sex problem, the following steps are recommended:

1. Ask your family doctor for a referral. Before beginning counseling for any sexual problem, a physical exam is in order and you may find your family physician able to help directly, since many of them are now trained to provide help in this area.

2. Check the therapist's certification and licenses through means described earlier.

3. Check his or her standing with their professional organization.

4. Ask if the therapist is a member of the American Association of Sex Educators and Therapists—the only recognized national association granting certification for sex therapists.

To do less than the light work outlined above is to take unnecessary risks which could lead to some very unpleasant results. Much worse than a waste of time and money on an unqualified therapist is the possibility that therapy will fail and you and your spouse or loved one will come away with a feeling of defeat, the sense that the problem (whatever it is) is not correctable, and because of the inept treatment, your sex life could even get worse. Once burned by an incompetent therapist, you're unlikely to gamble again, and if the success of the marriage or relationship hinges on a good sex life, failing in an attempt to get help could lead to separation or divorce.

Good Help Is Available

While it may be something of a chore to find a competent and responsible therapist to help with a problem, it's not impossible. If you, the concerned client, take a skeptical attitude in your search, you may find yourself spending what seems like an undue amount of time, but there are rewards for your caution. The following are five steps to finding a therapist:

1. Ask for a referral. (If you're embarrassed about asking someone face to face, make anonymous phone calls.)

After deciding to seek professional help, you'll need the name of someone to call. A referral is like a recommendation in that the name of the therapist given you by a third party—your family doctor, minister, crisis telephone worker, or a mental health center—is someone the third party believes to be good at what he or she does. Although no criticism is intended, physician referrals are often interpreted by clients as "orders," and too often, they are made exclusively to psychiatrists. This is done partly because psychiatrists and physicians are in the same fraternity, but often because physicians do not know qualified psychologists, social workers, or other mental health professionals who well might be of as much or even more help for the problem you have. By calling a number of people who make referrals, you will have several names (they often give three names) to choose from, and those that show up again and again are likely to enjoy a good reputation, which usually means that the therapist is respected by other members of the professional community. Professional communities have very active grapevines and any therapist who is a real jerk will rarely survive within the referral system.

2. Check credentials.

You can do this in two ways. One way is to call the state licensing board, the county medical society (if you are looking for a psychiatrist), the state or local psychological association (for psychologists), and the National Association of Social Workers (Appendix C). A second way is to call the therapist directly and ask questions about credentials, professional affiliations, licenses, and specialized training. Again, this won't guarantee anything, but it's a lot better than doing nothing.

3. Ask about the therapist's style or approach.

While you have the therapist on the phone, briefly outline your problem and ask how the therapist might be of help to you. Will she want to see you alone? Will she want your spouse or family to come in? Will she recommend using any medications? What kinds of techniques does she use, and what does she think would be most helpful for you? These questions and many others may be difficult to ask, but the answers will go a long way toward reassuring you in your quest for someone to be of help. If the therapist acts put off or sounds angry, keep looking.

4. Ask that the first visit be a consultation.

A consultation is different from therapy in that it does not imply a commitment to proceed beyond the first visit. You're obliged to only one appointment (and the cost of only one appointment). A consultation gives both the therapist and you a chance to discuss your problem and mutually decide if therapy should be undertaken, and does not automatically result in expectations that therapy has begun or carry the implication of a possibly long-term relationship. I strongly recommend this step, as it puts you in a much better position to negotiate therapy in terms of your needs, and makes possible a more equitable sharing of responsibility should you decide to continue.

5. If in doubt, get a second opinion.

Having secured a list of therapists' names and having seen one of them, you may feel the first therapist didn't quite understand you or your problem, was too cold or aloof, too lackadaisical, or too anything. If you left that first appointment feeling very undecided about continuing, you might want to seek a second opinion. Since you saw the first therapist only for a consultation, you are free to see another one to get his or her ideas and opinions before making a final decision.

Some therapists may view your seeking a second professional opinion as threatening to their knowledge and skill, and you may even be seen as "doctor shopping"—in fact, you are; but then, considering the importance of the purchase, you should. If the therapist discounts your need for a second opinion, you can bet the problem is his or hers, not yours. Never underestimate the fact that while you may be in dire need of help, the therapist is in need of money, and since you've got the cash, you've got the power.

The Isms

The isms that count in therapy and seem to weigh heavily on whether the first session is successful are racism, sexism, and agism. And, whether you've got the problem or the therapist does, the suspicion on either of your parts that the other guy is prejudiced is going to make working together nearly impossible.

Racism

Professional therapists strive for objectivity and most of them believe they hold no serious prejudicial attitudes. In my experience, totally objective therapists do not exist, and if I meet one who claims he can work well with anyone of any color or age or sex or sexual persuasion, then I figure he's just out of graduate school, a fool, or both.

Professional therapists are encouraged to deal with the ethnic and racial attitudes they learned as children and constantly to examine their feelings about the people they work with. Even so, if some are blatantly prejudiced, more are simply ignorant of their individual client's ethnic and cultural experiences.

Serious problems can arise when a therapist pretends he is not prejudiced or does not know he harbors such feelings. I once knew a drug counselor who claimed he was "color blind." "After all," he would say, "a lot of those niggers helped us win World War II."

In fact, no one is color blind and a therapist who is not aware of major racial, social, or cultural differences between himself and his clients doesn't appreciate the relationship of culture to personality. This doesn't mean that people of different races cannot be therapeutically helpful to each other, just that they need to know that there are differences and to appreciate them as differences (and different is not worse).

Ethical therapists know the sources of their racial prejudices. If their feelings represent a serious conflict for them, they will refer you on to another therapist. A good friend of mine grew up near an Indian reservation and, though he has no clear dislike of Indians, feels he cannot give them the same unbiased attention that someone else might.

The other side of the coin is, of course, your own racial attitudes. If you are a middle-class white and your first session in an outpatient clinic is with a black therapist, what goes on in your head? Do you trust a black person as quickly as you would a white one? An Oriental? Hispanic? Do you trust people from different races with equal ease? If you don't, talk to the therapist about it or find a therapist where initial trust isn't an issue.

If you detect negative and prejudicial attitudes, questions, or treatment or even "vibes" from a therapist, either bring it up for discussion or move on. A sensitive therapist will often beat you to the issue by bringing it up before it becomes a problem.

What you don't need in a therapy relationship is to be treated in a way that fits a prejudiced therapist's idea about how "people like you" should behave. Remember, there is no one exactly like you.

Sexism

There isn't room even to outline the scientific research on the topic of sexual differences between therapists and clients and how these differences and similarities affect the therapeutic relationship. And since no one can grow up in this world without having feelings, attitudes, expectations, and some pretty clear notions about how boys and girls are "supposed" to behave, therapists, like everyone else, are subject to sexist attitudes. In a way, therapist attitudes about sex roles are such an enormous potential problem I doubt if anyone wants to examine all the implications.

Not long ago I worked with a middle-aged couple who came to me with the hope that I might help them keep their marriage of fifteen years together. For a lot of reasons unacceptable to the wife, her husband had had an affair with a younger woman, and, upon finding out, she threw the rascal out. This is such a common occurrence in the midlife struggles couples go through that it hardly warrants mentioning except that the wife was the one who felt depressed and guilty. Her parents, friends, the rascal (of course), all agreed that if she hadn't started law school the year before she would not have driven her man into the arms of another woman. Some therapists would agree with this woman's friends and family and counsel her to get back into the kitchen. Others would counsel her to major in civil law with a special focus on divorce settlements.

The therapist's ideas about what boys and girls are supposed to do when they grow up can make a very big difference in how therapy is approached, who is included, and what the outcome might eventually be. If you think the therapist has strong sexist attitudes that don't agree with yours, bring it up, discuss it with him or her, and set it aside. If the therapist's attitudes remain a major issue, and the two of you cannot agree on what you had hoped to get out of therapy, set the therapist aside. After all, you didn't take him to raise.

If you are a woman, you should be aware that sexist attitudes (women are by nature dependent, helpless, weaker, hysterical, and basically inferior) are more prevalent than most male therapists are willing to admit. Until recently, the study of psychology was the study of male psychology, and research on the developmental aspects of women and the unique problems they encounter was very sparse. Also, some schools of psychotherapy, particularly Freudian schools, deemphasize the psychological makeup of women. So, in your evaluation of a potential therapist, make it a point to find out what sort of attitudes the therapist holds about women.

Sexual prejudices are at work from the client's side of the desk as well. I recall an intake interview conducted by a competent psychiatric nurse who, after an hour and a half of encouragement, history-taking, and thoughtful questioning, had no more idea about why the young man sitting in her office had come to the clinic than when he first sat down. Bringing the interview to a close, she asked if there was anything else he wished to tell her, adding that she felt she must have overlooked something. The young man blushed, shifted uneasily in his chair, and blurted out: "I can't pee in public!"

As embarrassed as he was by his fairly common problem, he might have told a male therapist what was bothering him within the first few minutes of the interview. The question is, who had the problem? In this case, I'd guess it was the client. Any experienced nurse knows how men feel about bedpans, but they can't read minds.

If you can afford a private therapist and one of either sex is available, then picking the same or opposite-sex therapist is your choice. If you make an appointment at a clinic or a mental health center and you think the sex of a therapist is an important issue, ask for what you want—all they can say is no, but usually they won't.

I personally feel that the sex of a therapist has less to do with the success or failure of therapy than do other therapist qualities—maturity, empathy, competence, and training. The most important thing for you to remember is that regardless of the sex of the therapist, almost any specific complaint or problem has been heard at least once before, and you can expect a professional not to wince, retch, become alarmed, or giggle at what you consider a serious matter.

Agism

When I was a young graduate student still in training, one of my first clients was a forty-five-year-old mother of five whose reason for entering counseling was to get some advice on how to cope with her fifteen-year-old sexually active daughter. This woman, not quite old enough to be my mother, took one look at me and asked my age. I stammered around and finally admitted I was twenty-five.

"How many teenagers do you have?"

"None," I smiled.

"Then how do you know how to help me?"

"I'm not sure I do," I said. "But I'm willing to try."

Reluctantly, she let me conduct the interview and when it was over, asked if she couldn't be assigned to an older therapist. Since we didn't have any older therapists in the clinic, she was stuck with me. She agreed to a second appointment but failed to show up.

My supervisor for this case, after listening to a tape of the interview, scolded me for admitting my age, stating that I should have evaded the question with another question like, "Do you think my age is important to your problem?" I accepted my supervisor's remarks (I had to if I wanted a decent grade), but I always thought that that lady had exellent judgment. What, after all, did I know about sexually active teenage girls except that there hadn't been any in the town where I grew up?

What was going on in this interview was both a legitimate query as to my qualifications and experience in working with problems between teenage girls and their mothers and the issue of agism. I'm not sure who was at fault, and I'm not sure it matters. I am certain that the woman's experience of "getting help" was not altogether satisfactory.

Agism, like other isms, is a prejudicial attitude toward people older or younger than yourself in which they are stereotyped, usually with negative characteristics. In general, older people receive more prejudicial treatment (because most of us are not yet old and therefore lack perspective). But both young and old are treated less as unique individuals than as groups of people who are assumed to share common traits or characteristics.

To one degree or another, all therapists suffer from agism—even the older, salty ones. Therapists have parents, some of them crotchety, petty, senile, or dying. All therapists have feelings about their parents—love, resentment, pity—and all these feelings about their parents can spill over into their feelings toward elderly clients. Though therapists may try to resist, these feelings are there and if you're a senior citizen, you may experience some of these feelings put on you.

For example, you may be interviewed by a middle-aged therapist who insists on helping you into your chair even though you just jogged the three miles to the appointment. Or, if you're one of those charming little gray-haired ladies, the therapist may continue calling you "dear" when you've twice explained your name is Mrs. Swanson.

These examples may be of small irritants, but a much larger problem may be in getting an appointment in the first place. Some agencies and practitioners reflect a more pervasive attitude that amounts to discrimination against the aged. Once your age is known, say you're sixty-seven, you may be referred to a senior citizens center, nursing home, or some other agency specializing in problems of old age. No doubt our society's preoccupation with remaining young and vibrant and beautiful has contributed to this prejudice toward the aged. It's something we could work on.

W. C. Fields said he didn't care much for dogs and kids and there are therapists who, if asked the question, would say they care more for dogs than children. I know one psychologist who begins counseling with parents of teenagers with the premise that it's "us against them." This may make the parents feel great, but their troubled adolescent often feels outnumbered. The point is that you should not assume that every therapist is skilled in working with children or adolescents, or that she or he is even sympathetic to the problems children encounter.

Most responsible and competent practitioners will refer clients they don't feel they can do well with and for some, working with children is not particularly satisfying or rewarding.

Agism is more subtle than racism or sexism, but it's there all the same. If your antennae tell you the therapist is treating you like a class of people rather than an individual, don't dismiss the feeling as unimportant.

What Kind of Professional?

A very logical question a troubled person might ask is: what kind of professional should I see—a psychiatrist, psychologist, social worker? I wish there were a simple answer.

In the broadest sense, people with the most serious problems—major depression, psychosis, extreme fluctuations in mood, disturbances in thoughts (hallucinations and delusions, etc.)—should begin with a psychiatrist. As mentioned earlier, only psychiatrists can prescribe medications that can have a significant impact on the symptoms that accompany these disturbances. Also, if the troubled person is functioning so poorly that carrying on daily activities—work, family life, recreation—is becoming impossible and hospitalization may be needed, a psychiatrist can usually effect this alternative with more ease than can the other professionals.

However, most psychologists, social workers, and psychiatric nurses are trained to recognize the full range of clinical problems clients can present and will, if the situation calls for it, refer out to other medical specialists, including psychiatrists.

But beyond this very general rule of thumb (that the more serious the problem the more likely one should start with a psychiatrist), it is difficult to specify what sort of professional works best with what sort of human problem. Within each profession, particular therapists often specialize in particular problems, or work with particular age groups. For example, in my experience, social workers tend to do more family-oriented work. But many psychologists and psychiatrists are now specializing in family therapy. Psychologists, depending on their training, are able to provide psychological testing and evaluation services to assess such questions as school readiness, intelligence, brain function, and personality traits, and, so far, this area remains the exclusive domain of psychologists.

Outside of the major mental health professions, there are many other qualified counselors and therapists available. And while most states now require some type of certification or registration to offer counseling services to the public, others do not—especially if those services are offered within a religious organization.

Several years ago I served as a consultant to a hospital-based Clinical Pastoral training program where clergymen and -women from a variety of faiths came to learn and improve on their counseling skills. Empathetic, caring, nondenominational in their approach, many were excellent, natural therapists who blossomed with a little formal training. However, not all priests, pastors, ministers, chaplins, or men or women in positions of religious authority have had special training in counseling or psychotherapy; so, if you can, try to determine if the person you want to see feels up to handling your particular problem. Many are more than able; the rest should be able to refer you on.

Unfortunately for the consumer, much of the confusion and conflict between the major helping professions swirls around the question of who is qualified to do what. Since all the modes of therapy—individual, marital, family, group (and excluding only the medical option of medication)—are offered by all the professions, none can claim special or exclusive expertise in any of these areas. There is, then, no simple way for a potential client with a particular kind of problem to select a therapist of a certain stripe solely on the basis of her or his profession. Again, a few questions to the practitioner prior to making the first appointment should help you decide which kind of therapist has the most to offer.

5

The Therapies–
A Brief Guide

Many years ago while working as a trainee in a state mental hospital, I was assigned a patient for individual therapy. He was a young man, about my age, who recently had been admitted for reasons I was yet to learn. At our first interview, he was nervous, tense, and unsure of himself. As I had only started the job two weeks earlier and was fresh out of graduate school, I too was nervous, tense, and unsure of myself. I asked him how he came to be admitted to the hospital.

"It all began," he said, nestling into his chair, "with the fact that my parents never wanted me. I was the last of three children. Mother was already in her forties and the pregnancy was a burden for her. Even as an infant I was rejected. She breast-fed my brothers, but I got the bottle—and you know the psychic implications of that."

The young man talked on for several minutes and I judged that at the speed he was approaching his first birthday it was going to take a year to find out how he got into the hospital.

I interrupted his monologue. "Have you been in therapy before?"

"Of course," he replied, somewhat perturbed. "Three years of psycho-analysis."

He was a bright fellow and we quickly came to a meeting of the minds. I explained that my job was to help him understand how he got himself into the hospital and how he might get himself out again. We simply didn't have the time for another round of psychoanalysis, even if I knew how to conduct it, which I didn't.

The fellow in this anecdote, it later turned out, had not actually had formal psychoanalysis. His familiarity with the terms and concepts of psychoanalytic theory and therapy came as much from his college coursework as from the counseling he had (unsuccessfully) received. But the point is that people often assume the therapy they begin with will follow a certain format and fit in with what they believe to be true about the nature of the experience. When these expectations are not met, clients often feel disappointed, disheartened, and sometimes foolish.

In this chapter, I will briefly describe the major schools of psychotherapy, their focus and goals, and the role the therapist plays in the different processes. I will also touch on the theoretical underpinnings of these schools, since their methods of psychotherapy stem from different philosophic views of how the world of human behavior is ordered. But first, it is important to remember that the quality of the relationship you develop with the therapist is more important than the particular brand of therapy he or she practices. If you can't develop a foundation of trust where hope can flourish and have a sense of mutual respect, it won't matter if the therapist is a genius at whatever kind of therapy he provides.

To the degree possible, it makes some sense to pick a therapist who thinks as you do. The more your philosophies about life agree, the more likely you are to hit it off in a therapeutic alliance. So, when making that first appointment, feel free to ask the therapist about his brand of psychotherapy.

What follows are descriptions of the major orientations to individual therapy and, although there are many others that warrant attention, most are offshoots of these major schools of thought. Some of these approaches have been expanded to encompass other modalities of therapy (marital, family, and group), but for now I will focus on them as they apply to the treatment of an individual.

Psychoanalysis

Analysis, by its shorthand name, is the granddaddy of all modern "talk" therapies. If you were to ask the average man on the street for a description of psychotherapy, he would come fairly close to describing psychoanalysis. Cartoons, comedy routines, and parlor jokes usually play off the key elements of a bearded psychiatrist with a thick Viennese accent juxtaposed to a lovely young client reclining on the inevitable couch. That this scene might actually take place in fewer offices country-wide than one would imagine says more about our need for a high-status comic target than about the practice of psychoanalysis.

The theoretical assumptions underlying psychoanalysis are many, but the key ones include a belief that the nagging, neurotic problems we wrestle with as adults are the result of early childhood experiences, usually unpleasant, and usually beyond the reach of conscious remembering. These unresolved conflicts (hatred for a brother, fear of a father, incestuous longings for a cousin) continue to provide the impetus for our failure as adults to learn, to love, and to work.

And, what is worse, all this pain and torment is busily grinding away in some unconscious psychological machinery where (because it is unthinkable that we ever had such yearnings or hatreds) we have now clamped a lid over these feelings, blinding ourselves to the reality of our own childhood, and blurring or distorting our adult perceptions.

As the theory goes, we can't win. Though we may be unaware of them, these desires, fantasies, and memories do not go quietly away. They are there, demanding attention through symptoms of psychological distress affecting our behavior, our feelings, our thoughts and dreams. Since all of this ugly business is unconscious, we can't know what to do to correct things. Somehow, we have to tease these conflicts out into the open so we can deal with them. Psychoanalysis promises to do this.

Analysis involves getting at these unconscious dynamic forces, events, and conflicts so that the client can understand them (shake hands with yourself if you will) and then begin to make informed choices about how he or she wants to live life. Getting through the psychological defenses we have employed to avoid knowing what rotten things we wished or did or saw, is the work of therapy. To make conscious the unconscious is the primary goal of psychoanalysis.

To accomplish what many skeptics consider impossible, analysts use the techniques of free association and, sometimes, dream analysis.

Free association requires the client to assume a comfortable position, usually lying with his back to the analyst so that the client is free from distraction and can more easily let his thoughts flow. The client is encouraged to say exactly, and without inhibitions, what comes into his mind. The dimly lit room, relaxed position, and seemingly indifferent attitude of the therapist provide an atmosphere for the regression back in time to occur. What bubbles up from the unconscious during these sessions, it is argued, is what the analyst is interested in.

For the few analytic clients I've talked with, this is no easy task. Talking basically to themselves, clients often become frustrated and angry at the analyst for not saying much, if anything, in the course of an expensive hour. Analysts expect this; it is part of the therapy.

Dreams are considered a direct route to the unconscious, and, with a little experience, clients come to remember them. After some passage of time, interpretations are offered as to their significance and meaning— but only when the client is ready. The timing of interpretations is considered absolutely critical since they are viewed as the decisive step for drawing up something unconscious and making it conscious.

The client's relationship to the analyst is also considered vital, as it is in most therapies. But there is often a greater degree of attention directed toward how the client thinks and feels about the analyst since, as analysis progresses, the client will react to the analyst as if he or she *were* the overly critical father, indulgent mother, or whatever.

As a treatment, psychoanalysis is expensive in that it usually requires several sessions each week for a period of several years and costs a small fortune. If you hold with the notion that you get what you pay for, then psychoanalysis is the Cadillac of psychotherapy. But, like many other forms of therapy, the research that would prove the effectiveness of this approach over another approach simply does not exist—although psychoanalytic therapists and their clients can readily cite hundreds of examples of positive outcomes.

The final successful product of psychoanalysis is, even according to Freud himself, not a perfect psychological specimen. Rather, it is someone who understands himself better than most, does the best with what he has, and has the freedom to decide how he will live life. The ultimate goal is not so different from other therapies.

There are relatively few psychoanalysts in America, most of them in New York City. All therapists know the rudiments of the therapy and many use psychoanalytic techniques in their work. As outlined below, shorter forms of psychoanalysis are also practiced.

Other Forms of Psychoanalytic Therapy

Many of Freud's followers developed ideas of their own, elaborated on the Master's work, or split off in directions that even the founder of the "talking cure" could not have anticipated. These schools of thought and theory include the Neo-Freudians and those thousands of therapists who practice psychoanalytically oriented psychotherapy in one form or another.

Without elaborating on this fascinating history of the development of ideas on the nature of human behavior and what influences it, let us say that, for many reasons, followers of Freud sought more to change the emphasis and focus of his theory and practice than the rudiments of psychoanalytic theory itself.

The core belief that early experiences color the direction and degree of normal human development is not questioned. Neurosis is still believed to be rooted in infancy and childhood, but the role of culture and environment is also emphasized. In any event, these fine distinctions do not matter much to the average troubled person, unless he or she is quite sophisticated in psychology and the development of the variations of dynamic theory.

What is important, however, is that the Neo-Freudians and psychoanalytically oriented psychotherapists generally do not provide therapy in the classic mode. Rather, there is more likely a face-to-face interaction (sans couch), a shorter expected time frame for the therapy, less frequent consultations, and, therefore, less overall cost involved.

These analytically oriented therapists do, generally, use all or some of the same techniques: listening, talking (less so than some other kinds of therapists), interpretations, dream analysis, and so forth. And, of course, they would argue their goals for therapy are the same—to rid their clients of troublesome neurotic conflicts and problems.

Client-Centered Therapy

The basics of this extremely popular therapeutic approach (founded by Carl Rogers) are taught to practically all therapists. The primary underlying assumption is that all human beings have within them the capacity for personal growth which, if unobstructed, will result in each individual achieving his or her maximum potential to become a mature, responsible, self-sufficient adult.

The ultimate goal of this therapy is something called "self-actualization"—a kind of psychological state in which a person accepts himself for what he is, learns to feel good about himself, and is able to move forward in the pursuit of his personal freedom. There is nothing objectionable about these goals, and rarely anything objectionable about client-centered therapists.

Therapists from this school try to bring about this state of psychological health by providing a relaxed and warm atmosphere in which the client feels comfortable, understood, and totally accepted for what he is. Every attempt is made to make the client feel worthwhile. It is less important that the therapist understand what is wrong and more important that the client (through a process of having his thoughts and feelings reflected back to him from an objective observer), come to understand himself.

It would be very unusual for a client-centered therapist to do things like give advice, ask the client to practice, for instance, making friends, specify any particular action or habits in need of change, or in any way take a know-it-all attitude about what the client should do.

If, for example, you wish the therapist to write you a psychological prescription for what to do to improve your life, you are likely to go home empty-handed. Or, if you say you feel guilty about swearing at your mother, it would be against the client-centered therapist's approach to tell you you should or should not feel guilty.

His belief is that the feelings you express are *yours* and that understanding, clarifying, and coming to grips with them will lead to self-insight and psychological growth. In a word, the solution to whatever problems you may have is believed to lie within you, and it is the therapist's job to help you find the solution, not to offer one of his own design.

Cognitive Therapy

The word "cognitive" is a term that summarizes various ways of knowing and thinking. It encompasses the studies of perception, memory, reason, imagination, and judgment. As compared to feelings or emotions, cognition is that aspect of human intelligence we like to think separates us from the lower animals, and it is our rational behavior (or lack of it) that becomes the focus of these therapies.

The basic premise is that if people can think their way into problems, they can think their way out again. The approach assumes that our thinking is not always perfect and that, to the degree that it is illogical or faulty, we are more likely to do or believe stupid things to make us miserable.

For example, a client makes a statement that "nobody loves me" and because of this belief, he feels worthless, useless, and inconsequential. He avoids friends and family, doesn't want to go to work, and begins to squirrel himself away. As he withdraws from people, the evidence that "nobody loves me" mounts. In cognitive therapies, his "erroneous" belief will be challenged.

It is with some certainty that the therapist assumes someone at least likes him (maybe his wife, but surely his mother), and the therapist will set about to challenge the illogical conclusion the client has reached. The therapist must further assume his client hasn't all the facts—and that once the client's reality is shown to him, he will arrive at a new conclusion and get better.

It doesn't matter whether or not the therapist finds the client unlovable, only that the client be shown the defect in the logic used to reach an erroneous judgment. Directed to seek new information about how others see him and confronted with the unreasonable way in which he processes facts, the client may conclude that rather than being "unlovable" by everyone, only *some* people don't like the way he does *some* things, *some* of the time.

All of this is not to say cognitive therapies are exercises in pure reason and cold logic; rather that the primary focus is on how people think and how wrong thinking can lead to problems. In fact, cognitive therapies produce lots of feelings and these emotions are seen as the energy that propels change in the client's thoughts, beliefs, and attitudes.

Existential Therapy

Operating more from a philosophical position than a defined body of techniques anchored in a structured treatment strategy, existential therapists tackle the big questions we all face from time to time. Who am I? What is the meaning of my life? What place do I have in this indifferent universe?

The goal of existential therapy roughly is to try to assist the client to answer for himself these philosophical and sometimes spiritual questions. The answers or even the quest for the answers is assumed to lead to personal freedom and contentment with oneself. It is based on the premise that when we face our most basic fears (to live fully or die bravely), we are freed from that which torments us. In the process, it is hoped that the troubled client will learn to step back from his painful reality and see it from a perspective that permits him to accept what is, sometimes even with a sense of humor. A change in attitude is also a major goal of therapy.

The emphasis in existential therapy is on self-exploration and discovery, learning how one fits within the world of people and things, and seeing where living for others can make one a slave to expectations. Openness, candor, sharing thoughts and feelings, and becoming acutely aware and sensitive to the here and now, mark the therapy as one in which the relationship between the therapist and client, on a moment-to-moment basis, becomes the vehicle of change.

Because there are relatively few existential therapists and little is written that specifically describes their therapeutic interventions, I won't try to characterize them here. But, because of their emphasis on the basic humanity of all clients, the commonality in our existence, and the importance of living as best we can in the present, they operate much like client-centered and gestalt therapists.

Gestalt Therapy

The word "gestalt" is a German term meaning "form" or "figure" and, as it is used in the therapy business, translates into a type of therapy founded by Fritz Perls. Compared to most schools of psychotherapy, little has been written about gestalt therapy and, if you were to watch a gestalt therapist work, you might see why. Theory is less important than action. The therapist is spontaneous, creative, active. He operates from intuition and instinct rather than deliberate, planned actions.

The basic notion underlying the technique and practice of gestalt therapy is that people become divided against themselves, fractionated into bits and pieces that no longer fit together into a harmonic whole. As so many musical notes indiscriminately scattered about a blank sheet of music, there is no meaning or melody to their arrangement. The client cannot make music of his life and is seen as disorganized, at war with himself, and unable to express himself either in word or action.

The goal of gestalt therapy is to help the client integrate the parts of himself with which he is not in touch—his feelings, thoughts, fears, and physical self. The client is seen as blocked, stymied, out of touch with his senses, with others, and with himself. To grow in therapy and as a person, the client must acknowledge his self-alienation, his phoniness, his self-defeating games of living life in the past or future tense and make his way to a less obstructed present.

Gestalt therapy is usually conducted in a group setting, the therapist working with a single individual at a time but using the group as co-helpers and as a kind of human backdrop against which the client's behavior will change. The focus of the therapeutic conversation is on the here and now: What are we saying to each other? How are we saying it? Do our words match our feelings? rather than: What did I do (ancient history), What will I do (fantasy). The therapist pushes for the moment, for that immediate expression or interchange that is viewed as the best crucible in which change can occur.

To help clients gain a sense of authenticity and honesty, rules apply during the session which force the acceptance of personal responsibility. Group members are not allowed to gossip, to talk before or afterward about what happened during a session, and only what happens in a session is of importance.

Clients are coached to take responsibility for what they say, to stop manipulating others, to stop playing at being helpless, lost, or weak. Gestalt therapists assume clients are strong and capable, and confrontation about one's behavior should be expected.

Since much of the work of gestalt therapy is focused on the here and now, "thinking" about one's problems is discouraged. It is even seen as a handicap. Intellectualizing one's problems is viewed as a barrier between the person and his senses, and special attention is given to facial expression, posture, and gestures. In recent years, there has been a blend of gestalt therapy with massage, physical restructuring, and other touching therapies, all in an effort to fully integrate the client within himself.

Hypnotherapy

Not formally a school of psychotherapy, hypnosis is gaining popularity and is used by all kinds of therapists. While a great deal could be written about hypnosis, I will only highlight its usual applications and caution you to be absolutely certain that any therapist who provides hypnosis or hypnotherapy has impeccable professional credentials.

A powerful form of influencing human behavior and probably greatly underutilized by professional therapists, hypnotherapy is also the shell game of therapy charlatans—"now you see the symptom, now you don't." Anyone who can read and has a modicum of common sense can acquire the hypnotic techniques to induce trances but, like firing a pistol, it's easy to pull the trigger but oh so difficult to hit your target.

Hypnotherapists, or therapists who employ hypnotic techniques within their practice, tend to focus on suggestions to remove specific symptoms or revive painful memories. To help the client deal with the emotional charges associated with such recollections, hypnosis is also used as an effective method of inducing relaxation to combat anxiety.

Well-trained and responsible therapists do not offer hypnosis, hypnoanalysis, or hypnotherapy as the end-all to emotional or psychological problems, and anyone who does should be suspect. Hypnosis, like aspirin, won't cure anything, but qualified therapists who are skilled in hypnotic methods have one more tool with which to help their clients.

Eclectic Therapy

"Eclectic" (meaning a combination of many things) when used to describe a form of therapy means employing a variety of techniques and approaches from many schools of psychotherapy. The idea is to use the best methods from each school so as to provide the client with a dynamite therapy program.

A couple of things need to be understood about eclectic therapy— partly because most young therapists say that's what they do (it's in vogue) and partly because it can be very confusing to the client should he or she have the misfortune to meet up with what I will call the "chameleon" counselor.

Fifteen or twenty years ago any therapist who said he was eclectic was generally considered, at best, to be poorly trained, lacking any sound theoretical understanding about anything, and, at worst, an undisciplined fool. Older men in the field thought this way because there was a good deal of rivalry and cultism between the major schools of psychotherapy. This is still true today but being eclectic is much more acceptable.

Because of a growing lack of reverence for authority, and the failure of research to favor one kind of psychotherapy over another, most university students in training to be therapists feel quite free to adopt whatever they choose from the various methods available. When asked in their first job interview to characterize their therapy approach, most of them say "eclectic." This eclecticism makes it very difficult to nail them down about how they conduct therapy interviews. And, for the client, it may sometimes be tough to figure out what the therapist is about, which leads me to the chameleon counselor.

The chameleon counselor changes his ideas willy-nilly. Having little real depth of understanding of human behavior, he is constantly in search of the "true" therapy which will succeed with the clients he wants so badly to help. Further, he seems to have the idea that he must and should succeed with every single client, and that to do less is a total failure. Moreover, people should get well quickly. Each book he reads, workshop or seminar he attends, fills him with new ideas and the hope of becoming a successful healer. One can speculate that these therapists (most are young) are insecure about their work and/or themselves. They can be a blight on a client.

From a client's point of view, this therapist is a constantly changing light-show of language, terms, concepts, and actions that renders making sense of therapy next to impossible. Some have argued that one of the most effective ingredients in successful therapy is the fact that the therapist is consistent, week after week, month after month. A therapist who flip-flops in his ideas and suggestions can make it very tough on a person who's having the same problem with his own decision-making.

On the other hand, some clients are seekers and never seem to tire of trying different therapies. They even have a willingness to experiment with almost anything new. A friend of mine conducts what he calls his "gimmick group"—a group therapy session for people who want to experiment with the newly developing therapies. It is an anything-goes setting and the customers (as he calls them) seem to like it.

In fact, probably most therapists use more than one approach and no knowledgeable expert in the field would dispute that there is a great overlap of techniques in what happens in offices of professional therapists. It may be that the eclectic therapists, compared to the faithful of some schools of psychotherapy, are more willing to admit that they don't have pat answers to people's problems, but are willing to try whatever works. There is nothing wrong with a therapist being eclectic, especially if he has a few gray hairs and seems to be more practical than speculative.

Behavioral Therapy

The basic assumption in behavioral therapies is that the majority of problems people encounter in life and identify as personal weaknesses, faults, or fears constitute learned responses or unfortunate habits. These learned responses persist because some payoff (reinforcement) follows the occurrence of the bad habit. After whining unsuccessfully for an ice cream, little Tommy throws a tantrum. Mother unwittingly picks him up to comfort him and the next day, he throws two tantrums. Soon he is throwing tantrums all the time because the behavior is reinforced and little Tommy is getting his way about all sorts of things. He learns to be a brat.

The job of the behavioral therapist is to analyze the habit patterns of his clients, to try to understand what sorts of rewards are maintaining the behavior the client wishes to quit. Once he knows what these are he will attempt, with the aid of the client, to change the reward system and the unwanted habits.

For example, if every time a woman's husband is late coming home, she begins to feel anxious and worried, and a trip to the refrigerator for a snack makes her feel better, she may begin to gain weight. Her habit of eating when she is alone leads to obesity and later to depression and guilt about being overweight. The behavioral therapist will study the chain of events, offer an explanation as to how she learned the habit of snacking, and suggest a course of action to alter and gain control of the harmful behavior. He might suggest relaxing to music instead of finishing off a pumpkin pie, taking up a rewarding social activity instead of a ham sandwich, and so forth.

This is an admittedly simpleminded example, and behavioral therapists have developed a wide variety of highly sophisticated techniques to deal with all kinds of problems, ranging from sleep disturbances to thought control, to phobias, depressions, and on down the list of so-called neurotic disturbances.

The major focus of the behavioral therapist, however, will be on changing the behavior as it is expressed in undesirable habits. It is believed that since most behavior is learned, it can be unlearned. There will be less attention paid to how the woman feels about her husband coming home late, or the kind of shape the marriage might be in. The underlying causes for emotional problems are seldom explored (except as they have a history of having been learned), and "why" someone does what they do is seen as irrelevant to bringing about therapeutic change.

Therefore, if you are seeking an explanation as to what unconscious forces are at work, what hidden motives may be impelling you to do things you want to stop doing, the behavioral therapist is going to be disappointing. As a rule, he is short on complicated theoretical explanations for human behavior and long on pragmatic methods for helping people change. When questioned, he is likely to tell our obese woman that she feels depressed *because* she is overweight, not that she is overweight because she feels depressed.

This view that bad feelings follow bad behavior (not the other way around) more than anything else sets behavioral therapists apart from their colleagues and other schools of psychotherapy. Behavioral therapists will tend to be active rather than passive, and will often ask the client to keep records of his or her behavior, make homework asssignments, and generally work as teachers and coaches in a reeducational approach to problem-solving.

Which Is Best?

The kinds of therapies listed here include some but not all of what is available. Because it takes only a small following of true believers to launch a new school of psychotherapy, it is impossible to catalog what's happening all around the country.

Some experts have expressed concern about the rapid increase in approaches to therapy, claiming most of them have no scientific basis in terms of proving their effectiveness and that the public has little more than testimonials on which to base the decision to enter a particular treatment. Also, even within established schools of therapy, effectiveness studies are few and far between (with the notable exception of client-centered therapy as developed by Carl Rogers), and almost nowhere can you find useful, direct comparisons between any two kinds of therapy.

Again, you as the consumer must make the most informed choice you can. How well you fit with the therapist in terms of feeling comfortable, respected, and understood remains the most critical factor. A therapist whose credentials are the envy of his colleagues and who has enough degrees to paper a barn door isn't worth one minute of your time if you feel you can't trust him.

6

Marriage Counseling, Family Therapy, and Group Therapy

MARRIAGE COUNSELING

When two people choose to share the rent they become a couple; sometimes nowadays they even get married. No matter how much they love each other they have problems like bath towels—his, hers, and ours. If one or both describes a problem as an "ours" problem and they can't seem to solve it together, they may consider getting outside help. This chapter has to do with that help—call it marriage counseling, marital therapy, or couples therapy.

First, a relationship is defined as much by its intensity as by a license and a marriage certificate. And, since many couples choose to live together without being officially sanctioned by church or state, what follows applies as much to them as to those of us upholding the tradition of duly recognized bondage.

In this section, I hope to outline some of the problems all couples face, when those problems warrant professional attention, what the therapy is like, and what you might expect should you make an appointment. But first, a word about the institution of marriage.

A lot of people today think that they are permanently married when they stand up in front of friends and family and repeat vows that, in that most solemn moment, they have every intention of keeping. Almost half of them are wrong.

Having made this once-in-a-lifetime commitment (who thinks about their next husband or wife while standing at the altar?), how, some weeks, months, or even years later, could either member of this once happy couple quit? No matter how I searched for explanations for divorce, I could not find an accounting that would make sense for everyone and, in my research, I was relieved to note that no one else had either. It seems there are as many ways to be married (miserable or happy) as there are ways to be in this world. Since most people are bound and determined to pair up (despite the mortality figures), and no one seems to be trying to talk people out of the institution, I guess we who take the risk are going to be stuck with someone at least as imperfect as ourselves.

Given that marriages are breaking like eggshells under the wheels of social change, single people are skittery about getting married. They're waiting longer to get married, experimenting by living together before tieing the knot, and generally stalling what seems to be, in the end, the inevitable. But people are getting married in droves—once, twice, three times.

Almost every month someone you know is getting a divorce or ought to. They're dropping like flies. The faltering state of marriage and family has become the focus of a troubled nation, some think the first symptom of a society's final illness.

For those who do get divorced, the dust and tears barely settle before you find yourself warning a friend to wait "at least a year, Roger, give yourself time." But Roger marries again anyway, and you cross your fingers. People don't seem to learn, they do it again and again.

Divorce statistics that make marriage counselors shudder don't faze starry-eyed teenagers. The kids honeymoon in Las Vegas, where their odds of winning a million dollars are little worse than those they face as a couple who will celebrate twenty-five years together.

Besides the yet-to-be married, the living together "as ifs," and the newlyweds, thousands of married couples stay together for better or for worse, with emphasis on the latter. They may keep their vows to honor and obey in a grim, loveless relationship, biting the bullet for the duration. Or they may share the burden of an unhappy marriage by studying geometry—building love triangles or even rectangles with people they pray will always be strangers to their spouses. Either way their lives seem unfulfilled, yet they stay married. There must, then, be something to this unique intimacy between a man and a woman—how else could you account for all this foolishness?

I don't have an answer, but because so many people get married, get disappointed, and find it hard to stay together, the marriage counseling business is booming. Like other therapies, it lacks a cohesive theory, scientific validation, or even extensive proof that it works. But this isn't slowing people down. And while we therapists don't know everything about how to help troubled couples, we do know a few things.

What follows, then, is one therapist's view (biased) about some of the causes of marital distress, concerns people have when reaching out for help, and the stumbling blocks they are likely to encounter should they choose this therapy option.

Marriage—A Crap Shoot

Getting married is always a package deal. When you stand up and promise to accept someone, you usually know there are a few items you could do without, but because you're love-struck, you're willing to overlook these little imperfections—at least for the time being. We all want to believe that love can conquer all or, as some interpret this, "my love can change the one I love." As a wife told me (her husband complained she was a relentless nag), "I thought I could grind off his rough edges over the years."

The great romantic movie that couples take starring roles in at the altar may enjoy a few reruns but, in time, fantasy fades and reality sets in. The hard work of making it as a couple becomes inescapable and the adjustments necessary to live together successfully unavoidable. Couples can and do still love each other, even romantically, but let's face it, mutual adoration and selfless devotion are rare.

Most newlyweds profess a willingness to die for each other. Later, they're not even willing to risk minor injury. What areas of life together, then, must be negotiated if couples are to feel about each other the way they did in Act I, Scene I?

In no order of importance, couples argue (fight, squabble, disagree, take your choice) about sex, money, children, friends, in-laws, careers, religion, leisure time, and every other imaginable topic that affects both of them, including the color they paint the spare bedroom. This is as it should be. I have yet to meet a couple (in trouble or not) who didn't differ on one or more of these topics.

The couples who don't seem to make it through together, over the hurdles and around the obstacles, seem to have lost or never had a couple of critical skills—the ability to communicate and the willingness to compromise.

"We can't communicate" is a common complaint couples present. In fact, people who say they can't communicate are doing so very well. You cannot *not* communicate. Communication is not necessarily plain spoken English.

For example, are the following people communicating?

After he makes a play for her at dinner, she goes to bed early with two aspirins.

He comes home late from an office party, having forgotten their anniversary.

He makes plans to go fishing for the weekend, knowing relatives from Ohio are due Saturday.

Of course they're communicating, they're just not talking. As a method of communication, talking is not even very reliable. Humans are notorious for saying things they don't mean (including and sometimes especially "I love you"), and often the *way* they say something means more than what they said.

"I do care about you," he snarled.

"I'd do anything to save our marriage," she sighed, filing her nails.

The point is that problematic communication is a constitutional human ailment, and couples cannot avoid the malady. Open, honest, clear, and congruent talk is a treasure and just because there isn't a lot of it going around in a marriage doesn't mean people are not communicating. The problem is usually more that the way in which people do so is ineffective, inefficient, misunderstood, or misinterpreted.

When couples find they can't talk together about important matters, these matters get shelved. In my own work with couples, I often use the metaphor that a marriage is like a big house, with many rooms and many doors. Behind each door is a topic of vital concern to the couple (how to raise the kids, what to do about Grandma, should he change jobs, should she go back to school, etc.), and the doors to these rooms must be kept open.

As couples are different people with different views, values, and histories, they will have different opinions about how these issues should be handled. If they communicate badly and their discussions deteriorate into arguments, complete with hostility, shouting, and tears, they may find some of these vital topics not worth the agony of controversy. A door gets closed.

Often couples agree not to talk about things so they won't hurt each other and, while these agreements may be unspoken, the doors get closed all the same. No longer can the couple talk about her mother, his job, Johnny's grades, their sex life, and so forth. One by one, the doors in the big house are closed and the key turned. In time, the couple finds itself locked out of every room except the kitchen, and the most significant interaction of the day is "Please pass the butter."

The marriage functions, but barely. Each feels alone, isolated, unable to reach out to give or get comfort. They wonder why they are married.

What communications still exist are either hostile or innocuous—the latter cordial because it is necessary to keep at least the kitchen open.

When couples get into this fix, there is little willingness to compromise. Concessions are interpreted as confessions. Trade-offs become unthinkable. Each is fearful the other will give no quarter if a truce is sought. Caught in a stalemate, neither is willing to risk being hurt. Healing cannot occur. But, despite their agreement to a standoff, sooner or later something will happen that forces open one of these closed doors, and they will be obliged to examine their marriage.

I once worked with a couple who had been married for twenty years and, except for a two-week honeymoon together in Hawaii, had been fighting with cold war tactics ever since. With their only daughter about to leave home, their excuse for staying together was no longer valid. "Our relationship has been civil," said the husband. "Now we both want more." The glue that had kept them together was going off to college. They had to turn their marriage (and themselves) inside out to find reasons to go on together. Grudgingly at first, each was willing to compromise and eventually they worked things out.

I often ask couples early in our sessions to take a few moments to consider what in themselves they are willing to change, what grievances they are willing to forget, what transgressions on the part of their spouses they're willing to forgive. I don't care what it is and I don't even need to know. They don't need to tell each other what it is either. What I hope happens is that each person understands that they individually, personally, and privately must make a decision to do something to help the marriage, and that they must take responsibility for that decision.

I believe most therapists working with couples do something similar, something to shift the responsiblity for change where it belongs—onto the people in the marriage.

In this vein, I would strongly suggest that before you begin marriage counseling, you need to ask yourself what *you* are willing to give up or change. If the answer is absolutely nothing, then an appointment with an attorney makes better sense.

One other problem couples complain about needs mentioning. This is the old "he outgrew me," or "she's not the same woman I married" theme. There's no getting around it, people change. If they didn't, they'd be pretty dull potatoes.

What seems to upset couples is not so much that their partner is maturing, growing, expanding their horizons, but that all this progress is leaving them behind. Behind what? The discontented members of the couples seem to view themselves as having missed the train or that they never even had the tickets. Again, you need to ask yourself, whose fault is

this? Isn't it too simple to blame your partner for what you have neglected to do for yourself?

To sum up, one could ask, is marriage a crap shoot? The answer is yes,
probably, more or less. What follows is some information about when
things are bad enough to think about getting help—before you roll
snake-eyes.

When to Get Help

As a rule, most couples start therapy too late. I always know I'm in
trouble with a couple when one of them has stopped by the attorney's
office on the way to the appointment. In my experience, many attorneys
openly discourage reconciliation (it may have something to do with collecting a fee), and I am less than optimistic when one spouse has made a
down payment on a divorce action. I figure the most I might be able to
do is rearrange the deck chairs on a doomed ship.

There are several reasons why couples wait too long, sometimes until
it's too late. First, no one wants to admit they've botched the most important relationship in their life. And, even if one spouse is ready to
admit the couple needs outside help, the other isn't—"You're the one
who needs help, not me!"

Second, it takes two people at the therapist's office to make a marriage
counseling session. If one spouse refuses to go, the other's courage is
likely to fail. It takes considerable guts to define your problems as marital
in the first place, but to go alone, outside the marriage, to a total stranger
and itemize your complaints can put what's left of the trust between you
and your spouse in real jeopardy. Things may be bad at home, but they
could become unbearable when you return from the appointment. Getting cold feet is often the better part of valor.

Third, since seeking outside help is at best a tough decision, and one
person probably won't want to go, talking about seeing a counselor often
leads to yet another argument. Since the couple can't agree about much
anyway, conflict about getting help is almost predictable. The ability to
communicate and the willingness to compromise are already in bad
shape, and couples often end the quarrel about "seeing someone" by
closing one more door in their troubled house.

Lastly, bringing in a marriage counselor may lead to divorce. If, in the
context of therapy, conflicts cannot be resolved, the more distressed
member of the couple may decide to call it quits. And although the therapy was effective in clarifying reality, the reality is unacceptable and the
couple splits.

However, when the pain becomes sharp enough, couples do reach out
for help. Just what that pain threshold might be is impossible to define

precisely, but in my experience there are several signs and symptoms that, if ignored, can lead to separation and divorce. Couples therapy may not help, but it might, and even though we all have our own ideas about what a marriage should be, most people will agree the following signals mean something is wrong.

1. One or more of the children is having serious problems and the parents quarrel about how the child should be handled.

2. Communication between the partners is almost always sarcastic and hostile.

3. Arguments about anything have led to physical fighting (slaps, punches, shoves, etc.).

4. Unresolved sexual problems.

5. The word separation or divorce enters the conversation (or even if one person is thinking about these alternatives as a solution).

6. Things have gotten so untenable that one spouse leaves home, even temporarily.

7. One or the other of the couple is thinking about an affair or has done more than think about it. If you want your marriage to make it, it's a good idea to find a therapist before you find a lover.

8. One spouse becomes depressed or withdrawn or sullen or begins drinking excessively or feels insecure and unable to talk to his or her mate about the marriage.

9. The moment a couple agrees they have a problem together and don't know how to change the way they're treating each other.

10. Any time someone in the marriage begins consistently to avoid the other. Spending long hours away from home to avoid conflict, willingly taking jobs or obligations that keep one away from home, hiding out in the den every night, taking (as one lady did) tranquilizers and romance novels to her bedroom every night after dinner to escape her husband.

This problem list hardly exhausts the possibilities and is not meant to be inclusive. Also, couples with average or better than average marriages where none of these things have happened might decide they just want to improve things, enrich their relationship via counseling.

But I want to underscore one point—it only takes one member of a pair to read the signals that help is needed and, if that happens, it is sufficient cause for action.

Therapy Expectations

Many couples are disappointed with their experience in marriage counseling. The reasons for this seem, to me at least, to lie in what I would call magical expectations on the part of people seeking help.

Despite their professional humility and meager tools, marriage counselors are often thought capable of working miracles. They are viewed as omniscient, powerful authority figures who somehow have access to secret formulas that can turn unhappy marriages into blissful ones. This expectation, I assure you, is a false one, and if a therapist believes he is as extraordinary as his clients want him to be, the therapy and the couple are headed for trouble.

For example, many couples begin the first session with a litany of complaints about the other guy—apparently on the premise that when the full indictment is read, the therapist will be convinced that the complainer is a saint and the one complained about a villain. Then the villain takes the stand and, lo and behold, the evidence points to the one who led off.

This pattern of mutual blaming and fault-finding is about standard for opening sessions and if the therapist accepts the role of judge, everyone's in deep trouble. I once worked with a couple where both were attorneys. They had developed their evidentiary proceedings to a high art. Halfway through the first session, I had to tell them my office was not a court of appeals and that while they were impressive in their arguments, I couldn't pass any final judgment except to say they were both right and probably deserved each other. We had a good laugh and the responsibility for change was put where it belonged—on them.

Disappointment also occurs in what I would call shotgun marriage counseling. The couple arrives at the office, one smiling, the other grimacing as if I were a hanging judge. I suspect the one grimacing has a gun poking in his ribs, and I can imagine the one holding the gun thinking, "I got him here, Doc, now you tell him what a rat he is."

The gun toter is always disappointed. Experienced marriage counselors never side entirely with one spouse and, if anything, go out of their way to make the person forced into therapy more comfortable and less defensive. While you can certainly lever your spouse into therapy (announce you're leaving, throw him out, or use some other threat), you would be wrong to assume the therapist is going to use the same tactics to try to help the both of you.

Finally, couples (or at least one member) often seek out a therapist to say a few words over a deceased marriage. One or both have already decided the relationship is dead and that what remains to be done is to hire an official to pronounce it so. "We tried everything," they explain to friends and family, "we even went to a marriage counselor."

This face-saving maneuver is such a common occurrence in the offices of marriage counselors that, for the therapist to save face, he renames the work he is doing "divorce counseling." This is not to say that counseling around the issues of an agreed-upon divorce isn't valuable, it is just to point out that the assumed goal of two people entering the office of a marriage counselor may have nothing to do with salvaging a marriage. But if you are entering therapy with the sincere desire to make your relationship work, say so—up front and out loud. Your spouse needs to hear it and so does the therapist. Therapists work hard where hope is explicit.

Goals

Other than keeping a relationship together, what goals might people have when they begin couples therapy? There is no simple answer—for our own unique reasons, we all want different things. Certainly we all want to hurt less, to be respected, to be loved and comforted, and to have at least some of our needs met by the person with whom we share our life. And most of us would like to be as happy as the happiest couple we know.

As in any kind of therapy, it is critical that some goal or goals be talked about, defined, and mutually understood by everyone involved in the therapy. In working with couples, setting up goals is often the grist of therapy and the focal point around which much of the work is done. It is rare that couples agree about what makes an ideal marriage or even what they want in their relationship. It is this disparity between what is and what "should be" that leads to disappointment and discouragement.

I often ask couples how much happiness they expect in their marriage—fifty percent, sixty percent, seventy percent and so on. As one man put it, "My folks fought all the time. I'd be content if half of my days with Susan were happy ones."

Susan, on the other hand, pointed out that her parents got along wonderfully and she expected to be happy ninety-five percent of the time. Her husband looked shocked.

"Really?" he said. "I never knew that. Hell, I thought we were doing fine when we only argued on weekends!"

The point is, our ideas of what constitutes a successful marriage stem more from our experience as the children of married people than from our memories of Ozzie and Harriet or Beaver's mom and dad. Try as we might to be happier than our folks, we are likely to expect no more in our marriage than our parents got from theirs. And unless we come from identical families, our fantasies about married life are not likely to be the same.

These differences in expectations, some conscious and some not so conscious, need to be explored and shared, preferably before getting married, but at least after the honeymoon. Once married and after the first ugly argument, it becomes very difficult to communicate and compromise about some issue on your spouse's hidden agenda. We all have "if only" wishes (if only he would stop this, if only she would remember that, etc.), and we usually don't talk plainly about what we want from each other. Therapy should help you get these hidden agendas out on the table.

Almost always what people want from each other requires the other person to change. And, since change isn't particularly easy, asking and being asked to be different is usually less than comfortable.

Not to say what it is you want from a relationship is to keep your spouse in the dark. "I can't seem to please her" and "I don't know what he wants from me" are examples of the kind of blind grope we put our loved ones through, hoping that if they stumble on the right solution and give us what we need it will somehow "prove" they love us.

Finally, it does not matter particularly what goals are finally hashed out in therapy, but they must be hashed out. People work best together who have a clear vision of the future and how they will try to get there.

The Therapy

After one or both halves of a couple decide they want to see a therapist about their marriage, one will call for an appointment. The therapist will ask a few questions to get the lay of the land and gather enough information to decide if an appointment is appropriate. If one spouse is refusing to come in, occasionally the therapist will agree to call the reluctant spouse—but not with much enthusiasm.

After introductions, most first sessions begin with the therapist explaining how he knows what he knows—who called him, what they talked about, and generally what was said. This is all done in an effort to let the couple know he is open-minded and still unbiased.

The therapist, depending on his style, will then ask the couple how they see things, what the problems are, what they've tried in the past by way of solving these problems, and, at some juncture, ask each for some personal history and background.

Often therapists will explain confidentiality and its limits, how he works with couples, and what he expects of them. He is not particularly interested in establishing a psychiatric diagnosis for each person, but rather will focus on how the couple relates, how they talk to each other, how they hurt or protect each other, and will try to determine the kind of motivation each has to be there, as well as the probable commitment each has to seeking help.

Most marriage therapists see themselves as consultants, hired to advise, suggest, question for clarity, coach, and even instruct couples on how to solve their own problems. They also believe the only workable solutions that will stand the test of time must come from the couple—not from the therapist. Because of this position, couples are often frustrated by the therapist redirecting the conversation back to a dialogue between the couple.

Susan: "Charles has been angry with me for weeks."
Charles: "She's right, and she knows why I was mad."
Therapist: "I wonder if the two of you could talk to each other about what happened."
Susan: "That's just it, we can't talk to each other."
Therapist: "I understand, but I'd like you to try. Give it a go."

This kind of transaction is very common and, in the begining, an irritating experience for couples. Still, if the couple is to learn to communicate successfully they must learn to face each other and begin talking.

As the sessions continue, the therapist tries to help the couple learn to speak for themselves. "He thinks I'm unresponsive," or "She knows I really love her" are examples of people speaking for each other by way of a mysterious process called mind reading. It's amazing how well couples believe they can read each other's thoughts and feelings. That they're wrong much or most of the time has a lot to do with their feeling misunderstood by their mates. Any time you think you know what someone else is thinking, you're taking a big gamble. Therapists are savvy to this problem and will usually discourage couples from analyzing each other's motives via clairvoyance.

It is practically impossible for marriage counselors to avoid siding with one or the other of a couple, at least momentarily, during the course of therapy. Absolute objectivity and neutrality is a myth. The candid therapist will acknowledge this dilemma to his clients and try to give assurance that while he may appear allied more with one than the other at some time, his ultimate goal is the same as theirs—helping the marriage. Experienced and competent therapists invite concerns about perceived bias because they know if one spouse feels outnumbered, the therapy will fail and the fees stop.

A marriage counselor has to be one sex or the other. If the therapist is a man, the wife may feel she is being double-teamed, and if the therapist is a woman, the husband may think "women always stick together in these things."

The only way out of this fix is to hire a man-woman team (which is done, especially in sex therapy) or admit it isn't a perfect world and rely on openness and candor. Cost inhibits the hiring of male-female teams and there aren't many around anyway. Therapy can't go far wrong if the therapist and the couple feel free to talk about possible bias and prejudice as they go along. But it would be foolhardy for an opposite-sex client automatically to assume that the therapist is totally objective about sex roles all of the time.

Couples are usually seen together, but either member may request an individual session and often the therapist will suggest splitting the hour or meeting with each of them individually. There may be many reasons for this and the usual ones include giving each spouse a chance to talk about things they are afraid to bring up in a joint session. Also, the therapist may want to get a more historical perspective on each individual member.

If the therapist doesn't make it explicit, you should ask if any individual session is completely confidential. It should be, but be sure you and the therapist *and your spouse* understand the rules for any individual sessions. Courts have held that what transpires between the therapist and the couple is not protected by statutes of privileged communication, but that what the therapist and the client talk about in an individual session is.

Quitting Too Soon

Many couples cancel their second or third appointment and drop out of therapy before much of anything has been accomplished. They may not have been interested in making the marriage work, lacked the energy necessary, were disillusioned when the therapist failed to side with them, or were disappointed that no sure-fire advice or ironclad promise was made that things would get better. For some, there just wasn't enough magic. For others, the therapist seemed silly or ineffective or prejudiced and no working alliance was established.

Therapists may be all of these things (or worse), but regardless of the reasons, people often quit marriage counseling before it starts. I'm not sure who's to blame (an inept therapist or an unmotivated couple) and I'm sure it doesn't matter except that the net result is a failure experience for the couple. If at all possible, try to hang in there for four or five sessions before writing therapy off as a bad idea.

If you and your spouse concur that the therapist isn't being helpful, that is hardly a reason to discount all marriage counseling; maybe you should try again with someone else. At least you will have agreed about something.

How Much Time and Money

How long a couple stays in therapy is a three-way negotiation. Since either member of a couple can quit at any time, the first session can be the last or the therapy can go on for more than a year. Sometimes, if the work is stalled and the couple isn't putting in much effort, the therapist may suggest a break in therapy, termination, or referral to another marriage counselor.

Many times a great deal can be accomplished in as few as six sessions, other times little headway is noticeable after a year. Since marriages arrive at the therapist's office in various states of disarray, it takes varying amounts of time to help couples get things back in order. As with other kinds of therapy, couples and their therapists should be reviewing their work together, assessing progress or the lack of it, and be continually alert as to how things are going.

The cost of marriage counseling will vary with the setting: private practitioners have the highest fees, counseling agencies and mental health centers take what they can get, and many qualified pastors, priests, and clergymen work for a minimal or no fee (they apparently get their rewards later).

Many see the fees they pay a marriage counselor as excessive. This has always seemed odd to me. A man I once worked with blanched when I stated my fees to him and his wife. They drove away in a Mercedes and left for a two-week "second honeymoon" in an effort to work out their problems after that first session. I later learned he drank up twice the fee each week trying to cope with his pain while she spent hundreds of dollars on shopping sprees trying to forget how miserable she felt.

By the time you've reached a marriage counselor, you've already blown thousands of dollars on the relationship—a few hundred more doesn't seem excessive to protect your investment.

Finding a Marriage Counselor

Not every therapist who hangs out a shingle is a marriage counselor or couples therapist. Check out the therapist's credentials, how much experience and training he or she has had working with marriages, and don't be timid about asking questions.

An untrained therapist is a threat to your marriage, and it would be a serious mistake to put you and the one you love (at least a little) into the hands of someone who might aggravate the situation. Of those couples who complete marriage counseling, about two-thirds are happy with the results, about twenty-five percent see no change and the rest, less than ten percent, report the marriage is worse. It seems then that the odds are with you. The odds improve if you happen to be mature, know how to give and take and respect each other. The odds rise sharply in your favor if you get an early start and both people are determined to make the marriage work.

Finally, most people who go through the agony of a divorce wish they had tried harder to make a go of their marriage. In their desolation and loneliness, and faced with the prospects of starting over with someone else or not starting over at all, some wish they had even tried marriage counseling.

FAMILY THERAPY

Families begin as couples, usually in love with each other. They learn to accommodate, to adapt, to adjust and then, just when John is comfortable with Mary's habit of forgetting to set the alarm and Mary can sleep through John's snoring, somebody gets pregnant and they have to start all over again. What was stable gets destabilized. Where there were two, now there are three, and the problems seem multiplied by four.

When little Scott starts school things change again. Jane is born, more changes. Scott gets a bad report card and Mother starts to worry. Dad changes jobs. Scott seems to be straightening out. Mother gets bored and spoils Jane. Suddenly, Scott gets sent home from the sixth grade for sticking a cigarette in his nose and lighting it. Mother blames Dad for not spending more time with Scott. Dad counters with an accusation that Jane is a demanding, selfish pill because Mother can't set limits. The children are busy playing off one parent against the other. Wondering if they've fallen out of love, the usual arguments flare into confrontations. People are crying in their rooms, pillows are getting pounded. Sullenness is rampant.

Is this unusual? No. Is family therapy indicated? If a flag of truce cannot be honored and the problems worked out, maybe.

Most often, initiating family therapy is the therapist's idea—rarely do people call a clinic or therapist to ask for an appointment for the entire family. The most typical sequence of events is that someone outside the family (school, church, juvenile court) has labeled Scott as disturbed, troubled, emotionally sick. Since most people think Mother is to blame, Mother gets the call. (How many times does the teacher call about little Freddy and ask for *Mr.* Jones?) Mother, then, in her role as caretaker for the family, reaches out for help. She may or may not consult with Father.

If Mother calls a psychiatrist or psychologist or any professional therapist without training or experience in family therapy, the therapist is likely to begin with the premise that the family has a child who needs fixing, and set out a course of therapy in which the child remains the identified patient. He will probably interview the mother, sometimes the father, but most of the therapy will be directed toward the child. Mother may also get some therapy, but Dad is often forgotten.

I've spoken with several adults whose parents took them to a therapist when they were young. Frequently, the parents were not considered to be contributing to the problem and were not seen in the therapy. Often the therapy was not effective.

When Is Family Therapy Indicated?

The following circumstances strongly suggest the need for an evaluation for possible family therapy.

1. A child or adolescent is having significant problems.
2. The parents are getting along so poorly everyone is suffering— Johnny runs away, Mary stops eating, Martha begins bedwetting.
3. A child is being neglected or abused.
4. Either parent is preoccupied with family troubles, so much so he or she can't work or play or relax.
5. Any recent or serious stress that has caused a family crisis they can't seem to move beyond—an illness, a birth, a death, Grandma moves in, Dad loses his job, and so forth.
6. A member of the family requires psychiatric hospitalization.

Although this is not an exhaustive list, these are the major crises that bring people into family therapy. However, any time a member of a family sees a problem faced by himself or anyone in the family as a "family issue," then at least an initial family evaluation is in order.

Family therapy has also been used for many specific problems, including drug abuse, alcoholism, gambling, incest, delinquency, and others. Often groups of families are seen together to learn how to cope with common problems. Again, this is usually on referral and sometimes is available from self-help organizations. Sometimes a combination of family therapy and group therapy for a troubled member of the family (like Alanon and Alcoholics Anonymous) are available to a troubled family.

How Family Therapists See Families

Family therapists assume families are structured in some meaningful way. They see boundaries, power arrangements, alliances, trust relationships, subsystems, communication patterns, and all see the family as a group, the members of which behave as an intricate and complex unit.

A family is seen as a structure whose balance is critical and, like those old playground merry-go-rounds where you needed someone opposite you to keep the thing spinning on its spindle, family members work and play together so that the whole unit goes around and around and forward through time. If someone has a serious problem and can't play, goes away to school, deserts or dies or gets sick or for any reason steps off the family merry-go-round, the balance is temporarily lost and everyone feels wobbly. And if they can't keep up the momentum or change positions to keep balance, the smooth circling slows, teeters, trembles, and comes to a halt. The family can be in trouble.

Since almost all families face the same problems, family therapists quickly recognize certain familiar struggles: birth of children, someone needing to grow up and away, fighting with in-laws, Mother takes a job, Dad retires, and the like. They know that if the family's balance is to be maintained, there will have to be shifts, changes in relationships, and a need for renegotiating how things will be in the future. Goodwill and clear communications are critical and family therapists emphasize these in their practice.

Family therapists also know that families, as we've known them for the last couple of hundred years, are under attack by forces beyond their control. Father as the sole breadwinner and Mother at home in the kitchen minding the apple pie and keeping an eye on the cradle are fast becoming part of a dated Norman Rockwell view of modern family life. The women's movement, experimentation in communal living, house-husbands, the mass media, daycare, peer group demands, and the constant push and pull of a changing society have forced family therapists to view families as entities caught in a period of cultural transition.

Since all families are trying to adapt to these forces of change, the family therapist cannot measure a given family against an idealized version of what families "should be" but rather has to take them as they are. A therapist has to view a family as a unit in a swiftly changing culture that, within itself, must go through certain developmental stages that will require internal adjustments, negotiations, and restructuring. Where he can, he will try to keep the merry-go-round going. "Nobody is doing what they're supposed to," lamented a middle-aged father about his wife and children. "They've all jumped the tracks."

The Therapy

As with all kinds of therapy, family therapy is an approach, a method, a collection of techniques woven together with largely untested theories and supported by few solid facts. Research on effectiveness is sparce. The standards for how family therapy should be conducted are nonexistent.

But among the therapists who advocate the approach, you can find plenty who will argue it's the greatest boon to helping people since aspirin.

Simply put, family therapy can be any counseling provided to two or more members of a family where the functioning of its members is the focus. If the problems expressed are almost exclusively between Mom and Dad, it's called marriage counseling, even though some experts feel that any time you work to improve a marriage, any children are likely to be affected.

Family therapy can be done with one parent, one parent and one child, just the kids, or everybody but John who's away at college. Meddling Aunt Minnie who lives next door could be part of the therapy and Grandpa George, who never comes to visit but sends ten-dollar bills regularly to spoil his grandchildren, could also be invited.

But regardless of who gets included in the therapy, someone gets elected as the I.P. (identified patient). This unfortunate—often a troubled teenager—is seen as the sick one by the rest of the family and often serves as the family scapegoat.

I once worked with a depressed mother and teenage daughter where this was exactly the circumstance. The girl, pushing fifteen but acting nineteen, was driving Mother to distraction with late hours, poor grades, the wrong friends, a messy room, and wearing a roach clip on her purse strap. With her heels dug in, Mother skidded her to the clinic where I worked. Halfway through the hour, I got a glimpse of the problem.

"It's my last chance to set her straight," said the mother.

"How's that?" I asked.

"You tell him, Cheryl."

The girl gazed out the window, sullen and unresponsive. The mother then told me that she and her husband were planning to separate in June (this interview was taking place in April) and that, while divorce was likely, they had agreed to a truce until the school year was over.

"Harold is moving to Arizona and Cheryl says she's going with him. I guess she's old enough to decide for herself."

As we talked, I learned that Harold took no responsibility for Cheryl except to give her what she wanted, when she wanted it. He had never disciplined her, never set or enforced any rules, and rarely backed his wife on issues of how Cheryl should be raised. Bringing Cheryl to a psychologist was Mother's last hope of gaining some influence over what she saw as a rapidly approaching, sure-fire tragedy.

"Will your husband come in?" I asked.

"He refused. He said I'm the one who's crazy and needs the help."

I asked Cheryl how she saw the problem. No answer.

"Well, Mrs. Jones," I said, "it looks like you've lost the battle. If

Cheryl won't talk and Harold won't come in, I guess you might as well throw in the sponge, too. I don't think there's anything I can do."

Cheryl was smirking.

"But what should I do?"

"Nothing," I replied. "Absolutely nothing. In two months, matters will be out of your hands anyway, so why not let go of your duties now?"

"Like what?"

"You could start by informing your husband that he is henceforth the responsible parent. He can tell Cheryl when she can come and go and how late she can stay out. You can refer further calls from the school about Cheryl's conduct and poor grades to him, and you can have him take her to her doctor and dentist appointments. He can shop for her clothes with her, be sure she washes the dishes and cleans her room before she gets her allowance. He can meet the boys she wants to date and give his approval. You can tell him . . ."

Mrs. Jones interrupted. "But that would be disastrous."

"Maybe," I said, "but if they move to Arizona, there isn't anything you can do anyway. At least this way you'll be able to watch what happens."

Mrs. Jones sighed. "I guess you're right. It's worth a try."

Cheryl's smirk had changed to an expression of alarm. The hour was ending. Finally she spoke.

"You can't stop being my mother," she said.

Mrs. Jones turned to her daughter, "I don't want to but I love you and you're not giving me any other choice."

A couple of days later I received a phone call from a very angry father. He accused me of mucking around with his family and upsetting the status quo. He said I had no right to force him into the mess he was now in and that, where he and his daughter had been the best of friends, she was now testing him, arguing with him to skip school, begging money for clothes he could not afford, and was generally driving him crazy. I invited him to the next session. He refused.

By the next appointment, Mother was much less depressed and Cheryl was a chatterbox. We worked with their relationship, how things would be in Arizona if Cheryl moved with her father, and generally what the future held. We talked about their feelings for each other and gradually, the two of them came together. Although the father held out and never came to a session, the parents renegotiated their marriage and the family stayed together. More often than not, if parents are not getting along, the children are hurting. Not always, but often enough the family therapist will try to influence the parental relationship, if not directly in counseling sessions with the parents, then at least by bootlegging changes in ways similar to those I used with Mrs. Jones.

And while it's nice to have all the players together in one meeting, it isn't always necessary or desirable. Family therapists will often work with family subsystems: mother-daughter, father-son, grandmother-grandson, sister-sister, or any other grouping that needs attention.

The purpose of the work is to bring about change, change in the way the identified patient feels and change in the way the family functions. Family therapists believe that to help one, you also have to help the others and, unless you were born under a rock and have no family, it makes pretty good sense.

Resistance

As experienced by family therapists, the greatest difficulty in attempting to help a family is the doubt, denial, and outright antagonism expressed by various members of the tribe when some "outsider" suggests everyone in the family needs to come in. The question, "Who is this stranger and why should we trust him?" is perfectly natural.

If you're the one setting up the appointment, you can expect something like the following from the rest of the family: "I'm busy Tuesday," "It's Joey's problem, make him go," "I haven't done anything," "Sorry, got a golf date," and so on. This kind of resistance is to be expected. It should not stop you. If someone is adamant about not going, leave them home. Curiosity about what happened will kill them.

There are, of course, real issues at stake any time a family decides to examine itself with the idea of changing something. Will coalitions be questioned and maybe broken up? Will the fighting get worse? Will someone spill the beans about Tommy? Can I count on Dad to keep quiet about our secret? If the whole truth comes out will Mom and Dad stay together? These fears and many more are activated when the friendly therapist makes the seemingly innocuous suggestion, "Let's sit down and have a family pow-wow."

There's no easy way around this resistance. A competent therapist is familiar with it, recognizes it, and knows how to work with it. If the family is motivated to stop hurting, the therapist can help everyone get around the obstacles that prevent the family from getting well.

Finding a Family Therapist

I have done very little family therapy and many traditionally trained therapists are neither qualified nor competent to conduct family therapy. And, even if a client presents a problem that is clearly the result of a dysfunctional family, the therapist who doesn't "think" family therapy won't recommend it. Worse, he won't diagnose the problem as a family problem.

So, if you feel the family ought to be the target for understanding and change, try to locate a qualified therapist. Besides checking out credentials to establish the therapist's professional status, ask if the therapist specializes in work with families. If he doesn't, he can recommend you to someone who does.

Another good place to look is the American Association for Marriage and Family Therapy (see Appendix C for address and phone number). They can provide you with names of members in your area. Not all qualified family therapists belong to the association, but those who do will have had at least two years of supervised work, a license (depending on the state) and will welcome your questions about their training, experience, methods, and fees.

GROUP THERAPY

The opening session jitters have passed (everyone suffers from them) and things begin to happen. Sarah begins to tell all, tears in her eyes. You want to comfort her. John, who hasn't said much, says Sarah deserves the mess she got herself into. You want to hold Sarah's hand with one hand and rap John in the mouth with the other. George says John is wrong to pass judgment on Sarah, but that Sarah needs to grow up. George talks like a professor, analyzing everything, and you want to ask him why he's in the group, especially since he's never said why he's there. You're wondering why the group leader doesn't ask John to shut up. And then, just as you're about to interrupt, Joyce offers a banal explanation for Sarah, stating that "women always get taken advantage of by men." The moment has passed. The therapist turns to you. "What do you think is going on here?"

For many people, the suggestion of group therapy is frightening. And yet, in your search for help, it is very likely someone will suggest you try a group. You would be right to wonder what you might be getting into, whether group is right for you, what risks there might be, and, even if it's cheaper, whether it works as well as individual therapy.

Are therapy groups as threatening as people say? Do I have to take my clothes off? Can I take a friend? What if I don't like someone in the group? What do I have to do in group? These questions and many more are raised by people referred for group therapy. I say referred because most people begin therapy in a one-to-one relationship with a therapist or see an intake worker who suggests they try a group. Rarely does a troubled person start out looking for a group of people to help him.

In this section I will try to outline what group therapy is about, how it works, how to select a group for your particular needs, the advantages and disadvantages. Also, I will try to make some suggestions about how to get the most from a group therapy experience.

It's one thing to risk revealing yourself to a qualified therapist in the privacy of her office and it is quite another to run out your emotional laundry on a clothesline for review and comment by six or seven or more people whose only reason for being in a group is that they, like you, have had to admit they couldn't seem to run their lives without a little help. Is this bad? Therapists of every persuasion and background say no, me included.

Still, nowhere in the field of therapy has there been more confusion, more speculation, more push, more experimentation, and, some would say, more tomfoolery than in the mushrooming growth of group therapy. Lack of definition about group therapy, unfounded claims, charismatic leaders who nurture their own cults of followers, and a Barnum and Bailey atmosphere in some parts of the country have rightfully spooked a lot of people away from what responsible researchers have shown to be a treatment modality every bit as effective for most problems as traditional individual therapy.

Now, what is group therapy? One simple definition is that group therapy is a form of treatment in which two or more clients (usually seven or eight) meet with a therapist to bring about individual positive changes in the members. The therapist is usually "in charge" and the group members will either have certain problems in common or share certain characteristics. Since therapists from almost every school of therapy (analytical, behavioral, gestalt, rational-emotive, or whatever) can and do conduct therapy groups, I'll skip the theoretical orientations of therapists and focus on what groups are like, how to select one, what you can expect will happen, and what will be expected of you.

When a Group May Not Be Right

There are three circumstances under which group therapy may not be your best choice.

First, if you're in the middle of a major crisis and the problems you're faced with are immediate and serious and the situation is changing rapidly, a group is often unable to take the time you may need to sort things out. A better choice would be individual therapy, although there are crisis-oriented groups that meet frequently and are designed for exactly these circumstances. Many mental health centers now have just such groups.

Second, if you're just too frightened to try a group, think you'll be too embarrassed, or are afraid you'll lose what control you have left, then opt for individual therapy. You can always try a group later, after you have had some experience with the helping process.

And third, if you are in individual therapy, it is not a good idea to join a group unless you have thoroughly discussed the decision with your therapist. A few people seek the haven of a group just when they are about to face some painful reality in individual therapy. If you feel you want to try a group, talk it over with your therapist. Most will help you get started.

Groups—The Good Stuff

Before seven or eight clients become a cohesive, trusting, risk-taking group of people trying to help each other, they are first separate individuals—accustomed to solitary confinement with their personal problems. Not much happens in a therapy group until the folks sitting around the room start to see themselves as something special. A group that never gels never works. How then, if you decide to join a group, do the good things happen?

First, *you* have to give to get. As in individual therapy, you've got to take chances, be open, expose yourself, and in a group, be willing to understand and help others. The therapist can't, won't, and shouldn't do what the group can, namely, give feedback, support, confrontation, and the priceless honest reactions its members give to each other. You have to lean forward, ask questions, interrupt, and basically want to help people like yourself. Ask yourself a question: "If I'm worth helping, isn't everyone?" If the answer is yes, you'll do fine in a therapy group.

Candid observations about ourselves are often unavailable in the daily course of our lives. Straightforward feedback about how we communicate our thoughts, feelings, and attitudes is a source of information we all need and want, but are usually afraid to ask for. Your fellow group members will give it—and all you have to do is give it back. If the only reflection you have of yourself comes from the bathroom mirror, it's going to be very hard to see yourself the way others do. A group can hold up different mirrors, several of them.

There's no mincing words—groups can be stressful. Sometimes people get their emotional batteries drained, sometimes they get them charged, and therapists (speaking for myself) often feel that after an hour and a half of group work, they've been pulled through the knothole both ways —twice. Because of this stress, group therapists often have cotherapists—someone to spell them, someone to share the work with. Therapy is never easy, especially group therapy.

One of the things a group can do is help people give up their basic wretchedness. In a group it is not easy to suffer in isolation, labeling yourself as strange, different, unlovable, and believe all the nonsense you're telling yourself if, at the same time, eight or so people disagree with you, sometimes vehemently. Groups have a way of undermining your negative self-appraisals, those rotten opinions you have of yourself. And, because the people in there with you may carry similar ideas about themselves, you get a chance to help them the way they help you. Learning to help others is itself a tonic.

Groups are a laboratory for change. After taking a look at yourself you may decide you want to be different (most of us do). The group and the therapist will encourage your experimenting with new ways of saying and doing things. With them you can risk, with them you can make mistakes, with them the errors you make in the trial and error of personal research are safe. You can venture and gain. At home, with the boss, with the girlfriend—maybe not. If anything, people who know you will resist your changing. Not that they love you the way you are, but at least they know what to expect. With a group, change is the purpose, the process, and the goal. Your changing for the better rewards everyone.

Lastly, a group functions best that functions on its own. For most therapists, a successful group is one in which he can put himself on automatic pilot and catch forty winks. The more the group handles its own problems, solves its own crises, and assists its members to operate independently, the more its individual members prove to themselves that they don't need therapy. And, as soon as someone reaches this startling revelation, they may terminate therapy, usually with the blessing of the group.

I recall one young woman who for years thought she was ugly, not just plain, but ugly, ugly. In fact, she was very attractive—high cheekbones, light complexion, long lashes, an hourglass figure, and big green eyes. Over several sessions, her individual therapist had been unable to convince her otherwise, and giving up, referred her to group. He believed she had arrived at this peculiar conclusion (of being ugly) as a child when she was beaten by her father and told she was an "ugly duckling."

For three months, the men in group assured her she was an eight on a ten-point scale and the women in the group flattered her as well. Then, as she could not break all the mirrors held up to her by the group, she caved in. "I guess I'm at least average looking," she sighed, "and I know how I got to see myself this way. Thanks to all of you." She quit the group amid hurrays and hugs.

Mixed Groups

In mixed or heterogeneous groups, what the members have in common is not their problems—your situation is not exactly like the guy's next to you and your reactions to life and its stresses are different. You come from different backgrounds, different age groups, have different symptoms, and in the beginning, it may seem as though this lack of commonality is a drawback. In fact, you share the most common of characteristics—your humanity. When such group members begin to build bridges of trust between themselves, the good stuff mentioned above begins to happen. A mixed group will generally be best for you if you are like any of the fictional people below.

> Mary is lonely, isolated, shy, and unsure about how to make friends. She feels unlovable, avoids mixing with others, and wants to find ways to let others get to know her.
>
> John is a businessman whose boss told him he's too abrasive, makes clients angry with his constant argumentative style of conversation, and seems to have trouble accepting criticism.
>
> Charles is twenty-nine years old, lives at home with his mother, and can't seem to break away. He wants desperately to be independent, but can't seem to make the transition.
>
> Florence is an attractive, twice-divorced woman who needs attention—more attention than most people seem to be willing to give her. She feels others don't appreciate or understand her, and her best friend accused her of being selfish. Twice burned by divorce, she wonders if she should try again.
>
> David acts before he thinks. In a fit of temper, he told his girlfriend to go to hell. Before she could explain what happened, he stomped off in a rage. He feels strongly but has trouble not acting immediately on his impulses. He doesn't know why he's always shooting his mouth off, but he wants to stop doing it.

While this is hardly representative of the kinds of people who do well in mixed-group therapy, they do characterize the problems many of us face—problems of shyness, loneliness, anger, immaturity, needing attention and affection, and learning to express our feelings so that we don't hurt others.

Finally, a mixed group is defined by its lack of a central theme, even though certain themes will be present throughout the life of the group. Any group leader who defines the purpose of the work to have a central focus (assertiveness training, independence for divorcées, separation from home or parents, house-husbanding, etc.) sets the main goal for its members and therefore the criteria for who should be included. Depending on your locale and therapist availability, a homogeneous group could be set up for any of the problems outlined above: shyness, loneliness, etc.

Getting Help from People Like Yourself—
Homogeneous Groups

The first homogeneous therapy groups probably date back to Roman times when small groups of persecuted Christians met secretly to give each other support, confess their sins, and work together toward a common purpose. With their focus on the evils of greed, intemperance, jealousy, and lust (today we call these selfishness, drug abuse, alcoholism, and fooling around), this method of working together toward common but individual goals has stood the test of centuries.

Such homogeneous groups enjoy tremendous popularity both within and outside the mental health movement. One has to conclude they're doing something right. Is one of these groups right for you?

What kind of special-focus groups are available? What follows is not an exhaustive list, and many of the groups may not exist in your community. But if they do, you may want to explore them. If your problem fits any of the following definitions, you may have something in common with people who can help you to help yourself.

1. Alcoholism
2. Drug dependency/abuse
3. Obesity
4. Gambling
5. Incest
6. Habitual lawbreaking
7. Child-rearing problems
8. Recently divorced
9. Being too passive (assertiveness training groups)
10. Chronic pain
11. Dealing with a terminal disease
12. Adult children of alcoholics
13. Making it through adolescence
14. Adjusting to retirement
15. Many medical problems—iliostomy, cardiac ailments, deafness, etc.

The list could go on, but these represent the majority of homogeneous groups where members enjoy an immediate sense of belonging and knowing that everyone there (sometimes including the therapist) is fighting the same fight.

Similar to self-help groups, these therapy groups, usually professionally led, provide a highly structured and powerful social network which cuts through the loneliness and isolation people with these kinds of problems suffer day in and day out. "Gees!" one client exclaimed to me at the end of the first session I held with a group of shoplifters, "I thought I was the only person in the world to make such a dumb mistake. Thank God, I'm not alone."

I cannot overstate the immediate feelings of relief, the sense of belonging, and the validation of one's humanity clients feel after joining homogeneous groups. The opportunity to hear others share the selfsame dilemma you have faced and to lay out to the group your fears and foolishness while people nod with understanding is something you just can't get much of these days, even from friends.

There are, of course, drawbacks. Some people don't like to join anything. One client I encouraged to try an Alcoholics Anonymous group came back after one meeting to report, "I'll quit drinking tomorrow before I'll stand up in front of a bunch of strangers and say I can't stop on my own."

Also, some people don't like to be painted with the same brush. To say you're just like a lot of other people—too fat, too passive, not taking your divorce well, or popping too many pills—runs counter to the client's need to view himself as a one-of-a-kind human being. And while I've no quarrel with individuality, it seems a shame to agonize over one's unique "plight" when dozens of people like yourself are willing to share the suffering.

A point well worth remembering is that many homogeneous groups have evolved because people have not gotten what they've needed from traditional individual therapy and from the professionals who provide it. And too, many of these groups cost little or nothing to join.

Making a Choice

Unless you're too frightened or think you'll be too embarrassed—or are neck-deep in an emotional swamp with the alligators snapping at your psyche—group therapy (mixed or homogeneous) may be your best option. You do have to ask yourself one simple question: "Can these people trust me, and can I trust them?" If your answer is a tentative yes, group therapy may be just the medicine you need.

7

The New Therapies–
Fads and Fashions

Compared to the known history of the human race, all psychotherapy is a fad. On the clock of human events, the whole enterprise began a few minutes ago. And if Freud and his early followers established the form and format of how the talking cure should proceed, the ritual of psychoanalysis is practiced in its original form by but a handful of the faithful.

Today the institution of psychotherapy is a bewildering array of conflicting ideas and notions, themes and theories, technologies and techniques practiced by an ever-growing army of healers who bicker among themselves about who should do what to whom and for how much. And since all claim success with the milder forms of emotional distress, it doesn't matter much what your problem is—they will all offer you a helping hand.

The less serious the complaint, the wider the variety of promised cures. For a simple tension headache, you could choose among any of the following remedies: autogenics, hypnosis, biofeedback, relaxation training, stress management, jogging, yoga, acupuncture, a host of individual or group therapies, chiropractic, pain clinics, dance therapy, minor tranquilizers, an opportunity to scream or be screamed at, a nude encounter group, and on and on and on. You might even take an aspirin.

It doesn't help much to know that practitioners of all these forms of treatment claim success, or that if one form of treatment is better than another for what ails you, one practitioner is unlikely to refer you to another who might help you quicker, cheaper, and at less risk.

How did this happen? How is it that new therapies can spring up overnight, each one promising more than the other?

And how does the average troubled person avoid being hurt, humiliated, or victimized in his quest for help?

In this chapter, I hope to describe the psychological environment that has nurtured the growth of the new therapies, characterize their leadership and methods, and suggest the kinds of questions the cautious consumer might ask.

The Atmosphere

It has been said many times that we live in the age of anxiety. Psychologists and psychiatrists have told us this is true so many times and in so many ways, it must be so—everyone is a little neurotic, everyone gets uptight, we all have an unresolved conflict here or there, interpersonal stress is commonplace, no one communicates, we need releases from the pressure we are under.

As a result, our language has changed. Now we talk like psychologists. Where once we had worrywarts we now have obsessive-compulsive neurotics. Where we used to cry at funerals, we now have grief reactions. Where once we were afraid of things, we now have phobias (some seven hundred by the last count). Does our use of language affect the way we see ourselves? I think so. And what if the language is unclear? When a client says to me he wants to "get it together," I ask get *what* together? If someone says they are "losing it," what, pray tell, is being lost? Thankfully these particular ailments are fading as clichés should. But now we have burnout—the latest in a long line of quasi-clinical terms that imply a new and unhealthy psychological condition. To illustrate the perils of language, let's examine this new ailment.

Experts would have us believe that burnout means a loss of energy, a feeling of being burdened, or a sense that one's reserves are exhausted. (Whatever happened to tired, bored, apathetic, stale, exhausted, depressed?)

We hear people say "my batteries are drained," and, remedially, "I need to get recharged." People get their "wires crossed" and "blow fuses." When I hear people talk this way I have the distinct impression we are talking about androids, not humans.

But being burned out implies something is clinically wrong, something can be diagnosed, something can be treated. And yet, like much of the vague language of popular psychology, the term lacks refinement. For example, is there a difference between someone who is slightly singed and someone who is well done?

The point of all this is that for whatever reason people are unhappy, disappointed, or discontented, we can, through the magic of labeling their feelings, create a new malady. And maladies require therapy.

It seems quite plausible to me that the one effect of our burgeoning psychological terminology has been to encourage thousands of people to search among their discontents for a psychological (and pathological) explanation for their woes.

Some mental health experts believe that at some time or other, one-third of the general population will be sufficiently disturbed to require professional help. The degree of disturbance may be slight, but the implication that a therapeutic conversation could benefit these millions staggers the imagination. With waiting lists at clinics, mental health centers, and in the private sector, and with psychiatric hospitals brimming over with patients, one has to wonder if we are becoming a nation of psychiatric casualties.

It may be that we are too quick to self-diagnose, too ready to conclude that our ordinary discontent is the result of some psychopathology. Or it may be that our society is a great machine whose noise and heat and stress raise our standard of living at the cost of our tranquility. We may be a self-indulgent people, babying ourselves with psychological explanations for our failure or, because we have achieved so much, we now have the time and money to search for our souls. It doesn't matter much what the explanation is—we are hungry for solutions to our perceived distress.

The New Therapies
If solid scientific advances are being made in the understanding and treatment of major mental illness, the steps are slow, painstaking, and costly. But for the problems most of us face, new cures are announced daily. The public's craving for psychological antidotes has proved a fertile garden from which fads and fashions and self-styled gurus seem to spring up overnight.

Given the short-lived nature of many of these therapies, any listing by name would be quickly outdated. And since today's fad may prove tomorrow's tradition, my intent is not to dissuade people from trying something new (which may be very effective), but rather to explore the characteristics of the new therapies and how you might decide whether to try one.

The first thing a consumer might do is take a close look at who's leading the parade. The modern-day messiahs of psychotherapy are rarely humble couriers of some new truth about what might help people, but

are rather mere horn-blowers of their own interpretation of enlighten-
ment. As their own front men, they discount the competition, dismiss established methods, and give no one intellectual credit for their ideas—as
if they had single-handedly invented the notion of human persuasion and
influence.

Often their claims of success border on the miraculous and, compared
to the scientist-therapist who avoids the press until all the data are in, the
new prophets relish publicity.

There is typically a cultish flavor to the new therapy, an air of worship
among the followers and, of course, leading the way an ego big enough to
be adored. "You had to have been there," a colleague once remarked
after a weekend marathon at a popular California therapy institute. "Just
seeing him was therapeutic."

This touching the hem of the "great one" leads to testimonials that, if
interesting from the viewpoint of a religious experience, fail miserably to
document the real effectiveness of a new therapy. And while I would
never minimize the importance of faith in a new believer, their glazed-
eyed excitement and open-mouthed gullibility cause the cautious among
us to wonder about the credibility of what we're told. We may want to
hear of wonder cures but in the marketplace of psychotherapy, modest
claims and reasonable rates are the prudent choices.

Besides the charismatic qualities of the new leaders, what are the characteristics of the therapies they propose? Since different is often equated
with better, not looking like any other therapy is important. Where
therapist and client used to meet in an office and talk to each other, they
now meet in the swimming pool, stripped of convention and clothing,
and yell at each other. Where physical intimacy cautiously follows the
development of a relationship, it is expected to occur spontaneously in
this new free-for-all atmosphere. Spontaneity, it seems, is a highly trea-
sured aspect of the treatment. Where humiliating a client was considered unprofessional, a crushing attack on her or his integrity is now justified—as if the more mortified the client is, the better.

In some of the new therapies, the tools of hatred are elevated to the
status of therapeutic interventions. Ridicule, mockery, satire, and sar-
casm are honed to a razor's edge. In group therapy, clients are orches-
trated and encouraged to attack each other's psychological vitals while
the therapist pins the victim's arms behind him with deft interpretations
about his neurotic defenses. And all within the guise of being helpful.

If some of the new therapies are potentially dangerous, others are
patently silly. Over a long group session, clients are forbidden to go to
the bathroom, to eat or drink, or use the telephone. They are directed to
express the deepest sentiments of love to total strangers and, a moment

later, to project their bitterest hatred on the same person. The setting demands a suspension of reason and sense of propriety, and the more outrageous the requirements for inclusion in the group, the more people seem to interpret their experience as significant.

Make no mistake about it, the leaders of the new group therapies are experts at manipulating their clientele into unique psychological experiences. If the threat of rejection by the leader or the group softens the best resolve to get up and go home, the fear of failing the cure and going it alone with one's troubles finishes the job.

The new therapies are replete with gimmicks, designed mostly to elicit feelings. Observed from a distance, much of what seems to be going on is the purposeful contriving of situations to produce displays of intense emotion. Getting a client to bawl like a baby, scream like a banshee, and shout vulgarities that would redden the face of an army cook seem to be the ultimate goals of the treatment.

Apparently operating on the premise that people are too uptight and need to "let it go," the therapies insist on tidal wave releases of emotions. In some therapies, a total loss of control is expected and rewarded and while some of us may need to lower our defenses from time to time and have a good cry or color up our language with a string of expletives, being asked to behave as if we hadn't a shred of dignity left leaves a lot of people cold. That the proof for the effectiveness of these methods exists only in the minds of the therapists who conduct the sessions should cause the unwary consumer some pause.

Finally, all therapies (new and old) promise the ultimate goal—the freedom to become an autonomous, self-directed individual liberated from one's fears and able to live contentedly, not only with one's fellows but with oneself. But for many, because the new therapies demand blind obedience to the therapist's directives, strict conformance to in-group rules, and the acquisition of a jargon in order to communicate with the healer, the quest for individuality becomes a travesty of the process. "Doctor," the client pleads while wringing the therapist's hand, "am I cured of my neurotic dependency?" is a one-liner that describes the too-frequent result of the ultimate psychotherapeutic remedy.

An Assortment of Groups

Much of what is fashionable in the people-helping movement has happened in the context of group work—not strictly therapy groups for people with significant emotional problems, but groups of people brought together to explore themselves and others under the leadership of someone trained to assist people to expand their consciousness, to learn to communicate better, to express themselves, to "connect" with others. What follows is a brief description of these groups, their strengths and potential risks.

T-groups, often called sensitivity groups, have enjoyed a lot of press (most of it good) and have been with us since the 1950s. As the cutting edge in the human growth movement, such group training in sensitivity has been used in private industry, government, hospitals, church organizations, universities, and hundreds of other settings where people are conscious of the need for better communication. T-groups don't necessarily turn insensitive people into sensitive ones, but the process is popular and, if some participants come away so sensitive, so open with their feelings that they drive their former friends batty, the effect doesn't seem to last forever.

The goals of T-groups are educational and encourage members to examine themselves and their feelings toward others—all in an effort to enhance self-awareness. Many see these groups and the techniques used as more artificial than real and scoff at them as games played by adults in a laboratory setting. Often seen as shallow and stylish, the movement has been parodied in films and books. "All right, group!" shouts the leader, "now we're going to practice this spontaneity until we get it right!"

Nevertheless, thousands of people have attended such workshops and if some regret wasting their time, others feel they have experienced a major life event.

Whatever the individual result, a T-group is not group therapy and not for people with significant problems in their lives; such training labs are a poor place to expect relief from emotional distress. Responsible T-group leaders publish disclaimers in their flyers to the effect that the focus and function of a scheduled session is not to provide therapy to participants. As you might guess, some people ignore the disclaimers, and some leaders forget to warn the public.

Encounter Groups

Like T-groups, encounter groups are not therapy groups, although the impact can be great and the results as powerful as found in more traditional group therapy. At the very heart of the human potential movement, encounter group goals include self-realization and self-actualization—two wonderful achievements by anyone's standards that no one in his right mind wouldn't want.

The problem for the troubled consumer is that such groups often promise more than they can deliver and there's considerable risk in assuming that your diagnosis of what's wrong in your life is the right one.

Encounter group leaders assume the client has the strength and personal resources to bring about change and that your decision to enter the group is the right one—no matter what kind of shape you're in. Usually, the encounter group leader does not interview you individually, does not make a professional determination about whether you would benefit or be hurt by the experience, does not offer alternatives to group, does not formulate a treatment plan, and does not follow up with you after the group is finished.

For those who don't mind beginning "where you're at" and feel they can handle the situation, encounter groups are an option. But, together with the fact that many encounter group leaders are charismatic, have powerful methods of influence (for example, orchestrating the entire group to break through some member's resistance), it is not surprising there are occasional casualties. A casualty from an encounter group is someone whose psychological condition is worse after the group ends.

Despite the occasional horror stories, the encounter group has attracted some very sound professionals and some very unsound gurus. The potential for adulation from followers and big money has created a climate in which the consumer should consider an extra measure of caution before taking the plunge. For those who want to play it safe, check the credentials of the leader as you would any therapist in terms of license, professional affiliation, etc. Better yet, consider a referral from a therapist who knows you well enough to recommend the experience.

A Word About Marathons

Widely used by group therapists for clients interested in personal growth, group marathons can run from six to forty-eight hours—sometimes with rest and relaxation periods, sometimes with rules against sleep, and no pit stops. Typically, they begin on a Friday night and end Sunday afternoon. Marathons are often held outside of cities in retreats or rustic settings which offer a relaxed atmosphere, freedom from jobs or kids, and a minimum of bothersome interruptions.

Therapists who favor marathons believe they are an improvement over weekly group sessions on several counts: there is enough time for the group to form a sense of cohesiveness and solidarity, clients' resistance wears down after several hours, people have a chance to "be themselves" and drop whatever role they usually play and, last but not least, the therapist has a chance to interact with the group in a context that doesn't demand he play the role of healer for the duration.

While many marathon leaders claim better results with these long-haul methods, research to support their claims is sparce. And since it is much harder casually to leave such a group once you've started, be sure you know the therapist leading the session and have a pretty good idea what you're getting into. My own feelings about marathons are that only healthy people need apply. You wouldn't ask someone who can't jog around the block to run twenty-six miles, and you shouldn't expect someone who isn't emotionally fit to wrestle with his reality for forty-eight hours.

But Do the New Therapies Work?
The answer is, who knows? What few studies exist suggest the effects of many new therapies are time-limited. While clients feel great immediately after treatment, within a few weeks they report feeling no better than comparison groups who skipped the therapy. Time, it seems, heals too.

Unfortunately, the public often accepts at face value what "experts" say. The scientific studies needed to prove the effectiveness of even old established methods of psychotherapy are mostly on a drawing table and, unfortunately, many of the new therapies not only avoid measuring themselves against more traditional methods, but attack the very idea of studied comparisons. It seems the antirational flavor of some of the new therapies coincides with an antiscientific attitude about proving effectiveness—in which case we are left to choose between heartfelt testimonials and must make a leap of faith not unlike that required to join a new religion.

If you ask someone who has just spent a hundred hard-earned dollars to be ridiculed, humiliated, and made to feel a fool in a room full of strangers, what would you expect him to say? I was suckered? No. People defend their follies with gusto. The very absurdity of their experience obliges them to do so. To the skeptic (which seems to me to be a healthy attitude to take toward therapeutic miracles), testimonials ring hollow.

We are left then with the question of facts. Did our friend George really change for the better? Did Sarah and Bob's marriage not only survive but improve after therapy? Is Aunt Rose more relaxed, more lovable, more considerate of others since she went to that marathon or is she still a bitch on wheels? Evaluation of positive change is often best made by others, not ourselves. Ideally, science could help us. One day it might.

Experiment versus Fad
Now that I have let off some steam about what I consider to be potentially dangerous vogues in the great therapy movement, I need also to address honest efforts at innovation in the theory and practice of psychotherapy.

There are, basically, two ways for a therapist to bring new ideas and methods to his work with troubled people—provided, of course, the therapist has an open mind toward change and perceives a need to upgrade his skills and improve his services to his clients.

First, it sometimes happens that a therapist stumbles upon some technique or phrase or interpretive statement that seems to help therapy move along, helps his clients to see something they didn't see before or opens up some territory of vital concern that heretofore had remained unexplored. For example, a friend of mine hypothesized that when a couple came to him for marital counseling and one of them clearly stated they wanted to leave the relationship, the other partner may have already reached the same conclusion but as yet had not said so. My colleague, experimenting with the idea that the partner who seems to want the marriage to stay together may, in fact, be the one who wants out the most, now routinely (and somewhat abruptly) asks the quiet spouse: "And when did you decide the marriage was finished?"

More often than not the quiet partner will blanch, show a little shock at the query, and then admit that they had decided some weeks or months ago that divorce was a distinct possibility. To this admission, the spouse who has requested a separation is often surprised, even floored. And, with the fresh footing that both partners are equally dissatisfied, therapy can move quickly forward.

This kind of experimentation by experienced therapists is altogether fitting and proper and reflects a healthy attitude toward the exploration of new ideas. It is, in a word, the application of the scientific method on a small scale: forming a hypothesis, testing the hypothesis, observing the results and confirming or disconfirming the original idea. It is how, probably, most therapists acquire skills and refine their methods of intervention. And this is good.

The second avenue by which competent professionals improve their abilities to help people is through education. They read journals, study the methods of other therapists in workshops, training seminars, and in actual practice. They seek out new knowledge and study techniques that have some measure of validity, some measure of effectiveness as demonstrated in practice or in research. It is, more than anything else, the therapist's attitude toward new ideas—a humble but skeptical attitude—that sets her or him apart from the charlatans. Professionals are genuinely interested in any new theory or therapy that holds promise for their clients, but will approach these fresh ideas with a degree of caution and suspicion. And they have a reason for this attitude.

The well-trained professional has been exposed to an enormous amount of information about the whys and wherefores of human behavior, as well as a solid grounding in the theoretical underpinnings of the major schools of thought about why humans act the way they act. They are not easily persuaded that some new and fashionable therapy is automatically better than anything invented heretofore and will carefully investigate the claims before launching off in some new direction with their clients.

Because the ethical standards of professionals hold that they should always treat their clients with respect and dignity, it follows that they would not subject those clients to patently experimental forms of therapy that may be dangerous or destructive to their clients' well-being. This is not to say, however, they would not experiment with methods or techniques whose effectiveness is promising, if not yet fully proven. But in no case should a qualified professional expose his clients to forms of therapy that are demeaning or degrading to the basic sensibilities of another human being.

It is also important to remember that some therapists are as subject to fads in psychotherapy as the clients they serve. In the business, a client who jumps from one therapy to another in a never-ending quest for contentment is called a "therapy junkie." When a therapist can't seem to settle on an approach that works and spends thousands of dollars playing follow the leader, we call it continuing education. If he can't explain what he does with his clients within a major theoretical framework of how humans behave, we call him, at best, eclectic. At worst he is confused about what he knows. He knows certain techniques work, but isn't sure why.

Since some therapists are unsure about how or why what they do with people is therapeutic, they too are hungry for solutions. When a favorite healer comes to town, they fill auditoriums with eager, hope-filled hearts—indistinguishable from those troubled people they will see the next day in their offices. Like everyone else, they need to believe in magic.

As a graduate student, I once met a psychologist in his early sixties who was about to retire. He said that when he started college he wasn't sure what he wanted to major in but that since human behavior seemed a complete mystery to him, he would take a few classes in psychology and collect some answers that might be useful in any future career.

"I knew they were teasing me," he said. "And after three years I guessed the answers I wanted were sure to turn up in my senior classes. They didn't. Then I figured they were holding back the good stuff until I got into the master's program. I was wrong again but I knew if I went on for the doctorate, I would surely discover the truths I was looking for."

He told me that by the time he had completed a major research project, trained in a hospital for his internship, and earned a Ph.D., it was too late to change careers.

"I never did find the answers," he said. "But now I know why—there aren't any."

Normals Need Not Apply

People with serious emotional problems would do best to avoid the pop or fad therapies. More often than not, a thoughtful and individual assessment of your problems will not take place before the therapy begins. It is when a careful screening is not done that people get hurt. There is always risk of emotional distress when these sometimes high-stress, intensive methods are used indiscriminately. The potential dangers are real.

In fact, many of these new therapies are offered and even advertised to the public as so-called training events. Often, the "training" is highly interpersonal, highly confrontative, and produces enormous amounts of anxiety. Any therapist/trainer who offers to work miracles with anyone, anytime, and for any problem is blowing smoke and is a potential menace to your mental health.

But what about the rest of us—those of us who believe our everyday problems are a bit outsized and might yield to some new kind of therapy? In the end, it's a personal decision. The benefits of some new therapy may outweigh the risks (or vice versa), but the intelligent consumer will always ask questions—about therapist's qualifications, about what will happen in the therapy, about how he will be expected to behave, about the methods to be used, about the rationale for what will take place, about the effectiveness of what he is paying for.

If the questioned therapist looks blankly into space and is stuck for an answer to these questions, maybe he doesn't deserve your fee. If he interprets your request for reasonable information as a sign of "deeper problems" or seems shaken by a query as to his proficiency, maybe he isn't all that proficient. If he says people like you who ask questions drive him crazy, maybe he's only a short putt away.

Finally, we are living in a time when change, any kind of change, seems better than what we now have. It is the season for cults, cults of curability that promise to free us from unhappiness, from anxiety and discontent, and from the pickles we get ourselves into. Let us not confuse our natural limitations with emotional sickness and then beg the healers to fix what only needs acceptance. Normality is broad and wide, not the narrow fiction some mental health experts would have us believe it is. It is no crime to be imperfect and no therapy, new or old, can rub out the self-doubt and fear we all know as the intimate companion to our dreams. Normals need not apply.

8

How Does Therapy Work
. . . Or Does It?

I f there's any one thing the reader and potential client would most like to know, it's probably the answer to this one question. And while it's a very good question and deserves a very good answer, I doubt very much if there is one, or at least a complete one.

In the simplest terms, therapy begins when two people (or more in the case of marriage or family counseling) agree to sit down together to talk about a problem that only one of them has. The one with the problem tries to explain what's wrong. The second person listens, asks questions, and says things. If the therapy is working, the two people often grow to like each other. When they are through talking some weeks or months or even years later, the one with the problem is not supposed to have the problem anymore and the one without the problem has some of the first person's money. So goes the talking cure.

Until a few years ago, this description of how therapy works was as good as any. It has only been in the last twenty or so years that any systematic research has been directed to the study of how and why psychotherapy seems to work or, for that matter, if it works at all. This really isn't so surprising when you consider the cost of conducting such research, the resistance of some practitioners to the idea that what they do with their clients should be examined under the bright lights of the scientific laboratory, and the Tower of Babel atmosphere that seems to characterize the field. And it's only been very recently that the use of audio and now videotapes has pierced the inner sanctums of the therapist's office to record what actually happens between a therapist and his or her client.

Part of the confusion is that there has been little agreement about what constitutes a "cure." The major schools of psychotherapy not only espouse different goals and objectives, but oftentimes radically different ways of achieving "cures." Therefore, though a few tentative answers about how therapy works have been found, general agreement about anything remains sparse.

Despite this general lack of agreement about how therapy works and an absence of evidence that when it does work, its effects are hard to predict, the fact still remains that people pay therapists to help them. And if you talk to the average consumer, he or she seldom feels therapy is a waste of time and money. *Something* is happening. What research is available provides a few probing fingers of light where once there was total darkness.

Believing It Works

Any time a client says to a therapist, "I know you can help me," the odds board lights up and the chances for a successful outcome rise sharply: If the therapist then says to the client, "I'm sure I can," you can make book on a happy result.

Over and over again research studies in medicine and psychology prove the importance of what is called the placebo effect. A placebo is a chemically inert substance that, once ingested, has absolutely no physiological impact on the patient, and yet psychologically has a powerful and measurable effect. People given placebos to counteract seasickness don't get seasick as often as people who didn't get placebos, and some studies show that as much as fifty percent of the benefit of medications is the result of a placebo effect, an effect that can't be attributed to the medicine itself.

As concerns psychotherapy, maybe it's a matter of optimism breeding optimism. Clients who believe therapy will help them tend to feel better quicker, function better, and get relief from their symptoms. Their belief that therapy is working may have an infectious but positive effect on their therapists.

With a client reporting "feeling better," the therapist gets excited about being helpful (Boy! Here's someone who really wants to change!) and might work at being extra sensitive, more attentive, and more creative. Like the effect of an enthusiastic audience on actors, the thrill of excitement works both ways, each feeding on the other until something extraordinary happens.

It seems, therefore, equally important that therapists believe in what they do. It isn't an easy task to determine if your therapist believes in himself or herself as a healer, but if your therapist gives off the message that she's pretty sure you're a hopeless case, then she too is probably a hopeless case. If you sense this is the situation, by all means find another therapist.

Psychotherapists, simply because they carry the title (and usually a degree or two), represent the voice of authority and, as such, are placebos in the same way that a capsule or tablet is—they symbolize a remedy. They may, however, like placebos, contain no active ingredients. If you must see a therapist, find one who is alive and well and believes in what he or she is doing. The popular one-liner among therapists, "do anything in therapy, but don't screw up your placebo effect," may be humorous to the professional helpers, but you as a consumer ought to expect some skill, experience, and know-how before you spend that hard cash.

It doesn't really seem to matter so much what brand of therapy or what kind of techniques the therapist uses so long as he or she believes, with the client, that what they are doing is working. So long as both parties have a reasonable idea about what they are shooting for and both feel they have the wherewithal to reach the same goal, then the goal—the client feeling better, doing better, getting better—is more likely to be achieved.

Just why the process works this way isn't understood, but probably has to do with psychological forces and energies that are yet unknown. It would be nice if we understood these dynamics and mysteries, but then, like the person boarding a jetliner to London, knowing how and why that monstrous piece of metal stays airborne is of less concern than that it gets off the ground when it's supposed to, and comes down when it's supposed to.

In a word, if you don't believe therapy will work for you, it probably won't.

Captains of Our Ships

A query common to all systems of therapy can be capsulized in the question, "Who's running the ship?" The ship in this instance is always the client or sometimes some aspect of the client's thoughts, feelings, or behaviors.

I have yet to meet a troubled client who said to me: "I've got everything under control. I just want to see if I'm doing it right." The need to be in control, to be on top of things, to feel a sense of power and mastery over one's life is so basic to human development and growth that without it, we can quickly feel helpless and inadequate. Without this sense of mastery, we can fall victim to despair.

All systems of therapy address this need for mastery in one way or another. Philosophically, therapists (from any school) cannot believe in fate or that chance governs the lives of their clients. They must tackle head-on clients' notions that they are the hapless victims of their environments.

Clients express this feeling of being out of control in hundreds of different ways. From the woman who suffers from stress and tension that delivers her a dandy migraine headache once a week, to a man who boils with angry resentment because everyone seems to be pulling his strings like a puppet, their problems can be viewed in terms of the common question, "Who's in charge?" On the one hand, the issue of control has to do with runaway physiological responses (I can't stop my headaches, ulcers, etc.) to one in which an angry man is unable to get hold of the forces that seem to be running his life. Since systems of psychotherapy are built around client needs, much of the variety in kinds of therapy may have to do with a common need for control expressed by people with similar symptoms.

Our culture places a premium on self-control and, in a way, the various schools of therapy amount to efforts to train people to get control of their lives. As a result, much of what is done in therapy—any kind of therapy—is to help the clients learn to master some aspect of themselves over which they feel they have little or no control.

From the psychoanalytic point of view, what's out of control are impulses that come bubbling up from the unconscious. These usually unwanted thoughts, actions, and feelings are neither understood nor governed by the conscious or rational mind. The therapy (grossly abbreviated) amounts to getting acquainted with the sources of these impulses and trying to understand just why the little nuisances are pestering you. Once you have met and understood them through therapy, you are supposed to be able to keep them in line and go about a normal, neurosis-free life.

For the behaviorist, the how of therapy involves understanding the circumstances under which you acquired all those persistent and nonproductive habits and then to begin a studied unlearning of them and, at the same time, a learning of new, more beneficial behaviors. The techniques can be elaborate or simple, but the goal is the same—getting control of your behavior.

The Rogerian or client-centered therapist begins with the assumption that the client does have control, although it may be a tentative hand on the tiller. By helping the client sort through his or her thoughts, feelings, decisions, and actions, a process of personal growth takes place and the client begins to take charge of the direction of his or her life.

There is no substitute to mastery and no joy comparable to its attainment. If you can recall the first time you straddled a bicycle, balanced it precariously, gave a pump, and went over in a heap, you have some recollection of how impossible a challenge getting going on two wheels seemed to be. With encouragement and Mercurochrome, you kept going. Within a month you were lapping the block and speeding by Mom and Dad with a "look no hands" shout and a self-satisfied grin. You had conquered a contraption you knew defied all laws of physics and the result was a sense of mastery that no one could take from you.

To gain this same sense of control over our interactions with others, our fear of public speaking, of failing exams, of asking for a raise, of coping with the loss of a job, or the quitting of drugs or alcohol amounts to a success by whatever therapy was tried.

A young man once came to see me at the request of his parents. We'll call him Charles. Charles was graduating from a major university with a degree in theoretical math and, while he was a straight A student with the books, he couldn't add two and two when it came to the opposite sex. His chief complaint was that he was lonely (his mother called it depression), and he thought he needed a wife. His equation for a happy life required a wife at about this time.

Since Charles had never been on a date, he was upset that he didn't have the necessary skills to get from point A (meeting someone) to point B (marrying someone). He also thought himself to be pretty dull—what with knowing a great deal about things nobody much cared about and almost nothing about anything else.

The therapy began with building a trusting relationship (I wasn't going to embarrass him) and setting some goals (getting acquainted with the opposite sex in case one of them took a liking to him). I should add that given his experience with mathematical formulas, calculations, and solutions, he believed therapy would work. I knew it would work too, but I was counting on chemistry.

For several sessions, we talked through his fears, hesitancies, and nagging self-doubts. He wanted to change, but, like most people, didn't know how. The first thing we decided to do was to have him practice meeting girls. He experimented in the university dining hall by seating himself opposite girls who were eating alone (I was counting on their being math majors) and who weren't so attractive as to scare him out of his wits. He was to introduce himself by saying "Hello," then make a comment about the food, or a book the young lady had with her and, at the first opening, introduce himself and learn the coed's name. He was not to ask for a date since we had agreed that was more than he was ready for.

At the first session following this dining hall experiment, he brought in the names of three girls and was quite pleased with himself. He knew three more females than he had known the week before, which made six counting his mother and two sisters. One of them said hello to him later in the week and, to his surprise, had remembered his name.

In the weeks that followed, we talked about sex, male and female roles, his history with girls, expectations, and what he wanted in a girl friend. We also set up a homework assignment each week that brought him closer to what he wanted. He learned how to draw people out, to talk about themselves and in so doing, learned he wasn't such a stump after all. I encouraged him to read things other than math journals so he could at least fake sophistication. Soon, he wasn't faking.

When Charles was ready for his first date, we agreed it should be a coffee date only and that he ought to avoid studiously any serious interchange, like kissing or proposing marriage. He felt particularly good about one of the several female acquaintances he'd made, and very cautiously hinted they might have pizza together. She accepted. Charles later told me they had sat in his car and talked until two A.M. All the while he was telling me this story, he was grinning like the kid on a new bike who coasted past his parents shouting, "Look, no hands!"

Charles and I met a few more times, but he was finding it difficult to fit me into his schedule—what with obligations at a social club he had joined, skiing on weekends with friends, dating, and job interviews. As he said at our last session, "I'll be in touch, but things are under control." I never heard from him again.

Emotions

When I first started out in the business of helping people, I was unaccustomed to clients crying. Men with the age and dignity of my father would come into my office, sit down, begin telling me of their troubles, and before I could stop them, begin to sob. Women, because it's culturally more okay, would drench themselves in tears when I would ask, "How do you feel about such a such?"

At first, I was alarmed at how I seemed to help clients lose control. I grew up in a family where emotional displays were rare but genuine, and to have all these clients weeping and wailing in what I had anticipated to be a relatively intellectual pursuit of the dynamics of their distress was unsettling. I was suspicious that I was making people worse, but my supervisor was reassuring and succinct: "No affect, no action." Translated, if the client doesn't experience some strong emotion while trying to change, not much is going to change.

Research has repeatedly shown that the experience of emotional arousal is essential to the process of successful therapy. And when you think of it, it makes perfect sense.

A bland and unfeeling discussion of the ins and outs of one's own personal dilemma is a contradiction in human behavior—we should expect people to be upset by what's upsetting them. How can you talk through your most intimate fears, personal failures, and most grievous disappointments without feeling something?

In many ways, therapy is a reenactment or at least a retelling of the hurts, pain, anger, and frustrations of life as experienced by the client. The experience of these emotions in the context of a safe, secure, and trusting relationship with the therapist working to make the reexperience one in which something can be learned, some insight gained, and something bad left behind, makes change and growth possible.

While no one understands emotions (there being some twenty different theories), all therapies promote the experience of them to further the client on the road to psychological health. While some schools of psychotherapy focus almost exclusively on devices designed to get folks to "emote," others deemphasize this effort to trigger feelings. But basic to *all approaches* is the understanding that emotional arousal is essential to change and growth.

How different therapists bring about the experience of emotions in their clients during therapy hours is a matter of training, experience, and intuition. Simple questions like, "How did you feel about being abandoned by your father?" to asking clients to pound a pillow to experience some rage they feel, or to talk to an empty chair where a deceased loved one is fantasized are but a few of the methods used to enhance the probability that the client will experience emotional arousal and begin to express feelings.

In many ways, therapy is a drama and the therapist the director. The client's construction of his or her role in life is at odds with the character he or she would like to be. Since the client is motivated to be someone different, the therapist must probe, persuade, cajole, and confront the client to try new actions, new modes of thought, new ways of being in the world—all the while directing the emotionally charged energy for these changes through the course of therapy.

There are doubtless a great many more elements and conditions necessary for therapy to be successful than the three highlighted here. But believing therapy will work, experiencing strong feelings in the course of that therapy, and mastering some aspect of one's existence seem essential to a good result. For any and all of these things to happen, the therapist must be good enough at his or her work at least to let it happen. I say let it happen because I personally believe people have great reserves of strength and a natural inclination toward self-healing. And from this point of view, the effective therapist is one who knows how and when to be helpful as well as how and when to stay out of the way when a client is struggling to get better.

In psychotherapy, the relationship between the person with the problem and the person without the problem is everything—it is the basis of influence and the only vehicle by which the person with the problem can change. There can be no change for the client if the therapist destroys that client's belief in therapy, shuts off the experiencing of emotions, or discourages a sense of independence or mastery.

9

The First Session

Imagine two total strangers meeting for the first time. They shake hands and sit down in an office. One of them has a sense of confidence and well-being, is comfortable with the surroundings, has read all or most of the books lining the shelves, and knows almost exactly what questions to ask, how to ask them, and generally what is going to happen for the next hour. The other person feels very little self-confidence, doesn't feel' well, is uncomfortable, hasn't read any of the books on the shelves and hasn't the foggiest idea about what is going to happen. Bewildered, upset, and not knowing what he or she is expected to say or do, the second person is feeling pretty miserable. This inequitable arrangement aptly describes the first appointment.

The person in whose office this scene is taking place has a job to do and the first part of this job is to make the second person feel less uncomfortable. Therapists have all sorts of ways of doing this: offering a cup of coffee, talking with the client briefly about what is going to happen, or offering to answer any questions the client may have as they go along. But regardless of how this is done, clients need to see therapists as empathetic, warm, tolerant, understanding, and at least capable of being helpful—if not immediately, then soon. If the therapist doesn't or can't communicate these qualities in the first session, it is often the last session.

If you were to listen to tape recordings of first therapy sessions, what you would hear is one human being trying to be helpful to another. The one trying to be helpful asks questions, gathers information, tries to understand and define the problem the second one is experiencing. The one with the problem answers questions, tries to explain what's gone wrong in his life, how he's feeling about this or that, and generally hopes to be able to get at least one human being to see his dilemma the way he sees it. Listening to the tape, this appears to be all that is happening. In fact, what they are saying to each other is almost nothing compared to what they are thinking or feeling.

While all this talking is going on, both people are busy sizing each other up—thinking, questioning, pondering, and trying to decide what kind of relationship they will have or if they will have one at all. For the moment, imagine a first interview between a thirty-five-year-old woman and a twenty-seven-year-old male therapist.

If you stepped inside the therapist's head you might hear some of the following:

> She looks more depressed than she's willing to admit, like she hasn't slept in weeks. She hasn't mentioned her husband. I wonder if he's got something going on the side? If he does, I wonder if she knows it? Maybe their sex life has gone to pot. Should I ask her about sex this first session? She looks like a first-class lady, even uppity, she might be offended. Maybe I should have her husband come in at some point. I wish she would talk about him. I wonder who pays the bills in the family? Who is going to pay my bill?

All of these questions and musings could happen within a few seconds and hundreds of others would occur in the course of an hour.

Now, across the desk, our fictitious client is busy with her own thoughts:

> He looks pretty young but he has a nice face. I don't see any pictures of a family and he isn't wearing a wedding band. I wonder if he is divorced? If he is divorced, what's his attitude about marriage? He doesn't say much. Why isn't he asking me about George? I'd think he could see George is the problem. And he's skipping over my sex life. Maybe he's too timid to ask. How can I tell him what's bothering me if he is shy? Oh, he can't be shy, he's a doctor. But aren't some doctors shy? This is costing me an arm and a leg. I wish he'd do something helpful.

The point of all this is that what the therapist and client *say* to each other in their first meeting is but a fraction of what actually happens. Changing postures, facial expressions, voice tones and quality, heart rates, and other visible and invisible goings-on are going on. What really happens between these two people is so subtle and complex as to defy simple description, and social science researchers sprout gray hair trying to figure out what ingredients go into the making of a good therapeutic relationship.

But from your standpoint, you needn't worry much about making the first session a success. Whether or not you "click" with a therapist is more his worry than yours—remember, he's the one getting paid to be an expert in establishing helpful human relationships.

In this chapter I hope to outline what seem to me to be reasonable client expectations about how they should be treated and how not, as well as what to do when certain problems arise. Also, there is a need to get a number of little things straight—things you need to know and understand before you make a second appointment.

Respect and Courtesy

It may seem obvious to expect to be treated with respect and courtesy. But, as sometimes happens, you may go to a therapist who comes across as cynical, demeaning, abrupt, condescending, or disinterested. I have heard clients complain, "He made me feel worse," or "I don't think he cares about my problem or understands me," or as one woman said, "He talked more about his problems than mine." If you spend an hour with such a therapist and go away feeling demeaned, belittled, or like a naughty child and the thought of making another appointment sticks in your throat, don't make it.

Nowhere is it written that you have to respect a therapist who is a jerk, even if he's a well-trained, experienced jerk. Unfortunately, many troubled people automatically assume the therapist is right and they are wrong. This gives some therapists just the setting they need to make themselves feel better while making someone else feel worse. As a rule, if a therapist makes you feel worse, find another therapist.

Paying attention to you is a basic requirement of good therapy and good interviewing. If you feel the therapist is preoccupied, daydreaming, or dozing (I've heard several complaints about therapists falling asleep during an interview), you should either say something or find someone with his mind on his work.

Clarity About the Therapy Relationship

Another thing you should expect is some clarity about what the two of you are going to do. Again, this is mostly the therapist's job. He should describe something about how he works, how many sessions the work might take, how often the two of you might meet, whether or not others might be asked to come in (wife, husband, children, etc.). He may speak briefly about his style of therapy, what he thinks is important, and how he will pursue what he intends. He may ask you to do homework (write down your dreams, keep a diary or journal, meet a new person each week, and so on). At the very least, you should have some kind of a road map about where the two of you are headed.

Many of these issues are negotiable, and you should feel perfectly free to express your needs around such things as when you will meet, how often you can afford to meet, and how you intend to take care of the bill. Confusion about the *how* of the relationship at the beginning can lead to all sorts of problems later on. If the therapist isn't clear about the how, don't hesitate to ask.

Money

Lots of therapists don't like to talk about money—as if they couldn't possibly accept cash on the barrelhead for their saintly endeavors. This attitude usually leads to problems for the client, so I'll spend some time on the topic.

First, if the therapist doesn't, someone (a receptionist or office worker) should present a frank description of the cost of the service you are buying. A therapist has nothing to sell but his time, and it is critical you understand that his time is what you are paying for. If you don't or can't know exactly what this help you are buying is, be sure you at least know what it costs.

Rates for therapy vary widely (from thirty-five dollars an hour in some rural areas to a hundred dollars or more an hour in the fox-fur trade in major cities). Many people seem to think that the more you pay, the better the help. In my own experience, this is not necessarily true. I've met a few mediocre therapists who inflate their fees because they know desperate people want the "best" and equate outrageous rates with effectiveness. As one client remarked to me as he was setting up an appointment over the phone, "I couldn't get to see Dr. Smith and I noticed that you charge less. How do I know you are as good as he is?"

If you are not told, make sure you understand the therapist's policy about missed appointments. Do you have to pay for these? How late can you cancel?

Another small issue is who is responsible for ending the session. Most therapists work in one-hour blocks—(although some don't and there's nothing magical about the fifty-minute hour). Often the hour ends at an awkward time or the two of you go past the time allotted. Generally, the therapist is responsible for the clock and for winding down the session. If you feel you want to continue beyond the agreed-upon time and the therapist is available, both of you can talk it over and decide to proceed or to save the issue for a subsequent session.

Most agencies and almost all private practitioners expect payment at the time services are delivered. There are many reasons for this, some fancy and psychological, others blunt and practical.

The simplest reason therapists and agencies want to be paid "up front" is that they need the money. To stay in the black, they need income. Experience shows that people will pay every other bill first (the grocery, the power company, the rent, the credit union) while doctors and therapists get paid last, if at all. So, to get their money, therapists and agencies try to get at the head of the line. Besides, sending out bills, waiting for payment, and writing off hundreds of thousands of dollars worth of bad debts each year makes therapists irritable and unpleasant. I know one psychiatrist who will not see clients unless the client has the fee in hand. This may sound unnecessarily harsh, but his collections are one hundred percent and his mood is excellent.

Among therapists there is also some generally accepted thinking that goes like this: The client will not benefit as much from therapy unless he or she is paying for it right along. While this may sound like a slick justification for the therapist to get paid immediately (most of us get paid once a week, twice a month or once a month), there are real problems with running up a big therapy bill.

First of all, therapy is expensive and just a few sessions will add up to a tidy sum. A large debt between a client and therapist confuses things and creates feelings in both people that can make the work of therapy more difficult.

If you, as a client, get behind in paying the bill, you may begin to feel guilty—another problem you probably don't need. You may also look for excuses to miss an appointment, and, if the bill becomes a big one, you may begin to question if you should pay it at all. Given that the results of therapy are uneven and sometimes slow in coming, getting into debt can influence your decision to stick out the work of getting better.

For therapists, not getting paid causes predictable sentiments: feelings of doubt, distrust, frustration, anger after second billings. Finally, they are forced to decide to continue seeing you with no hope of payment or terminating therapy unless you pay up.

As a rule, therapists have big hearts and soft heads when it comes to the business side of their work. They will often go on seeing someone for months or even years with no hope of collecting their fee. They may also be less than enthusiastic about your mental health.

So the therapist should talk to you about money. If he doesn't, be sure you do. You both need to trust each other and nothing builds trust faster than paying attention to the basics of the relationship. Prompt payment never hurts. An old joke illustrates the reverse—a frustrated psychiatrist tells a patient deeply in debt to him, "Pay your bill or I'll let you go crazy."

But what if your fortunes change and you can't afford therapy after you've started? An old ethical canon once obliged professional helpers to help even if they didn't get paid. However, as the helping industry has become commercialized, this ethic has largely fallen into disuse. Still, many practitioners adjust their fees downward and accept hardship cases outright.

Mental health centers, counseling agencies, university-based clinics, and United Way funded services are usually obliged to provide help to those who can't afford private care. One friend of mine sets aside a "workers day." He charges people the same rate per hour as they make at their job—a thoughtful practice that has not been widely adopted.

If you do suffer an economic setback, don't be timid about bringing it up. Talk it over with your therapist. If he's a professional, he will continue to work with you and make whatever adjustments are necessary.

A small thing but sometimes overlooked is who gets the bill. If you don't want a statement sent home, speak up. If the fee is to be paid through your insurance company be sure you know how the billing is handled, who will know that you're seeing a therapist, and how much information about you and your problem will be included in the form required to pay the claim. You should not expect interest charges on fees paid at a later time, and generally professionals do not reduce their fees for prompt payment. Any advertising for discount rates, special bargains, or "easy freeway access" strongly suggests the therapist is not a professional or doing so poorly he can't pay the rent.

Credentials
There are two kinds of credentials, the paper hanging on the wall in the office of most properly trained and licensed professionals and the kind that you feel. And almost everyone displays the first kind (I suppose out of tradition, or for the reassurance it provides some clients, or for the reassurance it provides the therapist). You usually don't ask about or question these parchment credentials. It is the second kind, the kind you feel, that gives you the sense of trust you need to get started on your problems.

Some years ago when my eldest son was a teenager he needed delicate thyroid surgery. Worried about the success of the operation, he asked the surgeon, "Exactly how many of these have you done?"

"Too many to count," said the surgeon dryly. Silver-haired and unoffended, he then went on to detail how simple and straightforward the procedure was, what complications might occur, and how he would handle these.

I later asked my son why he had asked these questions. "I don't want some guy that got D's in surgery cutting on my throat."

Even though trust is a soft commodity, therapy won't work without it, and you've got to have some trust by the end of that first hour, or at least the belief that trust is possible. There is more about the other kind of credentials in the chapter on "Choosing a Therapist."

Besides the thrashing out of the problem you made the appointment for and setting up some goals to work toward, several things should be clear between you and the therapist by the end of the first hour.

For openers, you should know how much the services are going to cost, how often you will meet, who will be included in the therapy, what therapy will be like, what you're expected to do or not do, and approximately how long the therapist thinks the therapy will take. Not so explicit, but every bit as important are your first impressions of the therapist. Your initial feelings, mutual respect, whether you think the therapist has any smoke on the ball, and whether you believe this stranger can help you, are all critical.

If you think the therapist is a racist, doesn't like young people or old people, or women or men in general, or for any reason holds attitudes toward you that are stereotyped and negative, then the two of you are off to a miserable start. Since you are not spending your time or money to adjust the therapist's attitudes, consider this first session a learning experience and try again. There is no point in throwing good money after bad.

On the other hand, if you like the person or even feel okay about him and think he is someone you can share your concerns with, then give it another session. Remember you're not looking for a friend, but someone who can help you out of a tough spot.

10

What Do You Want
From Therapy?

For a great many people their first visit to a professional therapist is a gross disappointment. So disappointing that a large percentage do not make a second appointment or, if they do, they later cancel it or simply fail to show up. While many people get what they want in one session, an even greater number come away feeling disheartened, disgruntled, misunderstood or, at the very least, that they got a wrong number.

For those who decide to continue therapy, other problems arise: they don't feel better right away, the problems they have are getting worse, not better—the therapist or clinic or mental health center is collecting their fee, but nothing is changing. What gives?

In this chapter, I hope to describe the importance of goal-setting and expectations, the need for clarity about what you and the therapist are going to try to accomplish, and to point out some of the things therapists can't and won't do. My reasons for doing this are many: people waste a lot of time and money looking for help that doesn't exist, agencies and therapists waste a lot of time and money disappointing these people, and clients and therapists waste a lot of each other's energy groping with one another about what to do.

Why a Goal?

When you hire a therapist, it is assumed you want something from her. If you could get what you think she has to offer elsewhere, you would have gotten it already. Most often you want the therapist to do something, say something, arrange something, talk to someone, help you stop doing something, or help you start doing something, or just make the pain go away. You may simply need somone to talk to, to share your thoughts with, to hear you out without being judgmental. You may not know what it is you want, but it *is* something.

Whatever it is you want, it is the reason you made the appointment. Setting up a goal for therapy may be easy or almost impossible—easy when you know precisely what you want but more often a perplexing challenge that takes two people (you and the therapist) some time to reach agreement about. You have your ideas about what you need, the therapist has hers. Often you may not agree.

"What does she want from therapy?" is an often-asked question in staff meetings where new cases are discussed. If the therapist presenting the case says he doesn't know, he is frequently asked to see the client again in an effort to find out.

Take, for example, a man who makes an appointment for himself, stating he is depressed and anxious because his fourth wife just left him. On his first interview the reasons for his being upset are defined. The therapist asks the client what he would like him to do. The man states he wants to feel better—a statement of a goal. The therapist offers therapy, pointing out that the man may need to examine his own behavior toward women.

"I just want my wife to come back to me."

"Have you asked her to come back?"

"I've begged her, but she refuses."

"Would she come to see me with you so the three of us can talk about a reconciliation?"

"I already asked her. She refused."

"What would you like me to do?"

"Call her and ask her to come home. She doesn't believe I love her. You could convince her that I do."

"I don't think that would help."

"Then *tell* her to come home."

The therapist pauses. "I won't do that. But I will talk with you about why she might have left."

"Forget it," says the client.

The therapist in this example is telling the client the limit of his willingness to intervene in the man's life and how he sees the goal of therapy. Since this is not what the man wants, he leaves, disappointed. What this man expected from his visit to a professional helper is not what he got. When offered therapy for himself, the man found the suggestion irrelevant. And since the two of them did not agree on a goal, therapy stopped before it began.

This contrived example illustrates that where there is no agreement about the purpose of therapy, there can be no useful relationship. It could have happened that the therapist never did ask the man what he wanted and they could have met three or four times before the client realized that the therapist was not going to deliver, i.e., call his wife and tell her to return.

Unfortunately, this kind of miscommunication happens all the time. And while it's nice to blame clients for expecting the wrong things or not making their requests clear, it is we therapists who are supposed to be the experts in communication.

Simple Is Best

I have often been accused of taking a shirt-sleeves attitude toward complex psychological problems. But in defense of what I would like to call a healthy pragmatism, I believe that if a therapist and a client can agree about one clear goal, there is at least a better than average chance their joint venture will pan out.

Good therapy goals are crystal clear—"I want to lose thirty pounds." "I want to be able to fly in an airplane." "I want to be able to ask my boss for a raise." These requests are straightforward and there is no doubt about having reached them—either you do or you don't.

But it is more often the case that people seeking therapy are not at all sure about what is ailing them and are even less sure about what it is they hope to change or achieve. Psychological complaints are notoriously vague. "I need self-confidence." "I need more ego strength." "I'd like to enjoy life more." "I want to be centered." "I want to put my life in order." "I want to be happy."

The goal the therapist and client agree on may have nothing whatever to do with the kind of therapy undertaken, and the therapy may or may not be successful, but at the very least, there will have been a shared understanding of what it is they originally set out to do together. If client and therapist have their sights set on the same outcome they have, by necessity, agreed about something, and they can both measure their efforts against that.

Very often the joint struggle to arrive at an agreed-upon goal for their therapeutic adventure leads to conflict—the client is willing to settle for a reduction in his level of distress, the therapist is hoping to turn the client into a masterpiece of mental health.

In my own experience I have sometimes found the entire course of a therapeutic relationship may involve no more than clarifying what goals might be tackled in therapy. In other words, the client needed and used the therapy to discover for himself what it was he wanted in life.

I once worked with a middle-aged woman who was married to a

wealthy stockbroker. While she did not want him involved in therapy, she complained that she no longer loved her husband, was depressed and without alternatives for the future. She wanted to leave him but was afraid of life on her own, what a divorce would mean to her children, and how her friends would react. For several sessions we discussed options, how she would manage, what she would do, could she make it as an artist, could she tolerate the drop in her standard of living a divorce would mean. In the end, she resolved to stay with her husband. "I couldn't give up the house, the country club and Mercedes," she said. "Besides, there are some lovable things about Fred."

The work of establishing a goal, simple or complex, is not yours alone. The therapist's job is to help you sort through the issues and alternatives, evaluating with you the possible consequences of decisions you might want to make. And while therapy styles and approaches vary, reaching a definition of what you want to change is essential to knowing how and where the therapy is going and when you get there.

Personal Growth Is Okay

Many people seeking therapy may not have specific goals for personal change. These folks seldom have serious or obvious emotional problems, and few are experiencing serious symptoms of psychological distress.

They may want to "realize their potential" or "get in touch with themselves" or otherwise use therapy to experience something they haven't experienced. This is all fine and dandy and there are lots of therapists who specialize in techniques of psychological liberation. A lot can be said for people who use therapy to improve themselves, their relationships, their effectiveness.

Things Therapists Won't and Can't Do

During the Vietnam War many young men presented themselves to professional helpers stating they thought they were unfit for military service. Some of them had genuine emotional problems, but many thought that to let yourself be drafted was a sure sign of mental illness. While some wanted and needed treatment, thousands more hoped to convince a doctor they were sufficiently disturbed to be classified 4-F.

At best, making such a determination of unfitness is a difficult decision, and many psychiatrists would not have given these young men appointments had this request been plainly stated.

A request for therapy is very different from a request for an evaluation—one is an appeal for ongoing help, the other is a petition that the therapist provide information about you to some third party. Some therapists will not provide evaluations, others are happy to—even specialize in this kind of service.

There are many circumstances in which clients seek out a therapist's professional opinion: child custody battles, insurance claims, statements regarding one's ability to work, certification for various kinds of licenses, and all sorts of legal problems. If you are not looking for therapy, try to avoid confusion, as well as wasted time and money, by being as clear as possible about what you are asking for. If the therapist says he'd rather not help you in the way you want, ask for a referral. He'll be happy to provide one.

Besides not being willing to conduct a clinical evaluation in order to provide information about you to someone else, many therapists will be reluctant or even refuse to try to influence your family or friends. They will not make phone calls to convince a spouse to come to therapy, they will not intercede on your behalf to convince Aunt Flora she needs help, and they will not defend you to your boss. It is more likely they will see their professional role as one in which they will help you to help yourself with these problems.

A mother and father once asked to see me about their daughter. The girl had joined a religious cult and temporarily vanished into New York City. Some weeks later, she surfaced with a request for a thousand dollars and the parents, distraught because their daughter had had a history of mental illness, wanted me to put in a phone call to the cult leader and convince him of their daughter's need for treatment. While I had the greatest sympathy for their anguish, their belief in my professional authority in such circumstances was unrealistic. I did put them in touch with a national organization of parents working out of the same grief and suggested a clinic where the girl might be evaluated and treated if they could get her there.

Lastly, many people believe a psychiatrist or psychologist can call up the boys in the white coats and have someone put away in a mental hospital. It is never this simple.

In some states, psychiatrists (usually it takes two concurring medical opinions) have considerable legal power to cause a person to be involuntarily detained at a treatment facility. In other states, complicated laws and procedures exist which, if frustrating to the person who wants someone put unwillingly in a hospital, are carefully designed to protect the individual's civil rights. Americans judiciously guard their right to be different. And, nowhere in the United States can an emotionally disturbed citizen be involuntarily detained and treated for mental illness without due process under the law.

Side Effects

One thing you should know about therapy is that you may not get what you want. You may not only get less than you bargained for, but may end up in a bigger mess than when you started.

Most therapists do not discuss the possible negative side effects of the treatment they provide—not because they are reluctant to point them out, but more because they don't know what they are.

Suppose you are a middle-aged housewife, married twenty-five years, and your husband is showing more interest in his work than in you. He spends two or three evenings a week out with the boys and when he is home, would rather watch reruns on TV than be with you. You become filled with self-doubt, anxiety about the future of the marriage, and begin to wonder about your adequacy as a wife and lover. The kids are out of the home and what you'd hoped would be the golden years begin to look like tarnished brass.

You tell your husband of your fears. He says you're an alarmist and insecure. You ask him to see a marriage counselor. To this proposal, he smiles and pours himself a drink. Things do not improve, and, as desperation and depression set in, you make an appointment for yourself with a reputable therapist. Even though the therapist strongly recommends your husband accompany you, hubby steadfastly refuses.

From that first appointment, the relationship between you and your husband will begin to change, for better or worse. With the therapist's help you may begin to feel better—at least you have a sympathetic listener. The therapist may encourage personal growth in terms of developing hobbies, returning to school, beginning a career and helping you find meaning in your life.

The therapist may refer you to an assertiveness training course where you will learn to express your feelings and make reasonable requests of others without feeling guilty. You may decide to begin to take risks. You may tell George how you honestly feel without dissolving in tears. It may even occur to you that the husband without whom you thought life was impossible has become more of a millstone than a mate.

While all this psychological growth is going on, your therapist and you have been unable to convince your husband to come to a single session and, despite your best efforts to encourage him, he remains unchanged.

As often happens in situations like this, the decision to separate or divorce is now more pressing than when you began therapy. At the same time you are feeling better and stronger, your husband may be feeling more angry and upset—blaming you and the therapist for rocking the boat and threatening to wreck twenty-five years of marriage. He may get over his anger and try to build a relationship with the new you, or he may want to call it quits. Divorces under these circumstances are not all that rare.

The point of this fictional case history is that it is not altogether clear who wanted what to happen. If George thought a little therapy couldn't hurt you, he is now surprised and dismayed. And would you have begun therapy knowing that divorce might be a side effect of the improvement you experienced?

In my experience, most therapists do not give warnings about possible negative side effects. Other than not knowing what they might be, there is the fact that what is a positive effect and what is a negative effect can only be determined by the client. The hypothetical husband in our example can hardly be expected to be overjoyed at the result of therapy. You, the fictional wife, could be very pleased with therapy. But what if a year down the road you feel you made a mistake about old George? For someone married twenty-five years, the single life is often a dismal reality.

The importance of negative side effects resulting from psychotherapy have yet to be examined in much detail in the professional literature. And while researchers and practitioners have taken notice of the fact that not all the results of therapy are positive, specific warnings (like those on bottles of medicine) are simply not available. Even so, it would be a good idea to ask about what might go wrong if you begin therapy, as well as establishing clear, positive goals.

A Word About Contracts

The idea of a formal, written contract between you and a therapist is gaining some popularity. The therapy relationship is unavoidably complex—involving time, money, commitments, obligations, guarantees or the lack of them, record keeping, good faith, confidentiality, legal responsibilities, and goals. In some areas of the country, consumer advocate groups are pushing for such contracts.

I basically haven't any quarrel with written contracts if both parties are agreeable. They certainly help clear up what is often unclear. I do, however, find written agreements unnatural in a relationship where mutual trust is the substance of the therapeutic alliance and the soul of a collaborative effort.

Still, a shared verbal understanding about what is to happen and what are the mutual obligations and expectations is unquestionably important, and I strongly advocate this kind of communication.

In the end, however, a therapist couldn't possibly guarantee positive results, and having him put in writing the limitations of his omnipotence seems, to me at least, sort of silly.

However it is accomplished, the goals of therapy must be worked out. Otherwise you have two people struggling with an undefined problem without understanding what each hopes will happen. It is therefore essential that you be active and feel that your participation in what will happen in therapy is not only desirable but absolutely necessary.

If you run into serious problems establishing goals for therapy, you might reconsider your expectations. You might also reconsider the expectations of the therapist. It may be that your expectations are unreasonable, or at least unreasonable for a particular therapist. There is no point in beginning therapy with someone who believes you can do less than you think you can.

Whatever happens, you will be the final judge—the one who decides whether what you sought was what you got. The only acceptable outcome is the one defined by you. Whether or not the therapist thinks therapy was successful couldn't matter less.

11

Getting the Most
From Therapy

Volumes have been written about why therapy works, how it should proceed, what it is like, what problems will be encountered, what techniques will cause change, and what constitutes a good result. Unfortunately, these books are written by therapists for therapists and usually in their own strange language. Almost nothing has been written for the person entering therapy about what he or she might do to get the most out of therapy. It is almost as if the helping professions have nothing to say to the people they help about how best to benefit from what they do. What follows in this chapter is a compilation of suggestions based on what clients who did well in therapy told me made their experience worthwhile. Who would know better what it takes?

Though most people don't know what part they are supposed to take in the therapy relationship, surveys of the research literature consistently indicate roughly two-thirds of those who enter therapy show improvement. However, the same reviewers find that from five to ten percent of clients experience a "negative effect" or are worse for the therapy experience. If the majority of clients are satisfied with their therapy, why bother suggesting ways to make therapy work better? First, while therapy usually produces positive change, it doesn't always do so, and for those folks who run from warm to lukewarm to being left cold about their therapy experience, some shared information might improve the odds of a successful experience. Even those for whom therapy will later be judged as being very helpful, knowing more about the experience might shorten the total time spent in therapy and, thereby save some time and money.

Let's assume you have found a competent therapist who, after your first visit, you feel good about—she seems to understand you, you're both in sync about values and belief systems, and you have agreed upon some goal or goals. Let's further assume that the therapist is without major prejudices, is competent, and seems to have her head screwed on tight. You realize you've got some work ahead of you and want to get on with it. What can you do besides do your share of the talking and pay the fee?

The Labor of Change

The first thing you should realize is that therapy is hard work, maybe the toughest personal assignment you can undertake. You are, basically, going to try to change the one person in your life who seems to be giving you the most trouble—yourself.

Clients who think the therapist is going to make their problems vanish without lifting a finger on their own are in for a disappointment. Whatever your goals in therapy (thinking straighter, feeling better, getting along with others, maximizing your potential, or whatever), all will require work. Therapists listen, coach, advise, suggest, reflect—you change.

No one can specify exactly what the work will be, but you can be sure that if changing something about yourself was easy, you would have done it already. With a stranger's help you are going to examine yourself, your personality, your strengths and weaknesses and, with effort, refocus your energies to bring about some change in yourself. There's no way around it—it will be a tad more difficult than falling off a log.

In therapy, effort is the coin of the realm. Changing yourself may be a slow grind or a happy flash of understanding that brings a new perspective to an old problem but, either way, it never happens by wishing, or magic, or waiting. You can, of course, skip working on yourself, avoid therapy, and make yourself feel better with drugs or alcohol. For a lot of people these days, this is the simplest solution. But it is, as they say, a long walk off a short pier.

Openness

You might think that anyone who pays a therapist from fifty dollars to one hundred dollars an hour to help them get at the nub of a personal problem would be the picture of candor. Not so. People hide all kinds of things from their therapist all the time, usually by omission. There may be as many reasons to be less than open as there are to tell the plain truth, but I can't imagine anything to be gained by fibbing to your therapist and keeping to yourself what might be haunting you.

All of us have done something, are doing something, or have something planned that could just as well be omitted from our list of credits. Some of us have skeletons banging around in our closets with such animation that if we opened the door just a crack the things would come charging out. They might even scare the therapist. Being human, skeletons come with the territory, and since experienced therapists spend years opening closets with their clients in search of these troublesome fellows, you might as well get right to it and drag out these fears, shames, guilts, and sundry sins so that the two of you can hit them with a therapeutic shovel. But even if you can't be completely open, tell the therapist you can't be, at least not yet. He'll understand.

I once had a young woman client who was afraid she was a homosexual because she was "extremely fond" of an older woman (who apparently considered my client her best friend). They had never talked openly about their feelings for each other and when I suggested to my client that she talk this through with her friend, good things happened. The friend understood, even knew she had such fears, and together they were able to work it out. My client's fears vanished. The problem as I saw it was that it took her four months to tell me she was afraid she might be homosexual. If she had brought it up sooner, we might have clobbered this old skeleton early on. The last time I saw her she was planning to marry.

In another example a colleague of mine was consulted by a middle-aged woman for several weeks about her depression and anxiety. Frustrated at the lack of progress, my friend took a long shot and asked the woman if she was involved with someone besides her husband. She fearfully confessed and quickly began to feel better, extricating herself from a no-win situation. Asked why she took so long to tell him she said, "I was afraid you would think badly of me."

People in therapy often hold back their most intimate fears, worries, and past deeds, and they do it with such regularity that a lot of therapy never gets started. They have their reasons for wearing a happy mask, probably very good ones, but if at all possible be as candid as you can— the sooner the better. I'm sure many people I haven't been able to help left therapy wishing I had asked the one question that would have enabled them to tell me something critical. A therapist can't know what you don't tell him.

Let's Not Be Friends

One reason people get into therapy is that they have no friends, no one to unload their woes to, no one to share the miseries we all succumb to from time to time. As friends, therapists aren't worth a damn. They won't loan you money, come to your house for dinner, go shopping with you, or ask you to go fishing. They're trained not to. If a therapist needs a friend bad enough to find one in his office, he is probably on the wrong side of the desk. Therapists make good listeners and may help you solve problems but compared to a friend, they are a poor and expensive substitute.

If you begin therapy by putting your best foot forward to make a good impression, you'll only confuse and befuddle the poor therapist, who is a lot more interested in your worst foot, the one you keep tripping over.

Trying to convince the therapist what a swell person you are leads to three unproductive results: (1) the therapist won't know how bad you might be hurting, (2) not knowing this he won't know what to do, and (3) he'll probably be disappointed that you don't trust him. To do his work well, he needs to know *all* about you, the good and the bad, the strengths and the weaknesses, what you see in yourself that disgusts you and what you like about yourself. You wouldn't try to strike up a friendship by chronicling your worst points, but those are precisely the things you hire a therapist to help you change.

Each time I interview a client who "became friends" with his or her last therapist, I have a pretty good idea why therapy failed and why this person is again seeking a helping relationship. The therapist's obligation to you is a professional relationship, a relationship anchored in a highly charged setting in which he is trying to help you change your life. He may even have to hurt your feelings to help you. He will respect you, maybe like you, and maybe even look forward to a friendship when therapy is finished. But to become a friend during the work of therapy spells failure for both of you. So if you don't want to neutralize your therapist or detract from the objectivity you're paying for, don't invite him home for chicken dinner.

Is Being Normal Okay?

Another good reason for telling a therapist *all* about yourself is that you may learn you are not as bad off as you thought. One of the best things you buy from a therapist is a storehouse of knowledge about people.

As a young intern in a hospital, I conducted the initial interview on a new admission—a forty-year-old woman who said she was too depressed to cook or clean house. With pleading eyes she asked if I had ever seen a case like hers before. I hadn't and I felt awful. A year later I had seen lots of people too depressed to eat, let alone cook food. I still remember that lady. She needed reassurance, reassurance I couldn't honestly give. A seasoned therapist gives reassurance, support that softens the unfamiliar into the familiar—no small source of comfort to distraught people. To get this support all you have to do is be yourself.

Therapists have the distinct advantage (or disadvantage, depending on your point of view) of having talked with thousands of people with problems. They've also read hundreds of books about what is normal and what is not so normal. It seems a lot of people feel they're somehow deviant, strange, or peculiar because they don't fit the definition of their own idea of what is normal. Normality is a statistical artifact and no one, to my knowledge, has ever met the perfectly normal person.

Being essentially normal is, after all, only a numerical achievement—it means that most other people are like you in some measurable way. The problem as I see it is that a lot of people simply haven't seen enough human behavior to realize that they are not really so different.

I once had a client who stated he was the original Casper Milquetoast and that no one on the planet was more passive, more manipulated by others, or more easily abused than himself. After talking with him for a while I learned that he had returned a set of faulty tires to an automotive store and had the unmitigated nerve to ask his boss for a raise. When I assured him that he made a second-rate passive male, he was at first dismayed. He thought the average guy bullied his way through the organization, threw vacuum cleaner salesmen from the front porch, and generally went around laying down the law and setting new precedents for the male prerogative. Relieved of this heavy burden to uphold some invisible and mythical standard, he made quick gains in therapy.

It is my own pet theory, but I think a lot of people would like to talk to a professional just to have their mental health checked—to find out if what they are thinking or feeling or doing is normal. I would also guess that a lot of fees are collected by therapists for pronouncing a finding of normality at the end of a life history.

In my experience, many successful therapists often do no more than give clients permission to be what they are. They do this by saying things like "Many people feel as you do," "What you're going through is pretty typical," or "I know you feel all alone in this but a lot of others . . ."

Since therapists have a much broader definition of what is normal human behavior and are generally liberal to boot, the client has a good chance of having his humanity validated.

It is a hopeless task to be perfectly normal (even if someone could define what that is) and if you ever found someone who is absolutely average in everything, he'd be pretty dull company.

Risk Taking

Once you've kept the first appointment with a therapist you've already evidenced a willingness to take risks, some would say even gamble. But is it enough simply to converse with a therapist? Can you really talk life's problems away? Probably not.

Risk taking is the essence of change. You take risks every time you step off a curb and certainly when you expose yourself emotionally to someone else. To show a therapist how vulnerable you are, how and where you can be hurt, what you don't like about yourself, your immaturity, pettiness, and prejudice, requires taking risks—risks that another human being won't reject you, think you're silly or stupid or immoral or turn your faults against you in some harmful way.

To take chances with someone, to trust them not to hurt you is the heart of therapy. But you must risk if you are to shed your natural defenses, your protective psychological armor, so that you and another human can together sift through the good feelings and the bad, the logical and the illogical, the things about yourself you want to keep and the things you would just as soon donate to the past.

To enter therapy and then not risk becoming a different person is to continue to trudge along neck deep in the rut you wanted out of when you made the first appointment.

In my own opinion, talking about change is never enough. Many therapists believe that without also *doing* and *acting* differently between sessions, therapy can be a colossal waste of time—a kind of intellectual calisthenic exercise in which the client tries to build psychological muscles by standing still in one place (the therapist's office). It may be that the risks taken outside of the office (telling a loved one how you would like things to be different, taking that first guitar lesson, interviewing for a new job) are the most important chances you can take. You may also stub your toe, but then who ever got a written guarantee life would be so much duck soup?

Finally, if your only goal in therapy is insight—a psychologically reasonable explanation of why you're miserable—you may achieve this dubious outcome with the assistance of a therapist. Cynically, some therapists will consider you have gained the miracle of insight when you agree with their particular formulations of how you got into such straits. What you then do with this new knowledge is, of course, your business.

The fact that you now *know* why you're miserable or stupid or depressed or ineffective or whatever may satisfy a gnawing curiosity, but *knowing* by itself is a pretty hollow victory. To *act* differently is to *be* different and this requires more than understanding your unfortunate circumstances and making promises to yourself to change or daydreaming about what it would be like to be free from wretchedness.

Getting Scared

You would be a very unusual client if, at some point in the therapy process, you did not feel anxious about some aspect of what you and the therapist are doing. Examining yourself, exposing your weaknesses, taking risks in talking about yourself and doing things differently, all can and do trigger anxiety. You might as well expect to be uncomfortable from time to time while you're going about the business of getting help.

For most therapists and for almost all schools of psychotherapy, anxiety is essential to the progress of therapy. It is an old tenet among therapists that clients who are not anxious about something make poor candidates for change and that unless some kind of fear or worry or source of anxiety can be found, you might just as well hang it up.

It is also true that a therapist who constantly helps you avoid anxiety by changing topics to matters less painful isn't going to be very helpful. If he can't tolerate your being upset, how then can you?

Anxiety comes in different forms—butterflies in the stomach, sweaty palms, rapid heartbeat, shallow breathing, being unable to relax, feeling as though something frightening is about to happen, vague fears that go bump in the night, and so on. We call these vague but unmistakable feelings anxieties, and a large part of therapy is learning about where anxieties come from and learning to call them by their right names—fears.

People prefer a specific fear to a free-floating sense of doom, since at least with fears you know who the enemy is. Feeling anxious, despite all the bad press it's gotten lately, is an emotional state without which we wouldn't know something is wrong—it can help us know something needs changing.

So, to be anxious during a therapy hour is not necessarily bad—it may mean you're working on the right things. Most therapists know how to help you combat anxiety if it gets out of hand, and besides, no one ever died of nervousness.

Resisting Change

Given that total candor, self-exploration, taking risks, hard work, and getting scared are prerequisites to making gains in therapy, it's not surprising that clients figure out ways to avoid all of this. When clients drop out of therapy before much has been accomplished, it's called resistance. Not making a second appointment after the first session is not considered resistance since, for a lot of reasons, you may not "click" the first time around. Like a lot of first dates, once is enough.

However, if you've gotten started in therapy and have been going for a month or more and begin to feel like throwing in the towel, you may need to do some self-appraisal about why you're feeling this way. If you don't find an answer, share these "don't want to" feelings with the therapist—the two of you may need a new footing to work from.

The interesting thing about resistance to therapy, and with it resistance to change, is that much of it is unconscious or at least not easily put into words. Therapists recognize it and try to deal with it before it becomes a serious problem. For some therapies, resistance is the focus of the work.

Resistance takes many forms, some of them are quite subtle. It's pretty obvious that someone who repeatedly misses appointments and doesn't bother to call or cancel isn't too excited about therapy. Whether the client is resisting coming to grips with a problem, doesn't like or respect the therapist, or just doesn't care all that much is difficult to tell. But therapists who get stood up often by a particular client interpret this kind of behavior as resistance. If you "forget" your appointment more than once it would pay to take a look at what's going on in therapy and to talk it over with the therapist—you may discover there are some real issues blocking your progress in getting help, that it's not the priority it once was, or even that you no longer need it.

Some clients resist the therapist's efforts to help them by finding fault with the helper. "He's too critical," "she makes me feel rotten," or, "I don't think he *really* cares about my problems" are the kinds of things clients say to their friends when therapy seems to be unproductive. It usually means they're ready to quit.

It's worth remembering that therapy is an uneven process and that if some sessions are great, others may be mediocre, and some a waste. During these middling sessions, it may be the therapist is less attentive or it may be you're just not up to a hardworking session. It may be you're getting close to making some decision, facing some truth about yourself, or arriving at a realization about something in your life that's going to cause you some sharp psychological discomfort. If you find yourself questioning the competence of the therapist you once respected or you're having negative feelings about therapy, ask yourself a couple of questions. "What's going on with me?" and "Why don't I want to continue?" If that doesn't help, ask the therapist; that's what you're paying her for.

Within any given therapy session, clients can resist the therapist's efforts to help them by such seemingly innocuous things as talking too long about the weather, politics, a movie thay saw—anything to avoid getting to work on what they're there for. Changing the subject of conversation, talking about the problems of a friend, rehashing old injuries and injustices from the past, or trying to get the therapist to talk about himself are all viewed as ways of not dealing with the job of therapy. Most therapists will call your attention to these shifts in focus. "We seem to be drifting," "I wonder why what we're talking about is upsetting you," or some such interpretation to help the client be aware that expensive therapy time is passing unproductively. Therapists want a fair exchange, namely to be of help for the fee you're paying, and therefore will assume responsibility for keeping the hour on target. Getting upset about these kinds of reminders only adds to the therapist's suspicions that for whatever reasons you don't "feel" like working, those reasons warrant explanation and understanding.

Lastly, being resistant to therapy and the change you hoped to bring about in yourself is a natural, even predictable, reaction. You should not be alarmed when it happens. Just remember, all the decisions you've made in life up until now were the best ones you could make with what you knew then. To rethink those decisions with new information about yourself means letting go of what used to work for you. Why shouldn't you be cautious?

Reassessment

In the job of supervising therapists for many years, I have frequently observed therapists and clients bogged down in a relationship where the therapist long ago ran out of ideas and energy and the client, once upset and symptomatic, is now feeling much better but is unable to separate from the therapist. The two of them meet weekly more out of habit than need, yet neither can broach the subject of quitting. The therapist may feel that to suggest termination is to abandon his needy client and the client, not wanting to waste the therapist's time, feels he must scratch around each week for a new and worthy problem. This needn't happen.

In one way, the goal of all therapy is a fond good-bye. Unfortunately, some therapists train their clients in everything but how to say good-bye. They convince them that they cannot function on their own, crippling them psychologically. I have met a few clients who were told in no uncertain terms that they would need therapy for the rest of their natural lives. The convincing of one human being by another that the former is incomplete and unable to live without the latter is a sad state of affairs. Any therapist who instills this kind of thinking in his client has no business masquerading as a helper.

To avoid the problem of excessive dependency on the therapist, the course of therapy should be evaluated from time to time. Some therapists do this routinely after a few sessions, others monthly, and, in line with my own biases, all should make it a point to spend some time evaluating how the therapy is going, whether the client is getting the help he or she wanted, and when they should mutually decide therapy is over.

If the therapist doesn't bring the matter up, you should. If you don't want to bring it up, you can gradually drop out by canceling appointments (until the therapist gets the message), but I would recommend talking about it. Talking openly about how you see the therapy going and whether you're making the gains you had hoped to will be easy if you have the kind of relationship and alliance most people want to achieve in therapy. Your questioning the usefulness of continuing the therapy or asking about termination should not threaten the therapist. I've never known a therapist to throw himself in front of a train because a client rightfully asked if he or she should end the relationship.

Another way to see if therapy is still needed is to take a "therapeutic holiday." This holiday can get you out and away from the weekly appointments and give you a chance to try the things you've learned. Most therapists will know what you mean and many now use such holidays to give their clients an opportunity to break from the routine. Oftentimes the client and therapist will schedule an appointment for some month or two or three in advance and this gives them both the assurance they might need to recap things at some future date.

When you both agree it's time to say good-bye, say good-bye.

12

Is This Matter Confidential?

Almost everyone assumes that what they tell their therapist is held in the strictest confidence and that there are ironclad laws protecting their right to private, even privileged communication. Such is not the case. People also believe that even if there aren't such laws, therapists would rather face a firing squad than violate their clients' trust to keep quiet about embarrassing or harmful disclosures made in the therapy session. This is also poppycock.

Maintaining a client's confidentiality is an article of faith for all professional therapists and, in fact, many have paid fines or gone to jail rather than disclose information confided to them by their clients. But what was once a canon—the guarantee of absolute confidentiality by the professional therapist—has been so riddled by new laws, government regulations, court decisions, and insurance company requirements to pay claims for therapy, that the only thing absolute about confidentiality is that it is not absolute. A few practitioners still promise complete confidentiality, but they may be fined or arrested for obstruction of justice or sued by injured parties for sticking to their guns.

Keeping a confidence is the essence of trust. Therapists and their clients can't work without it. Sometimes, however, the therapist is faced with situations in which the public good has to be weighed against the individual client's right to privacy. These decisions are extremely difficult. Take, for example, a situation where the therapist is evaluating a pilot whose job it is to fly hundreds of passengers around the world in jumbo jets. The pilot complains that he has been worried lately about periods of confusion and blackouts, after which he cannot remember what just happened and is, for a few seconds, "out of it." These lapses haven't happened while he's flying a planeload of people to Paris, but it might and he's worried about it. He tells the therapist that any word of this condition to his employers and the airlines or the Federal Aviation Administration would quickly put an end to his career. He has been promised confidentiality. What should the therapist do? What would you do?

Or let's suppose a client tells his therapist after a couple of visits that he would like to "assault some children." He hasn't done it yet, but he has a victim in mind. Or a mother confesses she is burning her new baby with cigarettes, or a teenager admits to holding up a liquor store and has, with the proceeds, just purchased a pistol with which to do a more effective job on the bank around the corner. These examples are admittedly dramatic, but they make a point—confidentiality is a complex issue.

Third Party Pay and Your Employer

Much more common are requests by insurance companies to detail why a policyholder entered therapy. Insurance companies vary widely on what kind and how much information they want before they will pay a claim. Many clients do not realize *any* information is expected by their insurance company, and are shocked to find out that the company will not pay the claim until they have a great many details about the nature of their policyholder's personal problems. In some cases, medical insurance claims (including those for therapy) are handled through the personnel office where you work and, people being what they are, your fellow workers may learn you're seeing a "shrink" and may even know why. You should also know that at least a few insurance companies feel people who use the services of therapists are poor insurance risks and may cancel your policy after you have filed a claim for therapy services.

The abuse of private medical information by employers may not be widespread but examples of such abuses include individuals being fired after their employers learned they were epileptic, people being denied promotions on the basis of having contracted venereal disease, and people being refused jobs on the basis that they had received psychiatric care. On the other hand, more enlightened employers encourage their employees to seek mental health services—some even pay for the initial visits to a therapist. But things can become complicated.

I once had an accountant as a client who, when he bought his medical insurance policy, signed a waiver or release for "all medical information" about him to be given to the company, when and if he filed a claim. I received a photostatic copy of his signed release. Attached to the release was a very detailed form requiring a complete psychiatric history and most of the details of therapy. To further complicate things, the client was an employee of the company who issued the policy. At our next session, I showed him the photostat of the release he had signed and the psychiatric history form. Justifiably, he became alarmed, feeling that his position with the company might be jeopardized when his supervisor learned the particulars of his problem. Together we agreed to tear up the form. He later left the firm and set up his own practice.

Whose Confidentiality?

The main thing to remember about confidentiality is that it is *yours*—not the therapist's, not the agency's or clinic's or hospital's the therapist works for, and not the insurance company's. Only you have the right to release information about yourself and only you can decide who you want to be in the know about your problems. Any time this trust is broken, you have grounds for at least a complaint, and, depending upon how damaging the results of the breach of confidentiality may be, you may have grounds for a lawsuit.

At the time you see a professional therapist (usually on the first visit) you may be asked to sign a form called a release of information or a request to release information. If your family doctor referred you to the therapist, it is generally accepted good practice for the therapist to write or talk to your doctor about how he sees your problem and to ask for any pertinent medical information or observations your doctor has made about you. These release requests are routine and should pose no problem, unless the doctor is your Uncle George and you don't want Uncle George to know anything he doesn't have to.

Since most mental health centers, clinics, and hospital outpatient settings receive some state or federal money to keep the doors open, you will almost always be asked to sign a release of information form allowing these folks to forward statistical information about you—age, race, sex, marital status, income, etc., to these governmental bodies so they can feed data about you (and thousands of people like you) into gigantic computers. These data are then compiled and routed to various health authorities, congressmen, and other people in control of tax dollars so that they can be convinced that taxpayers have emotional problems and need help.

As far as your confidentiality is concerned, with such agencies, you're well protected by rules and regulations, as well as automatic and stiff fines for anyone in the system who goofs up. Your name, social security number, or address should never go into the computer as these are personal identifiers. If, like some people, you consider the computer to be man's most Frankensteinian invention to date, and feel you can't trust your government not someday to use the fact against you that you once had an emotional or psychological problem, then simply refuse to sign the release. Services can't be denied you and the computer won't starve to death if you choose not to feed it tidbits of personal information about yourself.

If you choose to sign a release, the following safeguards should be included in the document you put your name to:

1. Date.
2. Place for your signature.
3. Place for signature of a witness.
4. To whom information is being released (doctor, lawyer, hospital, etc.).
5. That you have a right to revoke your consent at any time.
6. That you have a right to review materials sent about you to anyone you are authorizing to receive it.
7. An expiration date on the release or a statement that your authorization ends when you terminate your relationship with the therapist or agency.

Most good release forms also specify the nature of information that you are authorizing for release. For example, if you give the okay for the therapist to tell your insurance company you are being seen for marriage counseling and how often, that should not mean the very private details of your sex life will be forwarded to the girls in the claims office for a little light reading during coffee breaks. What you authorize by way of releases should be limited by a need-to-know rule, which would include only material necessary to pay your claim.

Complete Secrecy—A Misrepresentation

When you confide a deep, dark secret, it would be nice if, like hairdressers, you could count on the line that "only your therapist knows." In fact, this is seldom true. In most settings, therapists have supervisors, colleagues with whom they discuss their clients, and if they're in solo practice, they have wives or husbands. In many settings, your therapist is likely to get a consultation (share your problem with a colleague) or otherwise seek advice or suggestions on how he or she might best help you. To my own way of thinking, this is all for the good, since I'm convinced most therapists are hesitant to walk on water and need all the experience and knowledge their colleagues possess to do right by you. Most professionals do not consider talking among themselves about their work a breach of confidentiality when in their work settings. When they talk among themselves about clients outside their work setting, at a party, at a church social or wherever, they have to be extra careful—most won't do it at all.

I once was at a cocktail party held in honor of a local politician where there were a number of mental health professional types in attendance, as well as people from the community. A nurse working in one of the local inpatient psychiatric hospitals gave a colorful description of a woman patient's attempted suicide to a small group of attentive listeners. Her supervisor, a psychiatrist, was also at the party and was aware that the husband of the woman whose private life was making such interesting gossip had been invited to the party, but had not yet arrived. Having overheard the nurse breaking confidentiality, he made it a point to fire her on the spot. It may seem the psychiatrist's actions were severe, but every therapist knows that this kind of trafficking in problems of their clients is a professional hanging offense.

Exceptions to Confidentiality

Despite the therapist's commitment, both professionally and personally, to protect your right to privacy, there are a number of situations in which she or he is bound by law to suspend that trust. These exceptions to confidentiality are not universal since some states have not yet adopted regulations to circumvent the therapist's customary promise to his clients. Also, some of the exceptions noted here are not matters of total agreement among therapists or, for that matter, among the legal experts.

1. *Examination by court order.* If for some reason a judge has ordered you to be examined by a psychiatrist or psychologist (for example in a custody fight), you have no confidentiality. Since the judge ordered the therapist to provide him with a report and/or testimony and you agreed to the proceedings to bolster your case, you must live with the findings. If you feel the results of the examination might be harmful to your case, consult your attorney for advice. In no case will a reputable therapist alter his honest opinion of you. And he or she is bound to report the whole of the findings.

2. *The reporting of an individual intending to commit a crime.* Many states require therapists to report to the police any client who discloses a plan to commit a felony. So if you're a depressed bank robber, mum's the word. More seriously, any threat made on the President of the United States must be reported or the therapist is in violation of at least federal law.

3. *Child abuse or neglect.* Any time a client tells a therapist he or she

has physically or sexually abused his or her child or any minor, most states make it mandatory for the therapist to breach confidentiality and report these suspicions to state or county child welfare authorities or the police department. The same holds true when the therapist has reason to believe a child is being neglected, or not being provided with sufficient food or shelter. This law is a bit tricky since the client (often a parent) is not informed of the requirements to report until it is too late—after he or she has confided the problem to the therapist. The intent of the law is to protect children and those who cannot protect themselves; therefore, it is a good law. In some states (not enough in my opinion) neglect or abuse of retarded or elderly persons also must be reported. But to date, unfortunately, this is not a federal requirement.

4. *Suicide.* In some states, it's against the law to kill yourself. Legally, you just don't have this choice. However, people who attempt suicide are almost never prosecuted, but rather switched to the mental health system for treatment. It seems the majority of our society considers self-destruction pretty nutty. All states have involuntary commitment laws for the mentally ill, laws that deprive people of their right to do nutty things (including doing away with themselves). These laws force a suicidal person into treatment, usually in a private or public psychiatric hospital.

When a therapist feels a client is seriously suicidal, talks about it, has a plan, a date or time to act, a means to accomplish the task, and will not agree to stay alive while he and the therapist work on his problems, most but not all therapists will take whatever legal action necessary to prevent the client from committing suicide. This requires breaking confidentiality.

The therapist will notify whatever authorities exist in his or her community which will cause the client to be detained in a hospital. Most therapists consider an act of suicide a desperate plea for help and that people who feel suicidal have mixed feelings about living and dying and that, with a little time, their reasons for living will prevail and the permanent solution of suicide can be avoided.

There are probably a few therapists (poorly trained or lacking in compassion) who will not risk breaking confidentiality or in any way interfere with a client's self-direction, and will stand by and do nothing while a client completes his own suicide. The vast majority of professional therapists would consider this grossly irresponsible and if they knew about it, would take steps to have such a therapist drummed out of the corps.

I should add that almost everyone at some time in life considers this ultimate solution to life's problems. It is one solution. If you have felt this way or feel this way at the time you see a therapist, don't hesitate to talk about it. It is crucial for both you and the therapist to be on the same track about how badly you feel. He or she won't be surprised if you toy with the idea of suicide. Also, unless you're hell-bent to do away with yourself, he won't break your trust of confidentiality.

5. *Homicide.* Any time a client threatens to kill someone, it is very likely the therapist will take quick action to prevent this happening. Usually it requires him to have the client detained in a hospital for treatment, or picked up by the police. A recent California Supreme Court ruling now obliges therapists in that state not only to notify authorities of the homicidal plans of their client, but also to warn any victim if he or she knows who that victim might be. This ruling has not been tested in all other states, but most professional therapists I've talked with see the merit of warning the intended victim, especially if they might be sued if they fail to give warning.

Subpoenas

A subpoena is an order issued by a judge ordering a therapist to provide records or testimony or both about a client. A subpoena may be requested by an attorney representing you or someone else or simply issued by the judge because he wants to know something. For a therapist automatically and without resistance to obey a subpoena may violate your confidentiality. If a therapist feels his records or what he has to say about you as a client are not in your best interests, he may refuse to obey the subpoena and be held in contempt of court. A few therapists have gone to jail to protect client rights.

State laws vary on whether your communications with a therapist are privileged. If they are, the therapist may not have to comply. Therapists not protected by privileged communication laws are not fond of being held in contempt and may, as a result, obey a subpoena. If the therapist does not have your express permission to reveal confidential information and you feel what he says about you is injurious or harmful, you may have grounds for a lawsuit. In any case, your attorney will need consulting and the therapist, if he knows his business, will contact you the minute he receives a subpoena so that you can consider what course of action is going to be best for you. Remember, confidentiality is yours.

There are a few other areas where confidentiality cannot be guaranteed: testimony in civil commitments for involuntary psychiatric treatment, insanity defenses, competency hearings, instances where a client has died in therapy, and others; but these are out of the scope of a book of this kind and exceptions vary widely from state to state. Also, such problems warrant the services of a good attorney.

Compared to a few years ago, clients and patients whose emotional problems were so severe as to require involuntary hospitalization and consequent deprivation of their civil rights now have a great deal more protection. We all have more confidentiality and privacy than most of us realize. No longer can the authorities simply put crazy people away and lose the key and, in my opinion, our society is the more humane for it.

Confidentiality, Odds and Ends

There remain a few other situations in which confidentiality is less than a blood oath of secrecy and in which the therapist, although he makes his best effort, may not be able to keep the fact of your being in therapy totally confidential.

"If a man answers, hang up." An attractive married woman once gave me these instructions should I ever have need to call her at her home, to cancel an appointment, for example. She did not want her husband to know she was in therapy and so that I wouldn't have to masquerade as a vacuum cleaner salesman, she thought I should disconnect rather than give some screwy explanation. Luckily, I never had to telephone her at home. If for some reason whoever besides yourself might answer the phone is someone you'd prefer doesn't know you're seeing a therapist, a word of instruction to the therapist would be helpful, even though most therapists are sensitive about this.

The same holds true about billing. If you don't want whoever picks up your mail to know you're seeing a therapist, make arrangements so it doesn't happen.

It's not that all therapy-related transactions have to occur in a plain brown wrapper, it's just that if *you* are sensitive about being in therapy, you should be able to count on the therapist to make every effort to accommodate your right to privacy. It would be so much simpler if we, as a society, were more enlightened about therapy or could be as casual as one disc jockey client of mine who, upon my bumping into him in a restaurant where he was seated with a large group of entertainers, shouted for me to join them and introduced me as the guy who "kept my trolley on track."

Occasionally therapists, for research or training purposes or because their supervisors ask them to, will want to tape record or videotape a therapy session. Years ago confidentiality was often skirted and people were tape recorded without their permission. Recorders were designed and disguised so as not to alert the client that he was being taped and it was only after several studies were conducted that it was learned that taping a session made no difference to the average client. Your permission should always be asked before any recording occurs and failure to sign a specific and separate release for such recording is a violation of your rights. If a therapist tapes an interview with you without your express permission, I'd recommend you raise holy hell.

Nowadays, recorders sit on many therapists' desks and they're becoming more common than house plants. To the extent that the therapist reviews his work, seeks consultation about his interviews, and otherwise enhances his skills, the practice is a good one and you will be the benefactor.

Unless you're seeing a therapist in a university-sponsored outpatient clinic or a student counseling center, it is unlikely you'll be asked to participate in a psychotherapy study. If you are asked to be a subject for a research project or participate in any experimental form of therapy, you can be pretty well assured that your anonymity, as well as your psychological well-being, is being carefully protected. Professional ethics, rules and regulations on the use of human subjects, and research review committees composed of reputable scientists oversee virtually all such studies. If asked to participate, you will be invited to ask questions or opt out of the study if you choose. The services you are requesting should not be affected by your choice not to participate.

Only one other area of imperfect confidentiality needs mentioning— your privacy as a member of a therapy group. Without detailing the pros and cons of group versus individual therapy, it is a very common reaction of people seeking help to dismiss the suggestion of talking about their problems with a group of strangers. As far as confidentiality is concerned, a group therapist is bound by all the codes we've discussed, and in the opening session of the group meeting, one of the rules he or she will discuss is that "what is said here remains here"—asking the group members to keep confidential what each of the others discloses.

The problem is that the members of the group are not bound by ethics or law to keep their mouths shut about your problem. In my experience, confidentiality in groups is seldom a problem. The fear that someone in the group may purposely set out to malign your character or feed lurid details about your sex life (if you're lucky enough to have a few lurid details to talk about) to a gossip column is such a remote possibility that it might be best to reexamine your reasons for resisting your therapist's suggestion that you join a group. You may find a group experience the most valuable source of help available for the problems you face.

Finally, trust is the key element in any therapeutic relationship— without it, as in any other human relationship, there's nothing to build on and if there's nothing, we might as well go on leading lives of quiet desperation. We all need trust, privacy, and confidentiality, and therapists will do their damnedest to protect your needs for these. In a way, unnecessary intrusions by insurance companies, employers, government officials, and others who consider what you and your therapist talk about as public information constitute a common assault on all of our rights to privacy, and only together can we successfully defend these constitutional rights.

13

The Complaint Department

A thirty-five-year-old married woman asks her attorney to file suit against her psychiatrist because he told her to crawl around on the office floor and make gooing sounds like a six-month-old baby, after which she felt outraged and humiliated.

A forty-year-old business executive threatens to take to court a psychologist who told his wife that she was behaving like a "doormat" and since the psychologist also told the woman she was married to a "chauvinist," she is now threatening to divorce him if he doesn't start treating her fairly.

A seventeen-year-old boy cries bitterly to his parents that his therapy group—at the direction of the therapist—delivered him a spanking which, though more symbolic than real and leaving no marks, both embarrassed him and demeaned his adolescent pride and self-respect. The parents threatened suit.

The outraged but fictional people in these examples feel they or their loved ones have been wronged, hurt, or somehow injured and that they have grounds for a successful lawsuit. Most likely, however, their attorneys will tell them to forget it. Unless clear damages can be demonstrated, there will be no point in starting an action.

"He badgered me with questions and he made me feel stupid."

"He called me a 'hostile bitch' in front of my husband."

"She told me to take a soft pillow-like club and hit her with it, saying I was angry and didn't know it. When I refused, she hit me with one of these clubs and tried to provoke me. Then I really smacked her and now I feel rotten."

"He gave me a deck of cards and told me to build a house with them. When I was finished, he kicked it over, explaining I needed to see how futile my life was."

Not the stuff of lawsuits certainly, but are these things worth complaining about? Well, maybe. Aren't therapists a little weird anyway and who knows for sure that what they did wasn't okay? If the therapist did nothing clearly unethical (maybe what he said or did was only poor taste or poor judgment), most people will say that since you sought the help voluntarily, you asked for it.

Still, Americans have a low regard for bullies, exploiters, and anyone who takes unfair advantage by reason of position or power, and suits against therapists are on the rise. People are expressing their dissatisfaction with therapists, some publicly, most privately, and a few through the courts. In this chapter, I hope to accomplish two things—describe the kinds of therapist behavior that warrant a complaint or possibly a civil action and to outline the steps you can take to get satisfaction if you feel you've been wronged. I do this because the good-guy therapists need protection from the bad-guy therapists, and, in many cases, only the unhappy client can tell us if there is a bad apple in our barrel. Also, many people do not seek the help they need because they fear mistreatment, harm, or that they're going to be made to feel worse. Maybe if they knew beforehand what inappropriate or unethical behavior was and what to do about it, they wouldn't hold back about seeking the needed help.

Why People Don't Complain

There are several very good reasons why people don't complain about a bad therapy experience. In the first place, who likes a complainer? Our society doesn't like a whiner but registering dissatisfaction about professional services is another matter. Those therapists most interested in the image of their profession want to hear your complaints. Things are slow around most ethics committees and the members who volunteered for duty need something to do. Agency directors want to hear your concerns about their employees and though they may not like what you have to say, they would rather hear it from you than from a third party.

Secondly, people don't complain because to do so means they have to admit they made a poor decision in the first place. We all make mistakes and you certainly can't be blamed for assuming a professional therapist is not going to treat you with anything but respect and dignity. If he didn't, that does not make you stupid.

Thirdly, people often fear filing a complaint will expose them to ridicule or embarrassment or that, somehow, the confidential nature of their problem will become public. In some cases, the loss of confidentiality is a necessity if the complaint is to be taken to the parties who can do something, but I can assure you that extra caution is taken by those who hear your complaint to protect you from further injury.

Fourthly, people don't complain because they feel it won't do any good and in many situations they are right. The problem is that some very just grievances are never heard, and the rotten apples go on spoiling the barrel. The helping professions worry about their image with the public and are willing to discipline their members. But their responsible committees on ethical conduct and professional standards need your complaint before they can act.

Lastly, people don't know what channels of protest are available to them. Only in the last few years have the professional associations begun to inform the consumer about such channels and to make it known that they are willing to take their lumps.

Minor Gripes

The most common complaints about therapists with which I am familiar have to do with disappointment—the therapist doesn't do what the client expects him to do. "He talks too much," "he talks more about his problems than mine," "he never says anything," "she never gives advice," "I don't think he really understands me," "she isn't helping me" are all typical of the frustrations clients experience.

Most would agree that these are petty disgruntlements and yet they are the very reasons people fire their therapists (usually by canceling their next appointment or not making another one). The difference between how the therapist works and how the client thinks the therapist should work accounts for most of these disappointments, and there isn't much anyone can do about them, particularly if the therapist's style of therapy doesn't agree with the client's expectations.

Outside of the therapist's style (active versus passive, directive versus nondirective, analytical versus focusing on the here and now, etc.), there are other common complaints that, while not about unethical behavior, are viewed by clients as discourteous. Having their session interrupted by phone calls, the therapist being habitually late, canceling the therapy hour because of "higher priorities," and other signs and signals that the therapist does not view the therapy hour as importantly as does the client are sources of complaints that, if left unspoken, become resentments that impede therapy.

Misunderstandings about how client and therapist are going to work together frequently lead to complaints. If you have to miss an appointment must you pay for the hour? Will the therapist keep an appointment hour open for you while you take a vacation? Is he available after hours or for emergency appointments? These and other questions should be dealt with early on, preferably in the first session (see chapter 9), and will clear the way for a good working relationship. Your therapist has the obligation to lead the negotiations about these issues and you have a right to expect him to do so.

Before firing a therapist over these irritants, say something—most therapists will understand your feelings and make things right. When it comes to psychotherapy, you needn't feel the doctor is never wrong. A colleague of mine once had a client tell him toward the end of the therapy hour that he seemed "too tired" to pay attention. He laughed, agreed he was pooped, and cut the fee by half for that session.

Major Complaints

Serious complaints about therapists are rare but, in my experience, not uncommon. That sentence may sound contradictory but it is not.

Angry clients rarely take their complaints to the right people, people who can help them set the dogs on an unethical therapist. More often they complain to the wrong people—friends, family, pastor or priest, and frequently to another therapist in a different profession. Complaining to a psychiatrist about a psychologist or vice versa happens all the time and reinforces our long-standing sentiments that those "other guys" are an unethical bunch. You won't get much action by asking one profession to help you with a complaint against another since none of us wants to have his knives sharpened by the Philistines.

If you've talked to the therapist about what you consider unprofessional conduct and gotten no satisfaction, going over his head requires a commitment, a commitment complicated by many unknowns. And while it takes courage, I encourage you to act. But first, what are the standards by which therapists are supposed to conduct themselves? What can you rightfully complain about? While it is true that you can sue anyone for anything, a civil action is not always the best solution. Besides being very costly, you could lose your case and gain nothing but humiliation.

Basically, all the helping professions expect their members to treat clients with respect and dignity, to deal with them fairly, to represent themselves accurately, to limit their practice to their areas of competence, and to uphold the moral and legal standards of their community. Professionalism in all matters is the core of conduct. For the specific ethical standards of a profession, you may write any of the national associations listed in Appendix C.

Malpractice Versus Unethical Conduct

It is important to understand that unethical conduct does not automatically provide grounds for a successful malpractice suit. It may, but not necessarily. To collect damages for malpractice you must first prove you were damaged. To do this, you will need to convince your attorney, a jury, and maybe a judge that because of some specific action or negligence on the part of the therapist, you have suffered in some real way— lost a job, a wife or husband, a source of income, your reputation, or been hurt in some way that a panel of your peers can readily understand. If your damages have been psychological (you are more depressed, more anxious, have fears you didn't have before you started therapy, etc.) then you will very probably need an expert witness to testify to that in a court of law.

It is not an easy task to find a professional therapist who will stand up in court and say his colleague was negligent or that some specific action or inaction led to the psychological condition for which the client is seeking damages. Known as "hired guns," such expert witnesses risk ostracism from their fellows and sometimes demand exorbitant fees to offset the consequences of becoming a pariah within their profession. Additionally, since standards of practice are vague, effectiveness of therapy uncertain, and much of the work of therapy more art than science, no professional in his right mind can afford to be dogmatic about what is right and what is wrong with the way his colleagues work, clear violations of ethical standards notwithstanding.

Finally, it is probably impossible to sue a psychoanalyst successfully for being insufficiently analytical or a nondirective therapist for giving advice or a behaviorist for interpreting a dream or a cognitive therapist who failed to make you *think* better. To do so successfully, you would first have to find a therapist of the same theoretical persuasion to admit he could have done the therapy better. Given the enormous complexity of human behavior (especially as it occurs in the course of therapy), it would take a therapist with an ego the size of Texas to so testify against a colleague. And juries don't like big egos.

Sex and Therapy

It's called "exploiting a dependency relationship," but by any name and by any ethical standard of the major professions, having sexual intercourse with a client is wrong. The public agrees, juries agree, and, with very few maverick exceptions, all professional helpers agree.

No one knows for sure how many therapists have sexual intercourse with their clients. Studies show an alarmingly high incidence of sexual contact between clients and therapists.

An old mentor of mine once said he never encouraged social contact with clients until therapy had been officially terminated for at least six months. Even then, he was cautious. "You can't be a friend and a therapist at the same time," he said. "And if you can't be friends, you can't be lovers." That meant, of course, that he never played golf with his clients, never had lunch with them, never went to their homes for dinner, or in any way maintained a relationship other than one that was strictly professional. Some therapists don't see it this way and in smaller towns it may be impossible to avoid each other. It is when the nature of the relationship changes from one of therapist-client to one of friendship that things can begin to go awry.

Sexual exploitation in a therapy relationship is always a breach of ethics and every qualified therapist knows it. To be sexually intimate with a client is to risk everything—job, career, family, reputation, and often a lawsuit. It is the one clear hanging offense. Still, it happens.

The reasons it happens are as old as time—two people get to know each other, are attracted to each other, and things get physical. The consequences of their sexual intimacy may not necessarily lead to disaster, but the premise of the relationship is a false one. The victim, almost always a woman, is usually vulnerable—lonely, in doubt about her adequacy, upset and in need of empathy, support, and even love. She may have trouble specifically dealing with men and in particular with men in authority positions. If the therapist makes overtures she may feel that to reject them is to jeopardize getting the help she needs. But, for her own sake, she must reject such advances and, until more women do, what sexual exploitation does occur will continue.

It doesn't take a genius to see that when you put two people of the opposite sex in close emotional and physical proximity, the likelihood of someone's chemistry getting away from them is increased. But regardless of who may have given signals that sex would be okay, the therapist is responsible for what happens. He (it's usually men) always could have said no.

While some argue that clients are not necessarily hurt by intercourse with the therapist, that it might even be therapeutic, the question remains—therapeutic for whom? An ethical therapist does not look for dates in his office and if your therapist suggests a more "personal relationship," it's time to scram.

More typically, the unethical practitioner blatantly uses his position of power to disguise intercourse (delivered by himself of course) as a cure for sexual inhibitions. It is enough to say that no reputable professional endorses such nonsense.

All of this is not to say that clients don't fall in love with their therapists or that therapists don't fall in love with their clients. But again, the therapist is ethically responsible for dealing with his feelings and with those of his client in an open and frank manner, often suggesting a referral to another therapist or at least a decent interval at the end of therapy before they see each other socially. Therapists frequently put themselves under supervision or in therapy when such problems arise to keep their professional balance. I know of at least one happy marriage where exactly this sequence of events took place.

An area of some debate has to do with physical contact and whether such contact is always necessarily erotic. Touching is a distinctive aspect of some modern therapies and authorities agree that a hug or a kiss given a client to comfort them is not unethical. In fact, touching is so basic to healthy human functioning, you could argue that to not hug a distraught client and thereby deprive them of a powerful form of support is poor practice. In my own experience, I've worked with clients who needed to be touched, given a hug, and otherwise physically shown that I cared about them and did not see them as so repulsive as to be "untouchable." I've also known clients for whom anything more than a crisp handshake would have violated their sense of privacy.

As with so much of the art of therapy, it is a matter of the therapist's clinical judgment whether he engages in physical contact with his clients, although at least one state has outlawed touching by psychologists. I know a therapist who hugs everyone and a therapist who never hugs anyone and I've heard complaints about both—the hugger is a "phony," the nonhugger "cold." Neither one seems to know precisely what people need.

How to Complain Effectively

If you think you have grounds for a lawsuit, I'll leave that decision to you and your attorney. I'm not a lawyer and only you can decide if you want to take that form of redress. But if you decide that's what you want to do, at least find an attorney who knows the score about malpractice suits and something about what you are getting yourself into.

If your beef is a minor one, talk first to your therapist. There is no way around it, a complaint is a criticism. To minimize the therapist's defensiveness, make your criticism as clear as possible—be specific, describe what your therapist did or said that upset you, and especially say how you felt about what happened. Try to avoid generalizations (you don't seem to approve of me, you never really listen, you're always late, etc.), but rather spell out how an incident affected you and how this concerns you. And don't wait—deal with the problem at the next session.

The majority of problems in communication, differences in expectations, and troublesome irritants can be handled with a little candor on your part and a little humility on the part of the therapist. If the therapist gets defensive or uppity, you can always complain to his boss or fire him.

If you decide the problem has not been resolved between you and the therapist after talking about it, you can get another therapist or, if he works in an agency, ask to talk to his supervisor. This is always awkward and the therapist won't like it, but if you need the help, then it's worth doing. As an alternative, you can always get quick action by asking to see the director of the agency or telephoning him or her directly. Since stress has a way of flowing downhill, you can be sure whoever ends up listening to your complaint is someone who can do something about it. Neither of these approaches insures a happy resolution, only that more people will know you're upset, people with power to do something.

If the therapist is in private practice and your complaint is a minor one and, after discussing your feelings with him you still aren't satisfied, there isn't much you can do. I suppose you could tell your friends the fellow is rude, incompetent, or squirrelly or whatever but, in reality, there's little to be done. Certainly complaining to the person who referred you to the therapist is worth doing and may result in fewer referrals to the therapist, but there's no direct benefit to you.

Most often people quit the therapist and start over with someone else. I do not recommend you point out the apparent shortcomings of your first therapist to a second one. While the latter may agree with you that the fellow wasn't worth his fee, many therapists will automatically side with their colleague and immediately begin wondering about you.

Unless your complaint is a serious one (usually involving a breach of ethics or a violation of state law), nothing is likely to happen if you file a minor complaint with a professional association. The procedure takes time, is stressful, and you will have given up some confidentiality. The same is true if you file your complaint with the state licensing board. Licensing boards typically turn the matter over to the administrative arm of government for investigation and the attorney general will act only if there has been a clear violation of state law. Again, since there are no benefits to you personally, it probably isn't worth your time.

However, if you have a serious complaint of unethical or illegal behavior to register, then by all means do so, if not for yourself, then for the rest of us—especially the therapists who want to maintain the credibility and reputation of their profession.

Just where to complain is less clear. For example, a psychologist may be licensed to practice but not belong to a state psychological association or the American Psychological Association, in which case registering your complaint to either association may be a waste of time. These organizations usually have no jurisdiction over nonmembers and would risk a lawsuit if they tried to sanction a nonmember or in any way injure his reputation or interfere with his ability to earn a living.

You can quickly learn if a therapist is a member of a national association by calling the association. (See Appendix G for a list of professional organizations.) If he is a member, then ask for whoever it is that handles complaints and follow their advice. The national associations have state chapters and this is usually where the investigation is carried out, sometimes by regional chapters in your area.

You may also begin a complaint proceeding closer to home by contacting the county medical society (if the therapist is a psychiatrist) or the local chapter of professional psychologists or social workers.

If a therapist is not a member of a professional organization, you have no choice but to contact the state licensing or certification board (assuming you're seeing a licensed practitioner) and tell them the problem. Most often this leads to an investigation by the attorney general's office (the people who enforce state laws) or the licensing board and, again, the proceedings may be lengthy, time consuming, and possibly stressful.

The consequences to the therapist against whom a complaint has been successfully lodged may vary from praise from his colleagues, to nothing, to a verbal or written reprimand, to suspension or expulsion from his professional association or to the loss of his license to practice. Praise, you ask? Yes. I know one therapist who refused to provide therapy to a woman alcoholic who would not agree to try to stop drinking. The therapist said, "I don't want to hold your hand while you kill yourself with alcohol and you refuse to go into a hospital." The woman filed a complaint stating the therapist had abandoned her. The review board agreed the therapist had acted in the best interest of the client and told him so in a letter.

The severity of the sanctions taken against a therapist will vary with the offense, who's doing the punishing, and whether this is the first complaint against a particular therapist. I would be grossly misleading you if I implied swift and uniform consequences were sure to follow each complaint. The process of meting out discipline to erring therapists by any helping profession is at best a poor imitation of justice. Except where the evidence for bad conduct is clear, cogent, and convincing, most clients would be disappointed with the ounce of flesh most ethics committees extract from a wayward colleague. Often the transgressing therapist receives a recommendation to enter therapy himself. This may be a very good idea, but hardly rings true as punishment.

While some of my colleagues won't be happy with the suggestions, I think it's a good idea to complain to three groups: the national association to which the therapist belongs, the state association, and the state board which granted him the license to practice. If one group fails to act, another should, and at the very least you will have more than one responsible group on notice.

Should you decide to file a formal complaint, put it in writing. The letter should contain the following points:

1. Your name, address, and telephone number.
2. The name and address of the organization and/or person against whom you wish to complain.
3. The nature of your complaint: how you have been treated or wronged and how you feel you have been harmed.
4. A description of any efforts you have already made to resolve the complaint.
5. Copies of any correspondence or papers about the matter.
6. Any additional background information about yourself or circumstances that you feel might be useful in evaluating the complaint.
7. Your signature.

By all means indicate you expect an answer to your letter and keep a copy for yourself.

One final note is in order. A serious complaint against a therapist can wreak havoc with his professional and personal life. Know your rights but also be sure the action you take is responsible. We want the bad apples out of the barrel as much as anyone, but we don't want to throw out any good apples in the process.

14

Pills, Pills, Pills—
A Guide to Psychoactive
Drugs

It is very likely that in your search for help with a personal problem, someone is going to invite you into a medical candy store filled with brightly colored pills and capsules containing potions and promises. While you won't be able to pick and choose what looks good, it may be suggested that the remedy for what ails you is contained in one or more of those little tablets, and if you will but take some, you will begin to feel better, think straighter, sleep sounder, handle stress, relax, or in some way be able to press the wrinkles from your tired mind. And in large part, this is all true.

These little pills, called psychoactive drugs, are powerful agents and for the most part live up to their advertising. However, since these small friends from chemistry are so powerful, it may be worthwhile to know a few things about them before you pop them into your mouth.

The modern drugs used in the treatment of psychological and psychiatric problems have had a short history, but an enormous impact on the way we, as a society, view solutions to our problems. Many experts now agree we have gone too far in our search for happiness through chemistry, and that we have created a cultural attitude in which taking a pill has become an almost standard response to pain, physical or psychic.

So prevalent is this attitude that many patients feel their physician has somehow shortchanged them if they do not receive a prescription after making an office visit. Can you imagine someone with insomnia being satisfied when their family doctor asks them to stop drinking coffee after dinner, skip the detective story or late-night vampire movie, and suggests they have a warm glass of milk just at bedtime? That milk and a reduction in stimulation could possibly be a substitute for a barbiturate is unthinkable, and a predictable rejoinder to such a suggestion would be: "I know all that, doctor, but aren't you going to give me something?"

To deal with this characteristic demand of patients, some physicians now give placebos (inert substances with absolutely no active chemical ingredients) to their insistent patients on the premises that: (a) what the patient doesn't know won't hurt him; and (b) the psychological effect of taking a "pill" often nets a positive result.

Beyond whatever magical effects are inherent in pills, some psychoactive medications are extremely effective. Some mood-altering drugs can break up a depression that for months has made life a barely tolerable exercise in the struggle to keep going. Still other drugs can mitigate the severe symptoms of mental illness which, were it not for the medication, would result in hundreds of thousands of people having to live their lives in mental hospitals while their hallucinations, delusions, and fear-provoking behavior have to be supervised and controlled through physical restraint and prisonlike environments. There is no doubt about it, the psychoactive drugs that combat major mental illness are the miniature miracle workers of modern psychiatry. Chemistry for the mind is here to stay.

There is nothing inherently evil in chemicals. But what they do to you after they enter your body should be a matter of utmost concern to you. To swallow a capsulized chemical invented in a laboratory, tested on defenseless rats and mice and a few brave fellow human beings requires a fair amount of trust in the physician who suggests you take it, in the company that produces the drug, and in the Federal Drug Administration to have evaluated closely the risks of taking a particular medicine.

You've Got an Attitude Toward Drugs—What Is It?

If you didn't care about your health, you wouldn't be reading this book. If you're offered drugs to change or alter the way you think and feel, you'll have a decision to make. To be quite frank about it, there's no practical way you can evaluate the pros and cons of a particular medicine. You're neither a physician nor a pharmacologist and, therefore, you don't have the benefit of years of training in the business of what drugs are made of, how they are produced, what benefits the research predicts they will have, what interactions they will have with each other if you're taking more than one, or what particular effect a given drug will have on you as a unique biological entity. If you're going to take any psychoactive drug, you'll first have to take a leap of faith. For some, the leap is shorter than for others.

In many ways, it is easier for some of us to believe that what is wrong with us emotionally is biological, not psychological. If something is psychologically wrong, then the cause is unknown and the cure uncertain. If something is biologically wrong, then the practitioners of medical science can find it and fix it. After all, they have X-ray machines, blood tests, stethoscopes, and all kinds of shiny hardware to turn us inside out and find the source of discomfort.

Since people vary widely in how they view the source of their pain, including psychological pain, they are also going to vary widely in what they believe is the proper remedy. If you're the kind of person who believes emotional problems are the result of biological imbalances, an inadequate diet, tired glands, or crooked chromosomes, then a biological solution—a chemical solution—may be the only kind of help acceptable to you. And if someone suggests you take a pill for your discomfort, you'll probably take it.

If, on the other hand, you're the kind of person who believes the mind can conquer all and that pills aren't good for people, then a chemical solution is not going to appeal to you, and the leap of faith it takes to swallow a tablet is going to be an Olympian effort.

Unfortunately, the causes of emotional problems are not nearly so simple and clear-cut as are our beliefs about those causes, and just because we believe we know what the matter is doesn't make it so. The point is that each of us has an attitude toward drugs that stems from a belief about what is causing us all this misery. We need to examine our attitude if we are going to take pills, or if we're going to dismiss them out of hand.

The decision to take psychoactive drugs is a serious one, and what follows are some suggestions and information that should help you make a more informed choice. I can't overemphasize the importance of discussing your feelings and beliefs about medications with whatever kind of professional you decide upon, and to determine, as best you can, the feelings and attitudes of the therapist about psychoactive drugs.

See a Psychiatrist

If you've already decided that psychoactive drugs are something you want to consider, see a psychiatrist. Besides the fact that psychiatrists are the best trained in matters of psychoactive drugs, psychologists, social workers, and psychiatric nurses can't write prescriptions and so there's not much point in wasting an expensive visit to one of these professionals.

Some mental health professionals (including psychiatrists) have a distinctly antidrug attitude when it comes to the use of medications for emotional woes. Still, if a psychiatrist says you don't need drugs to get better, he or she is probably right. The same statement from a psychologist or social worker may not be true since, if in fact medications might help you, they would have to refer you to a psychiatrist for that service—a referral that may result in a lost patient and a lost fee.

If you need medications for a serious psychiatric problem, a competent and ethical therapist of any persuasion will refer you to a psychiatrist, and, as pointed out earlier, the importance of finding a qualified therapist is underscored.

Ask About the Drug

Not long ago, I was interviewing a client who had had emotional problems some years before. As she had been prescribed several psychotropic medications to combat her symptoms, I asked her what they were—a routine inquiry. "I took a bunch of little white ones in the mornings and some red ones at night. The red ones knocked me out!" The lady wasn't retarded, but it was painfully clear she understood next to nothing about the medication, what effect it was supposed to have, or for that matter, why she was asked to take it.

Increasingly, physicians and psychiatrists are required to give you information about the drug they are prescribing, and why they are prescribing it. You should feel completely free to ask questions about what you are given to ingest, and should at least learn the name of it, what effects you can expect, how long you should take it, and, if you're concerned about cost, its generic name and whether the doctor thinks a generic product (usually much cheaper than a trade brand) is a drug of equal quality. Your questions will not only net you some needed assurances, but should also increase the physician's respect for you as a concerned and informed consumer.

Side Effects

Most drugs have side effects—some worse than others. It may be unfortunate, but many of the most useful psychoactive drugs are also the most powerful and have the greatest side effects, almost always unpleasant. A dry mouth, a decrease in sexual appetite, sleepiness, and other symptoms are common. Most of these symptoms will pass with time, but you need to know that and not be alarmed when they occur. Too often, people discontinue a needed psychoactive drug because they are unsure, frightened, and uninformed about these almost predictable physical side effects. Be sure to ask what to do if any of these unpleasantries occur.

Infrequently asked, but every bit as important, are questions about how addicting a particular drug might be. Psychoactive drugs vary widely in addictive qualities and some are completely safe in this regard. Others are known to produce states of temporary euphoria or a sense of mellow relaxation, and some people might think that if one pill is good, two or three might be even better. Although unintended, getting hooked on prescription drugs is so common that the National Institute of Drug Abuse has launched prevention and treatment programs all over the country to try to stem the growing tide of prescription abuse.

Take as Directed

It does no good at all to take medication prescribed by a trained physician if *you* decide when, how much, and with what you take the pill. The biggest reason these medicines don't work for people is that they never have a chance. People forget to take them, take half as much as prescribed, double up to catch up or even discontinue them altogether—often without consulting their psychiatrists. Surprisingly, patients are disappointed in the doctor. You paid a psychiatrist for his knowledge—give him a chance.

Medical History

It is not up to you to offer spontaneously a complete medical history to a psychiatrist who is about to write you a prescription. You should expect to be asked some questions about your past health, current problems, major illnesses, and the like, or if you're being referred by your family doctor, the psychiatrist will already know much of what he needs to from a medical standpoint. However, never assume perfect knowledge in human beings, including doctors. They can't know what you don't tell them, and to sit back and hope they will ask just the right question (of all the possible inquiries a physician might make to determine the status of your health) is to create problems where there needn't be any.

If you're seeing another physician or therapist, say so. If you're taking some cute little blue pills Aunt Edith gave you a year ago, say so. If you have had an alcohol problem in the past, bring it up. Despite our cultural perception of physicians as all-knowing, they're only third-rate diviners and can't see in the dark any better than you and I.

It is especially important to let the physician know about other medications you are taking, including aspirins, contraceptives, and antihistamines. He or she will need to know if you've had any reactions to other drugs or foods in the past, and any allergies or special sensitivities you may have to chemicals in any form. If you're pregnant, or think you might be but haven't yet confirmed this condition, be sure to bring this up—even if you're only suspicious. The fetus is highly susceptible to drugs in the first three months of life and there's no point adding guilt to the problems you may already have. Many physicians will not recommend taking any drugs during pregnancy, unless the illness, including a psychiatric one, is a life-threatening matter.

More Than One Medication?

In the language of emotional and psychological distress, it is extremely common for distressed people to describe more than one symptom. We are rarely just depressed, simply anxious, or only have trouble sleeping. It is more often the case that when we have troubles, the signs and symptoms come in batches. Yes, we're depressed; we also have no appetite, but if we do have an appetite, we're overweight. We can't sleep, we don't have enough energy to get going in the morning, or we're tense and can't relax, or we're bothered by recurrent thoughts that hammer away in our minds all day.

When a patient or client presents a battery of psychological symptoms, some physicians and a few psychiatrists prescribe a battery of drugs—one for each symptom. This practice of writing multiple prescriptions, or polypharmacy, is not an uncommon practice, but it is increasingly frowned upon by competent psychiatrists.

The apparent expectation of the person prescribing one pill for depression, another for anxiety, a third to get to sleep, a fourth to get going in the morning, and a fifth to counteract the side effects of the first four is that somewhere in this barrage of medication is something that might hit the target and give the patient some relief. This approach to helping people with problems (aptly called the shotgun technique) suggests the practitioner can't figure out what is troubling her patient, or at best, reflects a sloppy professional response to what is usually a delicate matter. Besides resembling a high-school chemistry experiment, multiple medications can place the patient at higher risk than is necessary.

If on your first visit to a psychiatrist you come away with a fistful of prescriptions, you'd be well advised to seek a second opinion. Two, maybe even three prescriptions of psychoactive drugs may be indicated; but one, used on a trial basis, is more the rule. If a psychiatrist writes you a host of prescriptions and gives you a "tut tut" answer to your questions about why so many are needed—remember, he or she isn't taking the stuff.

Medications and Psychotherapy

Almost never is a psychoactive medication an end-all to the psychological problems for which you're seeking help. To be offered only drugs for what ails you should be a clear warning that the therapist's approach is both narrow and limited.

On the premise that the vast majority of psychological and emotional problems are the result of difficulties in living, getting along with other people and ourselves, maybe it doesn't make much sense to expect a pill to do what needs to be done. There are, of course, those kinds of major mental illnesses in which a biological basis for the disturbance is highly suspect, and clearly these have responded well to certain kinds of psychoactive medications.

Psychoactive medications are often used as an adjunct to talking therapy, and as such, have no doubt benefited thousands of clients. But as too often happens, the talking stops and the pills continue. Pills give quick relief where the therapist's questions, confrontations, and challenges to change will more likely cause painful self-examination, self-doubt, and resistance to making decisions that would alter the basic problems that brought the client in in the first place. If you've accepted a prescription for psychoactive medications, use it. Keep in mind, however, that by themselves, pills make poor psychotherapists and that you're probably getting shortchanged if that's all you're getting out of the therapeutic relationship.

Pills and Booze

The competent physician will give you ample warning about the possible side effects of taking psychoactive drugs and alcohol together. Many frequently prescribed drugs are known to interact dangerously with alcohol. Once in a while some drugs lose their effectiveness when washed down with alcohol. Some, interacting with alcohol, can cause the patient to lose effectiveness or even to die.

Since about 2,500 American lives are lost each year due to drug/alcohol interaction, never hesitate to ask what a psychoactive concoction and a cocktail would do to you. Too many perfectly normal people die as a result of their ignorance of chemistry and you shouldn't hesitate one minute to ask your doctor about the effect of drugs and alcohol taken together.

What Are All These Pills?

As I mentioned earlier, you can't expect to be an expert about psychoactive medication unless you're willing to drop everything and go to medical school, or better yet, get a Ph.D. in biochemistry or psychopharmacology. Despite the nearly endless variety of sizes, colors, shapes, dosages, and names, there are really only three major types of drugs in common use in psychiatry—antipsychotic agents, antianxiety agents, and antidepressants. Some others, namely lithium carbonate and amphetamines, are used less frequently and more selectively since they are designed to target a narrow band of symptoms. There are also some psychoactive drugs that are mixtures of major tranquilizers and antidepressant ingredients designed, apparently, for the convenience of those who like the pills blended before they reach their bloodstreams. There are also, of course, several sleep preparations.

Antipsychotic Agents

The antipsychotic agents are used to relieve symptoms of severe agitation and the anxiety experienced by psychotic patients. These drugs have a remarkably quieting effect and result in a reduction of the symptoms of disordered thought, feelings of paranoia, irrational beliefs about reality, and other symptoms that often require hospitalization. Their major advantages are a usually rapid reduction of these psychotic symptoms and the resulting ability of the patient to carry on a relatively normal life, remain out of the hospital, and enjoy the benefits of a society that might not otherwise have been available to them had they required continued hospitalization. Some of the negative side effects, considered by most patients to be worth the trouble, include occasional allergic reactions, some involuntary muscle movements, dry mouth, slight constipation, and a sensitivity to sunlight. Depending on how long someone has to remain on these medications, the side effects can be increasingly hazardous and close monitoring by a psychiatrist is essential. The trade names of the antipsychotic agents (sometimes known as major tranquilizers and the phenothiazines) include Stelazine, Thorazine, Mellaril, Haldol, and Prolixin.

Antianxiety Agents

The antianxiety agents (trade names include Valium, Librium, Xanax, and Ativan, among others) are used primarily in the treatment of anxiety. In terms of possible drug dependency developing, the antianxiety agents are the ones most in question. Though very effective in the relief of symptoms of anxiety, they are not magic happy pills, even though they have been indiscriminately used in this way.

Short-term use is usually okay, but long-term use can lead to physical and psychological dependence, and there is increasing evidence that serious addictions can occur. These drugs have additive effects with alcohol and sleep preparations, and therefore present some risk. Since they do what they say, namely tranquilize, they can interfere with things like going to work, driving, operating machinery, and otherwise getting around in the world in an alert fashion.

Professional therapists often have strong pro and con feelings about the antianxiety drugs, but there is no doubt about their popularity—they even sell well on the streets. Advice: take them with care and caution.

The Antidepressants

The most common antidepressant drugs (referred to as the tricyclics and by the trade names of Elavil, Tofranil, Norpramin, and others) are in widespread use primarily for symptoms of depression. These drugs take some ten days to four weeks before their effect is felt (although faster-acting antidepressants are now available), and because their side effects include dry mouth, constipation, rapid heartbeat, blurred vision, occasional fainting or sweating, and tremors, they are often discontinued before these symptoms fade and the beneficial effect of the medications take hold. Incidentally, the antidepressants are increasingly used to treat chronic pain, and for some cases of agoraphobia (fear of open places).

For a time, amphetamines, commonly known to the under-fifty group as "speed," were used to treat depression. This practice is now considered bad medicine since the drugs produced a lot of fast-talking and fast-walking depressed people. Therefore, if you're depressed, you shouldn't expect a prescription for any of the following: Benzedrine, Dexadrine, Desoxyn, or others. The side effects of the amphetamines include overstimulation, inability to sleep, rapid heartbeat, loss of appetite, and a very probable problem of serious dependency. Withdrawal from amphetamines is quite unpleasant, and the initial symptoms of withdrawal usually lead the patient to take even more amphetamines which leads to an unremitting cycle of drug abuse. It may be easy to get high on amphetamines and experience one's mood elevating at a blinding speed, but in the treatment of depression with amphetamines, cheap is expensive.

Lithium carbonate is a relatively new drug and has been used successfully in the treatment of people with manic-depressive disorders, usually more satisfactorily when the person has had very clear manic episodes. Lithium, a simple salt, is harmless in appearance and while its less unpleasant side effects may include occasional fatigue, muscle ache, slurred speech, hand tremors, trembling, nausea, and diarrhea, the worst side effects are convulsions and death. The amount of lithium in the blood must be carefully monitored and a precise amount of medication must be taken exactly as prescribed or very nasty consequences can follow. Still, for many people who experience episodes of extreme emotional highs and lows, Lithium carbonate may be the first real salvation they have found.

Sedatives

The sedating or sleeping drugs usually prescribed by physicians should be taken with caution and prescribed with caution. Their effects are powerful but usually only effective for a period of days or weeks. If your sleep habits have not improved to the point that you can sleep without the medication in a few weeks, it would be a good idea to discuss this thoroughly with the physician. With rare exception, all of these drugs are addicting; extreme caution should be taken in using these to excess or taking them with alcohol.

The above is hardly representative of all possible medications that might be prescribed should you decide that this is the route you want to go. Cautious and competent psychiatrists will be more interested in the best results from a particular medication than they will be from getting results quickly. Often, a period of observation and trial use of medication is undertaken before a final medication regime is decided upon. Additionally, you may be taking some kind of medication prescribed by another physican at the time you seek a psychiatric consultation, and this medication will have to clear your system before the new medication can be effective or will even be prescribed.

At times, other medicine you are taking may interact with the medication given to you by a psychiatrist, making both or either medication less effective or more effective. For example, some antidepressants increase the breakdown of some anti-high-blood-pressure medications, thus making the antihypertensive medication less effective. You may then need to increase the amount of antihypertensive medication *only* while you are on the antidepressant. Another medication, Tagamet (an ulcer disease medication), decreases the breakdown of Valium so that what used to be an adequate dose of Valium can become an overdose of Valium while you are on Tagamet. There are many drug-drug interactions similar to these examples and it is very important to tell your doctor what medication you are on so these drug-drug interactions can be avoided.

Medication usually comes in pill form, but occasionally is given by injection or in liquid form. The usual practice in prescribing medications is to give the average recommended dose and then see how the patient does, adjusting up or down depending on side effects and the apparent benefits the patient is receiving. You can also expect to have medications changed occasionally as it is often the case that the trial period failed to produce the effects that you and the psychiatrist hoped for. Since you are a totally unique biological system, one medication may not work nearly as well as another kind that is intended to do the same thing. You and your psychiatrist may want to experiment with a variety of medications to find the one most suited to your particular body chemistry.

The question of how long you might have to take medications is determined on a strictly individual basis. Some medications for major mental illnesses are taken for months and even years to help the patient remain symptom-free. Other medications, particularly the antianxiety agents and sleep medications, will only be prescribed for a brief period of time, during which psychotherapy and making changes in one's life or environment will be taking place. For many patients I've talked with, the taking of a pill every day or even several pills every day is a constant reminder that their emotional stability remains in jeopardy. No one can argue this point with them.

Patients and clients who are asked to take medications for any length of time and have a negative attitude toward taking strange chemicals into their bodies are, as might be expected, resistant to the idea of being dependent on these concoctions to maintain their mental health. Many enlightened psychiatrists are now recognizing this very strong need to be free of medications and will experiment with what are called "drug holidays" for those patients who want to try a life without pills.

No one, not even the experts, knows exactly how these medications work. However, if they didn't work, you can bet they would quickly go out of existence. If in your search for help with a problem you are offered a prescription, remember that only when there is an informed professional community and a knowledgeable consuming public can the benefits of these drugs be separated from their risks.

15

Helping Someone Who Doesn't Want Help

Aunt Emma has been so depressed lately. The whole family has been worried about her since Uncle Morris died. She refuses to talk to any of us about what's bothering her. How can we help her get some help?

My husband is about to be fired from the plant where he's worked for fifteen years. His drinking gets worse every day. When I suggest he cut down or stop, he gets angry and drinks all the more and then can't go to work the next day. What do I do?

A friend of mine at the office has been making some pretty weird statements—like "I don't think I'll be around next Christmas," and "I'd like you to have my golf clubs when I'm gone." I'm afraid he's hinting at suicide, but don't know what to say to him. I think he needs help, help I'm not qualified to give.

Getting someone else to get help is something all of us who care about the welfare of our friends and loved ones may one day face. It's a tall order, and for those who share a compassion for the plight of others, it's also a personal responsibility that is impossible to dismiss. Doing nothing is sometimes worse than doing something wrong. They say time heals, but does it really?

A colleague of mine once told me the story of how he decided to become a psychologist. While in college, he had a good friend who, for a lot of reasons, was not doing well in his studies. This fellow saw himself as a failure, a disappointment to his family, and when his fiancée jilted him for another man, he became depressed, morose, drank too much, and began talking about the "easy way out." On several occasions, the young man made statements about how quickly life's problems could be solved by a single bullet.

Just before final exams, the young man suddenly appeared bright and cheerful, almost serene, and my colleague, feeling better about how his friend looked, was not alarmed when the fellow asked to borrow a shotgun to do a little target practicing. You can guess the outcome.

The point of this story is not so much that a young man took his own life, but that my colleague felt responsible for not having foreseen the tragedy, thereby failing to do something to prevent it. Worse, he felt he had assisted his friend by giving him a lethal means to kill himself. Had he known what to look for, what questions to ask, how to use himself as a friend, he might have been able to intervene and would not have burdened himself with guilt for so many years.

To get involved in someone else's problems is always a risky business, but not to get involved is only a risk of another kind. What follows are some tips and guidelines about how to help someone get professional attention. This list is far from complete, but it's a place to start. How deeply you choose to get involved is always up to you. Before acting, you must decide how much you are willing to risk, since people who don't want help or seem not to want it are likely to resent your intruding into their lives. Bringing up the subject of getting help is going to test your relationship, so be prepared for some unpleasantness. As a rule, the more serious the problem, the more risk you'll probably have to take.

1. *Expect Resistance.* No one who is having serious personal problems is going to be red hot about accepting a friendly suggestion to see a mental health professional. If he or she weren't resistant to the idea, they'd have done it already and you wouldn't have brought up the subject. Your bringing up the subject will likely result in a display of anger, resentment, and questions like, "How can you do this to me if you're my friend?" You have, after all, made a layman's diagnosis that something is pretty seriously wrong, or you wouldn't have taken the gamble in the first place. Upsetting someone who is already upset isn't much fun, but it may be absolutely necessary. While the person you're worried about may be offended in the beginning, it's often the case that he or she is grateful you had the courage and understanding to perceive them as hurting and struggling alone with a problem that needed sharing.

2. *Set the Stage.* Since what you want to talk to the person about is a serious matter, handle it as such. Get her alone, in some setting where you won't be disturbed, and then lay it out. It will be tough enough for her to admit to you she needs help, and if there's even an outside chance

a passerby may see her crying, she may have to answer the phone, or in any way be caught in a vulnerable, emotional state, odds are she'll keep up her defenses and you won't get the work done.

3. *Take an Hour.* Plan at least an hour or more to get said what you want to say, and to allow the other person enough time to get angry and get over being angry, cry and dry up again and, in general, to react to your persuasion or, if needed, confrontation. Since the person you're worried about probably hasn't talked freely with anyone about his or her problem until you brought it up, you can expect a display and range of emotions from fear to anger, desperation to depression, and all sorts of strong feelings that are going to make you pretty uncomfortable. Don't expect gratitude—that comes later.

4. *Denial.* If the person denies he needs help (and many will), stay with him and find out what he is afraid of. The usual fears include being thought of as crazy, inadequate, or a failure. When confronted with the idea that someone needs help, very often people will minimize the problem: "I don't drink that much" or "everybody uses uppers" or "I'm not *that* depressed." Another frequent excuse for not seeing a mental health professional is a previous bad experience with a therapist or knowing someone who had a bad experience. Either excuse may be absolutely true, but it doesn't alter the situation. Let's face it, there's lots of self-esteem and self-respect at stake when someone has to admit that he or she is unable to handle a personal problem, and may have to see a professional. There's never much to be gained by trying to talk someone out of the way they feel and so simply agreeing with their feelings about being afraid or skeptical about professional help is a useful tactic.

5. *Be Specific.* Tell the person exactly what you've seen him do or heard him say that's triggered your concern. "You're drinking too much" is a value statement and implies you've made a negative judgment, whereas, "I watched you put away a bottle of Scotch every night for the past week and I'm worried about how much you're drinking" is more to the point and harder to deny.

"You're angry all the time" is not as good as "When you came home last night, you bullied the kids and said my lasagna was terrible. Are you upset about something?" When you're specific, the person you're trying to help will have trouble dismissing facts, whereas you can count on him to resist your observations if you make sweeping generalizations. If you know of other people who have observed things that are also worrisome, feel free to share their observations with the person you're worried about since, as a friend, you can be a messenger carrying the concerns of other people as well.

6. Define the Problem in Terms of How It's Affecting You. If you're worried, say so. If the person is making vague threats of suicide and scaring the hell out of you, say so. People with problems are often so wrapped up in themselves, they are unaware of how their behavior affects others, and finding out someone they care about is frightened for them, angry with them, losing sleep worrying about them, is often enough to tip the scales in the direction of their getting help.

7. Don't Give Simple Advice. Telling someone to change jobs, get a divorce, take up tennis or fly to Mazatlán for a couple of weeks is usually worse than saying nothing at all. Most people with serious problems have struggled privately with all those alternatives and a lot more. If anything, they're convinced there are no solutions and certainly no simple ones. Sometimes just agreeing with someone that their problem appears insoluble is a source of great relief to the troubled person.

I once worked with a middle-aged housewife who cried bitterly that she had been a miserable failure in life: her husband didn't love her, her children avoided her, and what few friends she had were disappointed in her. She was depressed, but not suicidal. On her better days, she felt her future was hopeless, and on her occasional "up days," it was bleak. When I quickly agreed with her, i.e., that she had been a failure (at least in some ways), and that from her point of view, life would look pretty hopeless, she sighed and said "Thank God, somebody finally understands me!"

The idea here is one of empathy and most people appreciate the fact that while you don't have a neat solution, you at least understand them and the problem. So, if you don't want to appear simpleminded, don't offer simple solutions.

8. Don't Try to Fix Blame. Very often when we are in an emotional jam, we try to find out who is at fault—the boss, the guys at work, the wife, or the very popular "the kids are driving me crazy."

To agree with someone that their problem is the sole responsibility of some third party seals off the opportunity for self-examination and the possibility of exploring creative solutions. Finding out who's to blame makes for an interesting investigation of who's right and who's wrong, but seldom leads to decisions to change.

One angry young client spent several sessions trying to convince me his mother was an unloving shrew whose wanton lack of maternal instincts had resulted in his maturing from a recalcitrant child into a rebellious teenager. He had spent several years building a case against her and argued his forty-seven speeding tickets amounted to incontestable proof of her botching her job. When, somewhat exasperated, I too agreed she was "guilty as charged and should not be nominated as mother-of-the-year," he laughed and began to see the folly of his argument. Only after this interchange did he begin to accept responsibility for his own behavior.

9. *Have Some Information Available.* Before broaching the subject of getting help with the person you're worried about, spend a little time looking into resources, clinics, therapists, and other sources of help so you can have ready some names and numbers to call if the troubled person decides to do something. People in a crisis are much more likely to respond to a suggestion to seek help if they have information immediately available.

Since the person you're trying to help has, after all, been cornered by your reaching out to her, it's a good idea to have two or three resources for her to choose from. No matter how desperate and trapped a troubled person may feel, she still has a need for autonomy and to see herself as capable of making decisions. Giving her the names of a couple of therapists and a clinic or mental health center does not place her in an either/or situation and allows her a chance to exercise the freedom of choice essential to the maintenance of positive self-esteem.

10. *Leave the Final Decision to Them.* In the last analysis, people have to decide for themselves if they want to seek help. They may say they're going to see a therapist for your sake and that's okay—it may be better than refusing help altogether. Making it clear that they are making the decision also leaves intact their self-respect, and if they do decide to seek help, they're starting out on the right foot as far as having made a personal decision to act on their own behalf.

How much pressure you apply to someone who needs help and doesn't want it is a matter of personal judgment and belief. Many professional therapists don't believe clients can benefit from therapy if they are forced to accept it. I don't concur with this opinion. Many clients are levered into therapy by families under threats that if they don't get help the wife or husband will file for divorce or some other dire consequence will follow. Sometimes such threats are the only things powerful enough to get the person's attention, and then the help they need. In many of these circumstances, it is not so much a threat as a prediction of reality, and to the degree that such measures are successful in getting the resistant person into therapy, the problem does get addressed.

There is also the very important fact that you, as a concerned friend or loved one, must feel you have done all you can to try to help someone with a problem do something about it. It is, after all, only when you've gone the extra distance with someone that you can relax and get a night's sleep. You have to look after your mental health too.

Special Cases: Suicide and Alcoholism

Suicidal people are the ones we tend to worry about the most. As a rule, anyone who is contemplating suicide, has every intention of doing himself or herself in, and never hints at his or her plans to do it, is going to be successful. If you never know someone is suicidal, there isn't a whole lot you or anyone else can do to prevent it.

The problem is that most people are ambivalent about dying and in their desperate battle to find reasons to live, will let on to those around them they are toying with the idea of self-destruction. Since suicide is a permanent solution to what is often a temporary problem, all hints, comments, jokes, references, and threats should be taken seriously. To pretend someone close to you is only threatening suicide to get attention is to believe the myth that people who talk about suicide don't do it.

How much you want to risk to prevent someone you know and care about from committing suicide is up to you. But if you decide to act, the following are some clues you will need to know in order to be reasonably certain you're doing the right thing. This list of factors, signs, symptoms, and situations is only a partial summary and more detailed information can be gotten from your local suicide prevention center or mental health center. Additional information can also be gotten from the National Suicide Prevention Center, American Association of Suicidology (see Appendix A for pertinent information).

Depression. Depressed people can and do commit suicide. Not all depressed people think about suicide, but enough of them do to make depression one of the critical signs. The more depressed people are, the more likely it is they have thought about death as a way to end their problems. Serious, or clinical depression—as opposed to being sad about losing a job or breaking up with a boy friend or girl friend—is determined by frequent crying, sleep disturbance (difficulty falling to sleep or waking up too early in the morning, or not feeling rested after a night's sleep), lack of appetite and weight loss, loss of interest in sex, and feelings of worthlessness and hopelessness. It is not hard to spot depressed persons; they're the ones with sloping shoulders, drooping heads, soft and unsure voices, and sad eyes. They don't all look that way, but a lot of them do.

Threats or Attempts. Most of those people who eventually kill themselves have tried to do it before, told people they were going to try it, and in a word, gave ample warning to others they were checking out. As a rule, those who have attempted suicide by some lethal means (jumping, shooting, hanging, and the like) as opposed to those taking a handful of aspirins, represent the highest-risk group in terms of later completing a suicide. So if the person you're worried about has a history of trying suicide before or made serious threats in the past, go ahead and get worried.

Drug or Alcohol Use. Since some drugs, and especially alcohol, put the best part of the human brain temporarily out of commission, anyone who is suicidal and using these chemicals is at a much higher risk of killing themselves. The judgment employed by people while intoxicated ranges from poor to miserable, and the odds run strongly against their winning an argument with themselves to stay alive.

While a friend who has been hinting at self-destruction may die in a car crash after a few cocktails or take one too many sleeping pills with one too many nightcaps, it won't help much to convince ourselves it was an accident—we've still lost a friend.

In fact, our friend may not have wanted to die. But in that fuzzy, groggy, stumbling world of booze and pills, a sudden feeling of self-disgust can be too much of a temptation to give up the struggle.

Anger. Self-hatred is a sign of high suicide risk. Someone who is angry with himself is more likely to act on a suicidal impulse than someone whose hostility is directed toward others. Expressions of self-disgust and self-contempt lead the way to self-destruction and make it doubly difficult to persuade such a suicidal person to help himself by seeking professional care.

Anyone who can convince you they are so rotten as not to deserve the friendship and concern you are showing them by trying to be of help is someone to do more than fret about.

This partial list of signs only highlights the need for professional help and intervention. Combined with advanced age, a recent loss (for example, the death of a spouse, loss of a job, or sudden loss of health, and/or being left alone in the world) add up to a lethal situation. People don't kill themselves casually—it takes a lot of pressure, stress, depression, self-anger, and terrible disappointment with life to arrive at the decision to die now, and it doesn't take a highly trained professional to recognize the kinds of factors that lead to a suicidal tragedy.

There are many other indications of suicide risks that can only be discovered by talking with the person who is considering suicide. These amount to thoughts and feelings as opposed to situations, age, immediate circumstances, and aspects of the person's history with which you might be familiar. If you talk with a suicidal relative or friend, and you find them readily admitting to wanting to die, that they can find no reason for living, that they feel a sense of urgency to "get it over with," and have picked a time, place, and method, and have attended to their will, bequeathed their favorite possessions, and have their house in order—it's time to act! Rarely will all these signs and symptoms be present in the same person or at the same time, but any one of them should alert you to look for more and be ready to help.

If philosophically you believe people with problems should give themselves time for things to work out, and that life, even as it is, is better than death, then you may be the only being on the planet who can prevent a suicide. You can't assume others know what you know about someone on the brink, or that if they do know, they will act. Your community, the human community, does not condone suicide and there are tax supported professionals immediately available to offer assistance to prevent such a death. Your local mental health center, crisis line, or police department will know what to do if you fail in your attempt to persuade the person you're worried about to get help.

Several years ago, before the new commitment laws were adopted, I worked with a middle-aged, divorced woman who twice attempted to take her own life. She survived two massive overdoses only because of heroic efforts by an intensive care unit team in a local hospital. Angry and disappointed at her failure, she insisted that she would one day kill herself—"nobody can stop me." The police charged her with attempted suicide and brought her before a judge. The magistrate, an acquaintance of mine, gave her a stiff sentence—six months in the county jail or therapy with me. She chose the worse of two evils, me.

We arm wrestled psychologically over the pros and cons of staying alive, and after a year she moved away to another state. During therapy, she repeatedly expressed her resentments about life and considered me something of a meddling nincompoop. For every reason I could dream up to stay alive and try to be happy, she could think up three for why it wasn't worth it. Still, we learned to like each other and the therapy was successful. Each year, I get a Christmas card from her—it makes my holiday season.

Alcoholism. Alcoholics are another special case: a group of people with problems who, as a rule, are the last to recognize their need for help and the first to deny they need it. In point of fact, denying one drinks too much is a symptom of the disease. People who drink in moderation (some ninety million) don't get confronted about their drinking and so don't get defensive. They enjoy alcohol without its sometimes evil consequences.

While there is a lot of debate among professionals about the best definition of alcoholism, most five-year-olds can make the diagnosis in a few words: "Mommy (or Daddy) drinks too much." A child can observe that when mother drives the station wagon through the back of the garage after an afternoon cocktail party, something's out of control. Or that the only time Daddy slaps him is when he reeks of 100-proof bourbon.

In a word, alcoholism is a kind of drug dependence that makes people sick in the body and the mind and leads to major losses: job, health, friends, and family. It's a predictable tragedy that haunts millions of American families and has only recently begun to get the kind of press it deserves. Most of the families in which alcoholics live know something is wrong—so wrong, they are afraid to talk about it. Yet, they also know that some action should be taken, but (like most of us) aren't sure if "things are bad enough yet," or if they are bad enough, what can be done.

There are dozens of warning signs posted along the route to chronic alcoholism, warning signs in plain English, which if the budding alcoholic doesn't see because he's drinking too fast, his boss, friends, and family can't help but read. What follows is a list of such warning signs in order of alarm. The further down the list you go, the more alarmed you should be. Any one of these signs does not an alcholic make, but more than a few and the person you're worried about can be headed for big trouble.

1. Drinking to relax or get relief from stress
2. Drinking more than usual or drinking more often than usual
3. Sneaking drinks
4. Gulping drinks
5. Drinking to build confidence
6. Feeling guilty about drinking
7. Acting touchy or defensive if someone suggests cutting down
8. Being unwilling to discuss drinking
9. Unsuccessful attempts to cut down
10. Having trouble remembering what happened after a drinking episode (blackouts)

This takes care of the early warning signs. They may develop rapidly or over a period of a few years. If you think the above list is picky or overly cautious, maybe it's time to take a close look at your own use of alcohol. But let's continue down the road.

1. Telling lies about drinking (or, is anything so good a person needs an alibi)
2. Drinking alone
3. Lost weekends. Getting a toot going Friday night and keep-

ing it going 'til church closes, complete with Monday morning hangovers
4. Missing work
5. Rather drink than eat
6. Resenting just about everything
7. Getting drunk unintentionally
8. Guarding and hiding the liquor supply as if it were gold
bouillon

With these warning signs past, the drinker has, as one recovered alcoholic friend of mine told me, "moved out of the amateur class and is
about to join the professionals." If the person you're worrying about
continues to drink, the following symptoms are increasingly predictable.

1. More blackouts and memory failure
2. Major disruption of family unity (separation or divorce)
3. Loss of friends
4. Loss of job
5. Physical problems—too many and too scary to mention
6. Hallucinations, tremors, unreasonable fears
7. Hospitalization for alcoholism
8. An early death

Hopefully, you will not have to witness act three of the alcohol tragedy. If you decide to try to help someone with an alcohol problem, you
may still be unsure about how to tell the difference between "drinking
too much" and alcoholism. Carrying a checklist of symptoms or trying to
recognize three out of four or seven out of ten signs may be cumbersome
and, in the end, not so very useful. To the practicing alcoholic, it's always
the person who "drinks more than me" who's got the problem; and since
ninety-five percent of the nine million or so alcoholics in America can always point to the skid row wino (a tiny minority) and say *they* are the
alcoholics, it's going to take some confrontation to be convincing.

The most important thing to recognize about alcohol abuse and alcoholism is that there is a direct relationship between drinking (in any
amount) and the occurrence of life problems. If a person drinks and gets
into trouble, he or she has a problem with alcohol—it's as simple as that.
You don't have to be a hot-shot diagnostician to see that anyone who
would rather drink than stay married, would rather drink than keep his
or her job, or rather drink than live to a ripe old age is very probably an
alcoholic. When alcohol becomes more important to a person than love
or money, he or she has a big problem with the stuff.

To the often-asked question about what causes alcoholism, I have a simple answer: who cares? It would be nice to know the answer to this question, and hundreds of researchers are frantically running around in their laboratories and hospitals in their stiff white coats seeking the answer. But in the meantime, the person you care about may be just as busy racing down the road to self-destruction. Whether a person is a bona fide alcoholic or a reasonable facsimile thereof, does it really matter if the ending is the same? The point is, alcoholism is a treatable illness and if we are to change the script in this singular tragedy, it requires action.

When to act is another frequent question and the best answer is *now!* If you've already been concerned, worried, or fretting about someone's drinking (or your own), *right now* is soon enough to do something.

What exactly to do is a bit more complicated. The ten steps of intervention outlined earlier in this chapter are a good place to start, and with luck, your honesty, candor, concern, and confrontation will be enough to get the person moving. Many people with alcohol problems simply stop when asked (or told) to. I've had several clients over the years who were at one time clearly alcoholic, and once they recognized they were losing the battle with the bottle, gave it up—nothing very dramatic or even painful, let alone heroic. But in my experience and the experience of hundreds of other therapists, these were the lucky or the smart ones.

Since a major symptom of the illness is denying one has it, it's more likely your first steps to help someone with an alcohol problem will fail. Who, after all, wants to admit they can't handle a few drinks or a six-pack, and must never take another drink for as long as they live? Denial of the problem when a child can see it and resistance to quitting drinking or seeking help should only confirm your suspicions that the person you're worried about needs worrying about—and more!

When it comes to helping someone with alcohol problems, some of the best resources are free. Your local chapter of Alcoholics Anonymous can be most helpful and is probably the best place to start. If the person you're worried about refuses to go to Alcoholics Anonymous, then you should take yourself to Alanon, a program sponsored by A.A. to help the families and spouses of alcoholics. Your community probably has an alcohol information and referral service as well as alcohol treatment programs, both inpatient and outpatient. All of these resources can provide information you'll need once you've decided to act. Some mental health centers will have alcohol treatment services available, and there may be practitioners in the private therapy business who are also savvy about working with alcoholics. You can't assume every therapist knows how to work with alcohol problems, and you should check this out very thoroughly before you refer or take your loved one to a therapist in the hope that the drinking will be addressed. There's a wry but awful truth that a therapist won't diagnose alcoholism unless the patient is drinking more than the therapist.

Helping Someone Already in Therapy

Sometimes it happens that the person you are worried about is already in therapy, already receiving professional help. From what your friend or family member or loved one tells you about the help they're getting (or you observe on your own), questions may arise. Is the therapist competent? Is the medication doing more harm than good? Is the advice given sound? Shouldn't there be more progress? and so on. This kind of doubt is troubling and it begs for resolution.

Questioning the quality, kind, or amount of help someone we care about is getting is a delicate matter for several reasons. First, who are you to second-guess a highly trained professional? Second, don't the professionals always know best? Third, do you have any business meddling in your friend's affairs? The answers, in my opinion are:

1. You can probably second-guess the professionals better than your friend

2. Professionals don't *always* know best

3. Yes, you should meddle (if it's okay with your friend)

So, if you do have a serious question about someone's therapy, how do you approach your friend or loved one or, maybe more importantly, the therapist? It is important to remember that no matter how much you feel you need or want to know what's going on, certain procedures have to be followed. Of these, the most important step is to solicit the cooperation of the person you're concerned about.

Since the therapist is bound by ethics *and* law not to divulge information about his client (even to a family member—unless the client is a child), there is usually nothing to be gained by placing a call to the therapist on behalf of the person you're worried about. At best, the therapist may listen politely to your observations, thank you for your concern, and then hang up. You will have learned nothing. Accepting your call to talk about anyone in his or her care is an acknowledgment (however oblique) that person X is a client and accepting the call can be construed as a violation of confidentiality. Therefore, many therapists will not even take your call.

Briefly, you will need the express and written consent of your friend or loved one even to get to first base. This request to permit the therapist to talk to some third party (you) typically would be made by the client during a therapy session—after which you may be able to call the therapist, arrange an appointment (you may be charged for the time), and/or expect a communication from the therapist.

More so now than in the past, families and friends do request information about the treatment their loved ones receive. This is a healthy trend—and one to be encouraged. People in therapy need support, and not just from therapists. They need friends and family. And while some therapists may balk at answering questions about the therapy they are providing, the secure ones won't.

In the past few years the National Association for the Mentally Ill (N.A.M.I.) has been active and instrumental both in advocating for the mentally ill and in expecting increasing candor from the professionals who treat people with emotional problems. State and local chapters exist in many parts of the country and can be of considerable help in assisting you to find out more about mental health services in general, and N.A.M.I. may be able to assist you in your particular efforts on behalf of someone you care about.

Getting someone help who doesn't want it is tough work, particularly for people who are suicidal, have an alcohol problem, or are addicted to drugs or gambling. Love, as great as it is, sometimes isn't enough.

In good old America where self-reliance and self-determination are the hallmarks of our psychology, many people tend to view those who would try to help someone who doesn't want help as some kind of neurotic rescuer with a self-proclaimed mission to aid the troubled. While there are few self-appointed saviors around, there aren't all that many, and it's a sad comment on our society that trying to help another human being can be construed as selfishness.

If you are still uncertain whether you should try to help someone, put yourself in their shoes. If you were frightened, depressed, miserable, dying of drink or drugs, and life stretched out ahead of you like a string of promises about to be broken, wouldn't you want someone to reach out to you?

16

Addiction and Codependency

Let's say a twenty-seven-year-old young, married, professional woman named Susan comes to see me because, while she thinks she would like to have a baby, she isn't sure if this is the right time. She makes the appointment for herself and comes in alone. Our opening discussion goes something like this:

"I made this appointment for myself," she begins, "but I'm worried about my husband, Jim."

"How so?"

"I can handle his drinking, but the other day I found a razor and a little mirror tucked in behind the aspirin in the bathroom medicine cabinet. Doesn't that mean he's using cocaine?"

"Sometimes. Do you know if he's ever used it in the past?"

"Well, yes. Before we were married. But when I asked him to stop all those other drugs and just stick to alcohol, he said he would. He promised."

"Do you drink?"

"A little."

"By yourself, or with your husband?"

"Just with him, you know, when we're out with friends or at home. We like to have a few cocktails before dinner and sometimes a couple of after-dinner drinks. A glass of wine at the end of the day really helps me relax. But sometimes when I come home late from a meeting, I find Jim completely loaded. So I know he drinks alone."

"Does he want you to have a drink with him when you find him like this?"

"Why, yes."

"And has a lot of money turned up missing lately?"

"Uh huh. But how did you know?"

"Lucky guess."

But it isn't a lucky guess. Having divided the majority of my professional life between the fields of mental health and addictions I have, usually the hard way, come to understand the nature of this most serious problem and how, too often, people, families, couples, and employers seem to fall into an unspoken deal wherein everyone agrees to agree that there is—even though it is standing there in plain sight waving its trunk around—"no elephant in this room!"

The elephant in the room is alcoholism and drug addiction. The unspoken deal among the players is to agree that the elephant stomping around the room and about to trample everyone really isn't dangerous—even if we could admit to ourselves he is there. This blinding of ourselves to reality is called denial and this chapter, if it is to be successful, will attempt to help you do something about denial—either your own, or someone else's.

Does He Really Need Help?

Admitting there is a problem is Job One when it comes to addiction and codependency. Owning the problem is the first, most important, and biggest step any of us takes. And since the field of addiction and codependency is a broad and growing one I can, in this short chapter, only accomplish a few things.

First, I will talk about the diagnosis of addiction from a professional and purely personal point of view. Call the latter an ant's-eye view.

Next, I will suggest why there is reason to hope and where to find appropriate help, what to expect, and how to get the most out of that help.

Third, I will talk about addiction and codependency and how we might, all of us, learn to lead happier, more satisfying lives.

Diagnosis

To the question posed by my fictional client in the opening of this chapter—"Does he really need help?"—we already know one answer. *Somebody* here needs help. Probably Jim, but surely Susan. If Susan is not at risk of becoming an alcoholic herself she is, clearly, in a troubled relationship. She may be married to an alcoholic/addict and, consciously or unconsciously, may be aiding and abetting his addiction. Whether she is codependent and enabling her husband's addiction awaits a few more questions, so let's continue our interview for a moment.

"So, you found a razor and mirror hidden in the medicine cabinet. What do you make of that?"

"I don't think Jim would lie to me. We had friends over the other night and maybe one of them used coke. They could have snorted some in our bathroom and just forgotten their kit."

"You're suggesting your friends hid the razor and mirror in your medicine cabinet?"

"I guess so."

"Has anything else about Jim's behavior bothered you lately?"

"Oh, well, I found a little stash of marijuana under the front seat of the car the other day when I was vacuuming it out. But it could have been there a long time. When I asked Jim, he said he didn't know anything about it."

"Jim used to smoke dope, too?"

"He was a real pothead back in high school. But he only used when he was under stress."

"Is he under stress now?"

"Yes. At work. He's been missing a lot of days for some reason. But Jim wouldn't lie to me. I love him. When somebody loves you they won't lie to you, will they?"

This is one of those questions we addictions specialists hate to be asked. Because of our training and experience, we can spot an elephant across a crowded auditorium and, because of this ability, people don't always like to hear what we have to say. But we have to say it.

"Yes, addicts lie to the people they love. They have to. If they didn't, those who love and care about them might insist they give up their drugs."

"Oh."

Susan's "Oh" is the beginning of the therapeutic process. If she is willing and able she may begin to accept her own denial that a problem exists; if she can't, she may first need help with her own issues of codependency. Codependency is a lot of things, but one of them is an unconscious willingness to jeopardize one's own health, happiness and welfare in the name of a relationship—no matter how sick that relationship might become. Helping codependents, like addicts, requires breaking through the denial that everything is okay.

Denial of an addiction problem is the soul and substance of the problem. Denial is at once diagnostic, life threatening, and crazy making. I say crazy making because, if you must distort reality day after day in order to continue the facade that nothing is wrong here and an elephant in the living room is as normal as apple pie, you eventually adapt to a world where black is white, squares are circles, and lies are truths.

But there are good reasons why people distort the reality of addiction through denial. We're not talking the joy of eating fig bars here—we're talking about the most powerful, concentrated, mind-altering drugs man has ever cooked up to put into his body so as to change his experience of reality. The immediate rush and pleasure from some drugs approximates sexual orgasm. The relief from tension brought on by a quick double shot of 100 proof is legendary. And, so I'm told, there is nothing so soothing as ending an evening with a high-grade joint and tall glass of wine. For some, their drug of choice makes them ten feet tall and bullet-proof. As an addict once told me, "They don't call it getting *high* for nothing."

Question: Does anyone give up this sort of pleasure seeking willingly? Not often. And seldom by themselves. The stakes are high. The risks of acknowledging the reality of alcohol or drug abuse are great. A confrontation could blow up the family, cause the loss of a much-needed job, and possibly destroy a marriage. Denial, sometimes, seems the better part of valor.

Getting help for the addict is never simple, seldom painless, and always takes more courage that any of us feels we truly have. Not only are we frightened by the elephant and hope denial will make it go away, we're not even sure this isn't one of those friendly elephants you see at the circus. Because we don't want to risk making a medical diagnosis of addiction (with all its attendant implications), we beg the question and go right on distorting reality until, with enough training and experience, we become codependent and part of the problem, not part of the solution.

So, when do you know you or someone you love has a problem with drugs, alcohol, or both?

Answer: the instant your under-the-influence behavior has a negative impact on the lives of those around you. You don't have to wonder if you're a grade A, first-class, certifiable, compulsive, craving, advanced alcoholic/addict at risk of ending up sick and dying in a hospital emergency room or on skid row; you only need to know that when you use booze or dope or both you worry, frighten, hurt or harm those who care about you, love you, rely on you, and need you.

Granted, this is a social–psychological diagnosis of addiction, but it works for me. Over my professional lifetime I have evaluated a couple of thousand alcoholic/addicts, many of them late-stage users for whom the medical diagnosis was, as the lawyers say, clear, cogent, and convincing. Their livers were distended and cirrhotic from alcohol, their brains damaged from sniffing glue and overdosing on various and assorted drugs, and they'd lost their families, friends, jobs, and self-respect. For some, the next drunk or OD would likely kill them. With the prognosis for recovery next to nil, the end of the road was just around the corner of one more fix or drink.

My point? You shouldn't have to wait until you're near death to know you're sick and need help.

Finally, I have had many struggles with clients over whether they were, or were not, alcoholic, or addicted to drugs. They didn't want to be, and I wished they weren't. But a counselor's job does not include joining in the game of Let's Deny the Elephant. So, if you seek professional help for an addiction problem, don't expect any game playing—for us, it's against the law.

Reason to Hope

To reach out for professional help with an addiction problem it might help to know that, in fact, treatment works. It doesn't always work the first time, but it works—sooner or later, and for most everyone willing to give up their denial. Inpatient or outpatient, the services are there and generally available—although some clinics have waiting lists.

More, there is a growing body of medical and psychological knowledge about the nature of addictions, how they begin, what maintains them, and what it takes to give them up. We know how to intervene in the addict's life in such a way that, although seldom a smooth transition, he or she has a chance to save a marriage or job or a life. Employers are more and more sympathetic to the addicted employee and many have employee assistance programs to facilitate the process of getting help.

Getting help for an addiction problem is more acceptable now than ever before. I can remember, in my own field and from personal experience, two very fine professionals (a psychologist and a psychiatrist) who were lost to drink while still early in their careers because none of us knew what to do about a problem a nice young doctor "simply couldn't have." Now we have recovery programs *just for doctors.*

So there is every reason to hope. People do give up drugs and booze, get clean and sober, and get well. It isn't easy, but it's a whole lot better than the alternative. I try to tell clients this: If you look at your life as a work of art, beginning recovery is like putting a fresh, clean canvas on your easel. Even better, this time around instead of black and white, you get to work in colors.

Whom to See

I have already written about the benefits, accessibility, and low-cost effectiveness of self-help groups. Alcoholics Anonymous, Alanon, Narcotics Anonymous, and others are always a good—and sometimes the best—place to start. But if these prove insufficient, then see a professional.

Most states now have a registration or certification process for drug and alcohol counselors. The requirements vary from state to state, but generally include a number of college courses pertinent to the physiology of drug addiction, the psychopharmocology of drug and alcohol effects, and the diagnosis and treatment of these disorders. Together with one or more years of supervised treatment work in an approved setting, and some sort of written and/or oral examination, the great majority of addiction counselors are well trained for their specialty. And since many chemical dependency counselors are in recovery from their own addiction, this is a bonus. Having been there, they can see the elephant better than just about anyone.

Social workers, nurses, psychologists, psychiatrists, general physicians, pastoral counselors, and others also specialize in working with alcoholics/ addicts. Please remember, though, that this is a specialty and that, without advanced course work and/or considerable professional experience in this area, ignorance abounds. We have an old joke that sums up the risk of underdiagnosis that attends a visit to an untrained, inexperienced or addicted/abusing professional: You can't get treatment for a cocaine problem unless you use *more* than your doctor.

Beyond finding someone, some agency, or some hospital with good credentials in the treatment of alcoholism and drug addiction, consider recent developments and how each might be beneficial to the recovery process.

Ideally, treatment works best when:

- the family and significant others are involved from the get-go
- it is culturally relevant
- staff members are culturally sensitive
- it is gender appropriate
- it is age appropriate
- it is group centered
- it includes networking with other community supports
- it is based on a careful clinical workup, including the possibility of a dual diagnosis (alcohol or drug addiction coexisting with another psychiatric illness—e.g., depression)

In most average-sized cities we now have enough treatment-needy clients to have exclusive self-help or professionally led groups for old white men, young pregnant women, Afro-American males, Native American females, lawyers, doctors, and just about any group of folks from any walk of life. Addiction being no respecter of class, race, religion, age, wealth or occupation, you and yours should be able to find a place to fit right in.

If you include the other addiction problems for which people can benefit from self-help group work (gamblers, sex addicts, overeaters, compulsive shoplifters, and such), you have, according to a recent *News-*

week report, a count that runs to 500,000 such groups across the country. With a total attendance of some fifteen million Americans *every single week,* that's a lot of therapy, a lot of help, and a lot of potential for recovery.

Beyond a given counselor's credentials in addiction work the same traits, characteristics, and responsiveness I've mentioned earlier apply to the goodness-of-fit issue between client and therapist. However, I should note that many addicts, because of their reluctance to give up their drugs or booze, may try to find fault with the counselor, or the appointment time, or, say, the lack of convenient parking. This is resistance, plain and simple. Expect it.

Codependency

I can't pretend to cover the whole and developing field of codependency in this chapter. However, because codependents and addicts seem to go together like cookies and milk, and frequently enter treatment together, it is often necessary that in order to understand the one you must understand the other.

But understanding the codependent phenomenon is not easy. At least it hasn't been easy for me. Early on I was enchanted with the concept and thought how nicely it explained why the wives and mothers and siblings and employers of alcoholics and addicts put up with so much outrageous behavior: because don't you see, they were codependent. Being unhealthy themselves, they enabled the alcoholic/addict by cutting him slack, making his excuses, paying his fines, and otherwise assisting him to deny reality and keep it from ever catching up with the plain facts of an out-of-control situation.

But it wasn't as simple as all that. Surely, I thought, not everyone who knows or lives with an addict is as pathological as the addict himself. And what about acts of love and altruism? Don't we humans help each other when one of us is down and out? Isn't caring the foundation of our major faiths? Isn't it by cooperation and self-sacrifice that we achieve a sense of community and society? Of course it is. So what, then, is codependency?

In my own view codependency is a number of things. And sometimes it seems to be a kind of necessary evil. For example, should the mother of six whose alcoholic husband manages to get to work each day and brings home enough money to keep the family off welfare be glibly labeled codependent? Should she share fully half the blame? Or is she doing what she must absolutely do to see to it that her children have shoes on their feet, bread on their table, and a father—however troubled and inadequate he may be? This is not to say she doesn't need help, but I personally don't feel it is fair to accuse her of somehow *asking* for all this pain and suffering.

From my own perspective on the human condition we, all of us, do what we must to survive. Sometimes it means getting along with, getting around, and getting by the alcoholic in our life. Children who grow up in alcoholic and drug-addicted families know exactly what I'm talking about: you do what you have to do. And even though you're all grown up you don't hand over your survival kit (the strategies that kept you alive) just because someone said they are no longer good for you—at least not without a struggle.

So what, again, is codependency?

For my part, I see codependency as, among other things, doing for others what they can and should be able to do for themselves.

For example, it is one thing for a mother to tie her two-year-old's shoes, it is another thing to tie her four-year-old's shoes, and it is codependent for her to tie her ten-year-old's shoes. Why? Because by age ten, a boy should be able to tie his own shoes. If he can't (and assuming he is physically and mentally able), he's been handicapped by too much help. The codependent mother, whose misguided devotion emotionally cripples her son, ends up living his life instead of her own. Worse, she can keep her "baby" bound to her forever by raging at the world, "How can you expect a boy to go out and face the world when he can't even tie his own shoes!!!?"

In adult relationships, codependency is many more things. Among these are:

- only being able to feel good about myself when someone else says they like me. As a result, I do dumb or stupid or self-harmful things just to maintain this positive appraisal.
- assuming responsibilities for others (while neglecting my own), when those others are perfectly capable of doing their share.
- living my life as an afterthought; i.e., all my attention, energy, joy, and happiness is put on hold while I help you with your life.
- only doing what you want to do, never what I want to do.
- fearing rejection so much that it makes me sick and causes me to change my values to avoid losing you.

And so on.

Frankly, what started out as a useful concept is, with so many people writing about it but so few willing or able to define it scientifically, now about to fall upon hard times. Like so many other passing good ideas, codependency has lost much of its early utility—especially since it now explains just about everything wrong with the American psyche and still doesn't tell us just what, exactly, we should do about it.

But people do make mistakes in their relationships with addicts and others and counseling and therapy seem to help them stop making them.

If these poor choices and/or unconscious harmful decisions can all be handily captured under the rubric of codependency—and the self-diagnosis helps get people into productive counseling—then so much the better. After all, none of us wants to experience what the classic codependent experiences when going down for the third time while drowning: someone else's life passes before your eyes.

The central point about codependency and addiction is that one should never, consciously, aid, abet, help, enable, or otherwise assist an alcoholic or drug-dependent person with his or her addiction. This means, as we say in our field, "raising the bottom." You can't soften the fall into the sickness and compulsion of addiction, but you can shorten it. And one of the quickest ways to shorten it is to get help for yourself. In so doing you will, necessarily, help the addict. And at the very least you will find confirmation for your actions and consolation for your trials. Self-help groups have some of what is needed; professionals should have the rest. My advice: get all you need, anywhere you can.

Recovery

The common goal of this chapter, for addicts and codependents alike, is recovery—whether through a combination of self-help efforts or with the assistance of a professional, or both. And what is recovery? This is like asking what is the good life?

From that ant's-eye view I mentioned earlier, I see it this way: recovery is not simply abstinence from drugs and alcohol or, for the codependent, steering clear of abusive relationships. Rather, it is learning to live without having to resort to mood-altering drugs in order to enjoy this banquet called life. It is getting and growing psychologically tough and able enough to handle the bumps, rough spots, and sometimes tragic events that go along with being an ordinary mortal—and I mean without having to get sloshed first. It is, I suppose, growing all the way up and deciding to stop injuring ourselves. A physical, psychological, social, and spiritual journey, we need the fellowship of others for some of the trip, but must take most of the scariest steps on our own.

Clearly there is much more to this recovery process and there is, as always, much more to learn. So let me end here by noting something that may make a difference in deciding to get help.

Don't wait. Don't let your ambivalence stand in your way. If in doubt, act. If you *think* there's an addiction problem with someone you know or love (or even yourself), you don't to wait for the Denial Police to show up and arrest you. All you have to do is pick up the phone. Start asking questions. Contact a self-help group, call a hotline, walk into a clinic or chemical dependency hospital, make an appointment with a counselor—just, as the saying goes, DO IT!

P.S.

If you're wondering what happened to Susan—the not-so-fictitious woman we met at the opening of this chapter—things turned out okay. The daughter of an alcoholic father, codependent and possibly at risk of addiction herself, Susan was, with some help, able to admit to herself a simple and painful reality: her husband was in trouble again with drugs and alcohol. From this starting place, she was able to accept that Jim, despite her love for him and his for her, was lying to her. And so long as he was lying to her, she could not trust him; and if she couldn't trust him, how could she have a baby with him? And if she couldn't have a baby with him, how could she save the family and the life she always dreamed of having?

Answer: she couldn't. But she got some help.

And so did Jim.

And so can you.

17

The Other Side
of the Couch

Many people think psychiatrists and psychologists and other kinds of therapists are crazier than their patients. Many more believe these modern-day healers are at least "mixed up" or, as one father asked his psychiatrist son: "Couldn't you get into some honest kind of work?" Still others hold the psychological practitioner in awe—sometimes respectful awe, sometimes fearful. Often there is envy of what is not enviable or hostile rejection of what is not very objectionable.

People often ask how therapists got into this line of work, what it's really like, and seem to have a measure of curiosity about life on the other side of the couch. This chapter is one man's view.

Not long ago, I was waiting to meet some friends for dinner. As I was enjoying the view from an eighth-floor cocktail lounge and browsing through a magazine, two women sitting opposite me offered to bring me a plate of hors d'oeuvres from a happy hour serving table. As we struck up a conversation, I had an ominous sense that, as often happened, things would turn out badly.

There are typically three pieces of information exchanged by total strangers that, depending on the kind of information traded, make people decide to continue conversing or find some excuse to terminate a budding relationship. These bits of information include name, where you are from, and most importantly, what you do for a living. It is this last disclosure that often finishes conversations for therapists. Consider the following dialogue:

"You looked hungry."

"Thank you," I said, "that was thoughtful." The older of the two ladies set a plate of shrimp and crackers in front of me.

"Are you from Spokane?" asked the younger one.

"Yes," I said, "and you?"

"We're both from here. Our husbands are in business together. My son's visiting from Colorado. They're late for dinner."

"What do you do?" asked the older lady (the killing question).

I paused a moment before answering. "Just for fun, why don't you guess my occupation?" It was a ploy to keep the relationship going.

The lady smiled and accepted the challenge. "You're a used car salesman."

"No."

"A bank auditor."

"No."

"An English professor."

"Sorry."

"A professional."

"Yes." The ladies named a couple more occupations and then gave up. "I'm a psychologist."

The reaction was immediate. The older lady nervously straightened her chair around, and the other gave what I would consider a consoling smile, as if I had confessed to a misdemeanor.

"I know a very nice psychologist in the school district. Maybe you know him?" said the younger woman.

I didn't know him.

"I didn't think he was so nice," said the older woman. "After all, he said Johnny needed more discipline at home."

The younger woman—apparently the older woman's daughter—insisted the psychologist was a nice person.

"My son and his wife saw a psychologist," the older woman began. "They were having a few marital problems and when he finished with them, they got divorced."

"That's too bad," I offered.

"They'd have been better off if they had handled it on their own."

"Counseling can't help everyone," I said.

"You said it!" The older woman turned her chair even farther, and, within a few seconds, the ladies were discussing an upcoming summer vacation. I was left with my shrimp and crackers.

This particular scenario is not all that unusual and so familiar to professional therapists as to be something of an occupational hazard.

A colleague of mine was playing pool in a neighborhood tavern and joined in a competitive game of eight ball with a truck driver. Midway through the championship game, the truck driver asked my friend what he did for a living. When my friend said he was a psychologist, the other guy's game promptly came apart. The previously confident and skillful pool shooter began making self-deprecating remarks, wondered aloud if he was being analyzed, and missed a series of simple shots. My friend felt as badly about winning as the truck driver must have felt about losing. They obviously weren't headed for a friendship.

Experts When We Meet

Of all the "meeting the public" experiences shared by therapists, being asked for advice is the most common. If a therapist is to give competent advice, he or she must collect a lot of information: history, sources of stress, kinds of personalities involved, and an accurate understanding of the problem—otherwise, the advice may do more harm than good. Most professionals won't work from the curbstone, but it seems the public never tires of trying to get them to.

Against my better judgment, I was maneuvered into participating in a local TV talk show—the subject to be discussed was the midlife crisis. Having been introduced to a few people in the studio and while waiting for our turn on the air, an attractive, thirtyish blonde woman, a total stranger, came up to me and said she had just divorced her husband and was planning a career in graphic arts. What did I think of that? Before I could answer that I didn't have the foggiest notion, the host of the show arrived and laughingly announced he was turning forty and was dead certain he was having sympathetic hot flashes to his wife's menopause, and what did I think of that? Almost simultaneously, a studio cameraman offered that his father was an alcoholic, and did I have some advice on what he should do.

I was rescued from all these questions when the on-the-air light began flashing.

The show went okay and when it was over, I was anxious to be on my way back to the office. To all the questions I had been asked before the show, I pointed out that for me to give advice under such circumstances amounted not only to poor practice, but to poor judgment. I gave out some phone numbers where better information might be obtained.

On my way out of the studio, a tall, attractive receptionist offered to walk me to the parking lot.

"What I'd like to know," she began, "is how to get someone to go and get help when they need it."

"That's sometimes very difficult," I said.

"My husband is sick. He wears my nylons to bed. Isn't he homosexual?"

I took a few minutes to arrange a referral to another therapist and tried to reassure her as best I could, thinking all the while that this morning's foray into the public sector had been like running through a psychiatric mine field.

I may have troubled over these experiences too much, but it strikes me that in no other line of work do so many people (and I mean total strangers) begin conversations by disclosing the most intimate details of their personal lives and problems. Sexual hangups, wife beating, homosexual panic, alcoholism, you name it, and people will tell all to a therapist they've just met and, what's more, may expect some advice or relief on the spot. It's no surprise to me that some therapists keep a low profile in public while others disguise their occupation to strangers.

Intimate Strangers

Just suppose you are in therapy with a particular therapist. You are walking through a large department store with your mother-in-law, two cousins, and Aunt Bertie in tow. You and your therapist spot each other at precisely the same moment and are on a collision course.

The therapist (if he or she has any sense of ethics or savoir-faire) will completely ignore your existence. Please do not interpret this as rudeness—your relationship is confidential and you must acknowledge your therapist first. If you say hello, the therapist will say hello and introductions may be in order. If your mother-in-law and Aunt Bertie are like my mother-in-law and Aunt Bertie, you might just as well skip the social amenities and laugh about it together at the next session. Any therapist who would embarrass you by greeting you and forcing you to explain your relationship to him or her is missing at least one professional marble.

The Training

Without detailing the specific training requirements or the years of experience and supervision people go through to become professional therapists, a couple of things could be said about their shared backgrounds. First, to become a psychotherapist one must have no qualms about prying into people's lives or, for that matter, having one's own life pried into.

Many therapist training programs require the novice to undergo psychotherapy as part of the total learning experience. And from two-thirds to three-fourths of all therapists will have been in therapy prior to or during their early years of training. Having had done with you what you will eventually do with others is not a bad idea and can give the trainee a valuable perspective on the process not otherwise available.

Whether in fact being a client oneself makes a better therapist is debatable, and not all training programs require it. Some critics within the professions even argue that undergoing therapy oneself may be harmful to being eventually an effective therapist. Overall though (and in my experience), most will seek psychotherapy for themselves if they are having problems—so much so that some insurance companies consider them poor risks in terms of filing claims for therapy. At least, it seems, they believe in their own magic.

The general public is sometimes suspicious about the motives of therapists and curious about why someone would choose to work in this field. The old gag that "you don't have to be crazy to work here, but it helps" has more application to doing therapy than, to say, selling shoes. But I won't pretend to understand why therapists end up therapists or, for that matter, why shoe salesmen end up selling shoes. Still, having worked for many years now with all kinds of therapists, I'm convinced that many of them took an interest in psychology for purely personal reasons.

In some cases, they may have felt their own psyches weren't wrapped all that tight and hoped that by taking a freshman primer in general psychology they would learn something about just how tight a psyche should be wrapped. Or they may have taken that first course because it was a requirement and discovered that what they thought was tightly wrapped had actually come loose and was waving in the breeze. Or they may have taken Psychology 101 in the hope that now, at last, Uncle George's bizarre fetish for cowboy boots could be explained to the family over Christmas vacation, and Dad's underwriting of a college education could be justified. For all these motives and more, rarely is this thirst for knowledge quenched by a first psychology course. If anything, the effect can be like salted peanuts.

For whatever reasons people take an interest in human behavior, it strikes me as unfair that they should be automatically suspect for taking a *serious* interest. A serious interest would, after all, lead to more classes in the field, a major, graduate training, and eventually a job as a therapist. The fact is, college courses in psychology have been at the top of the popularity poll for several years and psychology was once the number one major for undergraduates across the nation. Are all these people a little unhinged?

To become a bona fide professional therapist (despite motives as dark as voyeuristic tendencies or as light as love of humankind) requires a heavy commitment of time, money, and energy. Most therapists are going to be in their late twenties or early thirties (and very likely in debt) before they ever sit down and talk with a paying customer. They'll have read several hundred books, thousands of journal articles, and been put to sleep by as many lectures as fired their imaginations. And before it's all over, they will have been put before at least one firing squad of "old pros" for an exhaustive oral examination—the final rite of purification.

And when they think they're through, they're not. As licensed independent practitioners or agency employees, they must continue to train, to learn, and to be tested, not so much by the institutions that molded them, but by their colleagues and clients. All of this learning may not make them competent, but it's hard to see how it makes them incompetent.

The Money

Most people think doctors are the rich princes (and now princesses) of our society, and most people are right. But "doctors" is a big category and if some make more than a thousand dollars in a morning removing cataracts, reshaping noses, or excising brain tumors, most struggle along on less than five hundred dollars for a whole day's work.

Among the mental health professionals, only psychiatrists are doctors/physicians and, compared to their fraternity members in medicine, their average income can be relatively embarrassing. Psychiatrists who work in mental health centers or state hospitals earn, depending on location, between $75,000 and $100,000 per year (occasionally more if the duty station is in the Alaskan tundra or some other outpost). If in private practice, psychiatrists tend to gross considerably more (up to $200,000) but they also tend to work longer hours as they must be on call and ready for emergencies.

Psychologists and other kinds of therapists, like psychiatrists, are thought to make outrageous salaries. Few of them do. A doctoral-level psychologist with several years of experience can expect to earn $35,000 to $80,000 per year working in an agency or hospital, and usually a lot less in a university setting. Private practice is more lucrative, but also more demanding. Social workers tend to make a bit less than psychologists, but not much, again depending on the area of the country.

Of the major professions in private practice in this field, psychiatrists make the most, psychologists and social workers second, and psychiatric nurses the least, although because of scarcity the latter are quickly catching up. As a colleague of mine once remarked about the practice of psychotherapy, "The major difference between a psychiatrist and psychologist is about fifteen dollars an hour."

In the public or nonprofit sector, there are thousands of therapists working in service agencies who hold bachelors and masters degrees who make consistently less than schoolteachers, policemen, truck drivers, and carpenters. Maybe that's as it should be, but as one distraught woman bitterly complained after a dear friend committed suicide despite a therapist's best efforts to prevent it: "They don't pay you people enough." I agreed, but added that bigger paychecks didn't necessarily make better therapists.

For the private practitioner, there is no ethically sound formula to double, let alone triple one's income. Clients pay by the hour and there are only so many hours in a week. A therapist may offer group therapy, but then usually charges less. There are therapists who offer weekend marathons, week-long encounter groups, and other "treatment packages" which carry a hefty price tag and, to the extent they get takers, can turn a tidy profit.

Within the ethical standards of the therapy professions, it's okay to charge people less than your standard fee, but never more. A friend of mine was once offered a flat $10,000 by a wealthy businessman if my friend could somehow get him to "love life." When my friend explained that therapy didn't work that way, the disillusioned man offered to triple his usual fee, arguing that he wanted the therapist to work extra hard on his case. When, after another explanation of how therapist effectiveness is not contingent on so many pieces of silver, the man sagged back in his chair, apparently accepting the reality that here was someone whose opinions and perceptions were not for sale.

Many therapists also do charity work, and they are generally stout supporters of United Way efforts and other humanitarian endeavors. Some critics argue that mental health professionals are only in the business for the money. Some are, to be sure, but the vast majority couldn't possibly justify the work they do for the money it brings them.

Taking the Work Home

People often ask me if I take my work home with me. Do I worry about the people I'm working with in therapy when the therapy hour is finished? The answer is an unequivocal "sometimes." Certainly, there are clients who need worrying about more than others, and most therapists agree it's well nigh impossible to throw some mental switch and shut off the concern and thoughts associated with a particular client. But it's also true that if therapists fret and stew about the problems faced by everyone they're seeing (as many as twenty or thirty clients) they would soon end up on the couch themselves—and occasionally do.

Therapists must care deeply about their clients, but never so deeply that they lose their professional balance or perspective on who is ultimately responsible for what happens. Assuming total responsibility for the actions of others is not only illogical and impossible, but a surefire way to undo oneself as a people helper. From a therapist's point of view, it is better to give someone a handful of apple seeds, tell them when and where to plant, how to cultivate and harvest the fruit, than it is to reach in their own bin and pass out apples. Not only do you quickly run out of apples, but you leave people ignorant of how to grow their own.

If you were to ask the husbands and wives of therapists if their spouses bring their work home with them, you would probably get a more affirmative answer. As the wife of a friend of mine once complained, "David was so sensitive before he became a psychiatrist. That's one of the reasons I was attracted to him. He was such a good listener." David, like most psychotherapists, spends his work day listening attentively, asking carefully thought-out questions, and mustering up sensitivity, empathy, and understanding for several hours at a stretch. After a ten-hour day of talking to, at, and around human problems, he's pretty well tapped out by the time he reaches the front porch. Then, when his wife greets him with, "How was your day? Mine was rotten. Let's talk," a muffled scream doesn't seem all that excessive.

And sometimes therapist's spouses don't fight fair. Having worked with several couples where one is a therapist, I've noticed the therapist member of the couple is expected to argue by the Marquis of Queensberry rules, follow their ethical standards, and abide by the Hippocratic oath. The nontherapist spouse can kick, scratch, gouge, and throw any number of illegal punches, and if the therapist/spouse responds in kind, the nontherapist spouse will shout, "I bet you don't talk to your clients that way!"

But if a therapist/spouse uses listening skills, makes interpretations, and otherwise brings in the heavy psychological artillery—this isn't fair either. To this "professional" approach to problem-solving, the nontherapist spouse will reply: "Don't pull that psychological crap with me. I'm not one of your patients." Some days you just can't win.

Personal Problems

Of all the problems faced by therapists, their own personal ones, like yours, are the toughest to deal with. Oh, and they do have problems. I worked for a short time with a very depressed psychiatrist whose marriage was coming apart despite his best efforts to keep it together. On the morning his wife finally left, he had several patients scheduled and, professional to the core, he kept his appointments. One of his depressed patients stopped me in the hall after coming from her session with him and said she was very worried about Doctor H: "He's lots more depressed than I am," she said.

Right or wrong, clients expect their therapists to be hitting on all emotional cylinders and are usually disquieted if this isn't the case. For the most part, therapists are trained to keep their personal woes to themselves and it's considered bad form and countertherapeutic to load a client down with one's own problems. Still, it happens and especially with young and inexperienced therapists. Years ago, I came in late to a supervision meeting and listened to a tape recording of a graduate student in psychology counseling another student. It was several minutes before I was able to discern who was the client and who was the therapist.

Whether they want to be or not, therapists are models to their clients. They are expected to act and behave in an exemplary fashion and to exercise supreme control over their feelings and actions. If a client is provocative, challenging, and nasty, therapists are to remain understanding, empathetic, and most of all, calm and cool. I've seen therapists in mental hospitals spit on, their teeth broken out by punches, and in one case, stabbed in the arm, and never so much as raise a hand in anger. In fact, to strike a client or patient, even when grievously provoked, is usually grounds for immediate dismissal. To be sure, therapists are not made of stone, and if they are hurt, frightened, insulted, threatened, or otherwise upset, they are going to feel it like anyone else. And when they are, they get help. One of the basics of the business is to support each other, talk through feelings, and to share the stress of the work.

A special difficulty arises when a therapist has or has had a problem similar to that of his or her client. In that case, the easiest and most natural thing in the world to do is to tell the client how you personally overcame a similar difficulty. Right? Wrong! How you overcame adversity, triumphed over the same symptoms, and succeeded where the client has failed has practically nothing to do with being helpful. In fact, telling such "how I did it" stories generally backfires. The client may become more miserable and more resentful of what must come across as boasting. Besides, the therapist's problems are not on the agenda, even the ones he or she succeeded in solving.

If a therapist is currently struggling with a problem similar to the client's, maintaining an objective point of view becomes even more important. As you might guess, it's rather awkward for marriage counselors to keep a stiff upper lip if their spouses are suing them for divorce. In my own experience, there's nothing more unsettling than to have an argument with my wife for breakfast and then trot off to the office to work with couples who want to learn how to avoid fighting at breakfast. On those mornings when I lose one of those arguments (I much prefer winning), I have to redouble my efforts to not be judgmental about a couple's problems, especially around the wife's point of view.

It doesn't always follow that because therapists have personal problems similar to their clients, that they will automatically be ineffective. You could argue (and I've heard this interesting logic) that since therapist X has been married and divorced four times, he or she is exceptionally qualified to do marriage counseling. I guess the proof's in the pudding—how many satisfied customers has he or she?

From another perspective, I know some very fine therapists whose work with clients is more enriched, mature, and empathetic because they have personally endured what the client is going through. This is, in my experience, true of many alcohol counselors. This shared experience is also the common link that makes so many of the self-help groups and peer counseling programs so effective.

In supervising therapists in their work with clients, much of the focus of supervision is on personal feelings therapists have toward their clients, what these feelings are, and where they come from. If a therapist is having a personal problem that corresponds to one the client is having, the work of therapy may get stalled.

A young therapist once brought a case in for supervision in which the problem, as he described it, centered around the client's unwillingness to accept social invitations from men, claiming she had no interest in dating and was content to be a lady-in-waiting. When the therapist asked her what she was waiting for, she became flustered and reluctantly admitted she was waiting for the therapist to ask her out.

The therapist (a very ethical practitioner) was alarmed that his client had been entertaining such fantasies about him and was upset that he had not seen this lonely and sexually frustrated client was developing feelings for him. When I asked him to review his own feelings toward the client, he could not account for why the client felt this way: he had not been flirtatious nor given messages that he was in any way "available." Only after considerable probing did I learn that some three months earlier he and his wife had experimented with a trial separation of some three weeks duration.

During his separation, he had been out of sorts with himself and, like his client, lonely and sexually frustrated. I instructed him to review this period of therapy with his client and try to learn what had happened. He later came to tell me that it was indeed the case that he had been more transparent with his own feelings and that the client had gotten the "distinct impression" that something more than a professional relationship was possible. The therapist and client managed to talk this through, and therapy continued to a successful outcome.

It sometimes happens that the personal problems of therapists render them not only ineffective, but can make them dangerously neglectful or dangerously overprotective. I once supervised a novice therapist (we'll call him John) who, within a matter of two weeks, had two clients kill themselves. Now, there's nothing more devastating to a therapist than to have a client successfully commit suicide. No matter how well he or she knows the client or how long they have worked together, the therapist is predictably going to feel guilty, angry, and incompetent. In John's case, he felt all this and more. He questioned his basic abilities and skills and wondered if the Ph.D. he had just earned was a fluke. His reaction to the suicides was to begin to refuse to see depressed clients or clients who had any potential whatsoever for self-destruction. His colleagues recognized his changed attitude and insisted he continue to see depressed patients, since his inability to do so meant he might as well get out of the field.

For several weeks John's work suffered. He was so worried about another suicide that his clients became the target of a relentless pursuit of clues for suicidal intent, thoughts, feelings, methods, etc., until it became clear to them that John's fears about their suicide potential were all out of proportion to the way they felt. He was, in a word, going to save people from self-destruction even if they weren't self-destructive.

The problem as a couple of us saw it was that John was expecting every patient to commit suicide and, since people tend to live up (or down) to expectations set for them, he was increasing the odds that yet another client might not disappoint him. No amount of supervision or counseling could deter his zeal or alter his thinking and, upon some stiff, joint recommendations, he was encouraged to get into teaching—which he finally did.

To work effectively, therapists, like everyone else, pretty much have to come to grips with themselves and their problems, whatever they might be. At least this is the way it ought to be. They don't all take good care of themselves psychologically and it's only been in recent years that the professions have assumed some responsibility to help their troubled colleagues.

All in a Day's Work

I would like to say that the work of the professional therapist is pretty much like any other kind of work. You put in your eight hours, punch the old time clock, and stow the burden of the workaday world like most other people. Except that it isn't the way it is. There are these nagging details, this unfinished business for so many clients, and a constant barrage of human predicaments scheduled on the fifty-minute hour.

Like everyone else, the typical therapist begins his or her day by reading the newspaper. Since depression is America's emotional common cold (as many as fifty percent of a therapist's clients may be depressed), and since depressed people sometimes contemplate suicide, talk about it, or threaten it, the average therapist reading the morning paper is also scanning the local news for familiar names. Keeping your client's name out of the obituary column is not a job requirement, but it's essential to enjoying your morning paper.

Therapists work in lots of different settings—hospitals, mental health centers, group and solo private practices, social service agencies, and clinics—so it's impossible to characterize these in any descriptive way that would make sense. What is similar about these settings is that as a rule, they are busy places with clients or patients coming and going in various states of emotional disarray. When a therapist enters a waiting room full of distraught people and says "Good Morning," it may be that the therapist is the only one who is feeling reasonably good.

After a cup of coffee and maybe a chat with some fellow staff member (if the therapist is not in solo practice), he or she begins to see clients. Each client requires something different—but never less than your undivided attention. While one needs warmth and support, another needs confrontation, and a third may need something the therapist wasn't even trained to provide. For every client who's poised on the brink of psychological health and well-being and needs but a gentle shove or a well-spoken word of encouragement, there are ten who are bogged down in self-defeating habits, mired in miserable feelings, and immobilized by illogical thoughts that would require a team of six therapists pulling for all they're worth to extricate them from their dilemma. Most of the work therapists do is hard work.

Burnt Out and Black Humor

"Burnt out" is a popular term these days among mental health professionals and while I don't have a nifty definition for it and am not sure I even accept its usage, it seems to refer to a state of mental or emotional exhaustion in which the therapist lacks energy, feels used up, apathetic, and tired.

Some consider the work of doing therapy so psychologically stressful that more than four or five hours a day will drain the therapist's batteries. My own observations on this matter lead me to believe that for some therapists this is true (especially those who lack a sense of humor). In point of fact, more and more therapists are leaving the field to become writers, forest rangers, chimney sweeps, or to take any job that will take them away from people and their problems. Enter the need for humor.

If you, as an invisible stranger to the private world of the therapist, were to observe an average diagnostic staff meeting in which clients are discussed, you would probably be outraged. You would be outraged to observe that human lives could be discussed so callously, without apparent regard for the overwhelming emotional significance of, say, a young woman confessing to her therapist that her father had raped her at age ten and forced her to commit sexual acts with him until she was seventeen. To the experienced therapist, such tearful and anguished admissions by women clients are practically mundane. You might be shocked to hear a distinguished-looking doctor refer to a World War II veteran with chronic anxiety, knee injuries, a plate in his head from a combat wound, and severe alcoholism as "crock" or a P.M.B. (poor miserable bastard).

In a typical hour-and-a-half staff meeting, a half dozen or more cases are presented, discussed, diagnosed, and have treatment plans drawn up for them. Therapists participating in these meetings two to five times a week for months and then years simply do not and cannot maintain a keen edge on their sense of sympathy—at least in such meetings.

When you consider that during a week's work a therapist may have encountered a man who beat his wife so badly she committed suicide; an alcoholic woman whose children are being removed from her custody because she did not feed them for three days; an elderly gentleman whose wife of fifty years just died; a twenty-four-year-old woman going through her fourth divorce; a heroin addict; a troubled homosexual; and a depressed and out-of-work Indian chief, you begin to see why it's so important that a therapist maintain a sense of objectivity, distance, and balance.

For several years, I conducted such meetings three mornings a week. In the course of an average week, we would often hear twenty to thirty separate cases presented for diagnosis and therapy assignment. As chairman of this group, one of the central tasks was to keep the therapists' spirits up, joke with them, encourage and reassure them. No one ever felt malicious toward clients personally, but if there was any humor anywhere in the case presentation, it was worth exploiting. That this humor ran in shades of gray and black may be understandable.

Appendices

APPENDIX A
Self-Help Organizations

Al-Anon Family Groups
For families of alcoholics
1 Park Ave.
New York, N.Y. 10016
(212) 481-6565

Alateen
Part of Al-Anon, for the teenaged
    children of alcoholics
1 Park Ave.
New York, N.Y. 10016
(212) 481-6576

Alcoholics Anonymous
For adult alcoholics
468 Park Ave. South
New York, N.Y. 10016
(212) 686-1100

American Association of Retired
    Persons (Action for Independent
    Maturity)
(National Retired Teachers Association)
1909 K St., N.W.
Washington, D.C. 20049

American Association of Suicidology
Box 59 S. Ash
Denver, Colorado 80222
(303) 692-0982

Emotions Anonymous
For persons with emotional problems
P.O. Box 4245
St. Paul, Minn. 55104
(612) 647-9712

Families Anonymous
For relatives and friends of youth with a
    variety of behavior problems
P.O. Box 344
Torrance, Calif. 90501
(213) 775-3211

Gam-Anon
For families of Gamblers
P.O. Box 4549
Downey, Calif. 90241
(213) 862-6014

Gamblers Anonymous
For compulsive gamblers
P.O. Box 17173
Los Angeles, Calif. 90017
(213) 386-8789

Narcotics Anonymous
For narcotics addicts
P.O. Box 622
Sun Valley, Calif. 91352
(213) 764-4880

National Alliance for the Mentally Ill
Support advocacy group
1234 Massachusetts Ave., N.W.
Washington, D.C. 20005
(202) 783-6393

Neurotics Anonymous
1341 G St., N.W.
Washington, D.C. 20005
(202) 628-4379

Overeaters Anonymous
For overweight persons
2190 West 190th St.
Torrance, Calif. 90504
(213) 320-7941

Parents Anonymous
For parents of abused children
22330 Hawthorne
Torrance, Calif. 90505
(300) 421-0353

Parents Without Partners
For single parents and their children
7910 Woodmont Ave.
Washington, D.C. 20014
(301) 654-8850

Pills Anonymous
Box 473, Ansonia Station
New York, N.Y. 10023
(212) 874-0700

Recovery, Inc.
An association for former mental
   patients
116 South Michigan Ave.
Chicago, Ill. 60603

TERRAP
A self-help program for people phobias
1010 Doyle St.
Menlo Park, Calif. 94025
(415) 329-1233

Weight Watchers
A weight reduction program
800 Community Dr.
Manhasset, N.Y. 11030
(516) 627-9200

**For a more complete guide
to self-help groups see:**

*HELP: A Working Guide
to Self-Help Groups*
Alan Gartner and Frank Riessman
New Viewpoints/ Vision Books
A Division of Franklin Watts
NY/ London 1980

OR, contact the following:

National Self-Help Clearinghouse
33 West 42nd St.
New York, N.Y. 10036
(212) 840-7606

National Self-Help Resource Center
2000 S St., N.W.
Washington, D.C. 20009
(202) 338-5704

APPENDIX B

Voluntary Mental Health Associations

National Association

Mental Health Association
National Headquarters
1800 North Kent St.
Arlington, Va. 22209

Affiliated Divisions

Mental Health Association in Alabama
901 18th St., South
Birmingham, Ala. 35205

Arizona Association for Mental Health
341 West McDowell Road
Phoenix, Ariz. 85003

The Arkansas Association for Mental
Health
424 East Sixth St.
Little Rock, Ark. 72202

California Association for Mental Health
901 H St., Suite 212
Sacramento, Calif. 95814

Mental Health Association of Colorado
1001 Jasmine
Denver, Colo. 80220

Mental Health Association of
Connecticut
56 Arbor St.
Hartford, Conn. 06106

Mental Health Association of Delaware
1813 North Franklin St.
Wilmington, Del. 19802

District of Columbia Mental Health
Association
2101 16th St., N.W.
Washington, D.C. 20008

Mental Health Association of Florida
Suite 207, Myrick Bldg.
132 East Colonial Dr.
Orlando, Fl. 32801

The Georgia Association for Mental
Health
85 Merritts Ave., N.E.
Atlanta, Ga. 30308

The Mental Health Association of
Hawaii
200 N. Vineyard, Room 101
Honolulu, Hi. 96817

Idaho Mental Health Association
3105½ State St.
Boise, Ida. 83703

Illinois Association for Mental Health
103 North Fifth St., Room 304
Springfield, Ill. 62701

The Mental Health Association in
Indiana
1433 N. Meridian St.
Indianapolis, Ind. 46202

The Iowa Association for Mental Health
315 East Fifth St.
Des Moines, Ia. 50309

Kansas Association for Mental Health
1205 Harrison
Topeka, Kans. 66612

The Kentucky Association for Mental
Health
Suite 104, 310 West Liberty St.
Louisville, Ky. 40202

The Louisiana Association for Mental
Health
1528 Jackson Ave.
New Orleans, La. 70130

Maryland Association for Mental Health
325 East 25th St.
Baltimore, Md. 21218

The Massachusetts Association for
  Mental Health
38 Chauncy St., Room 801
Boston, Mass. 02111

Michigan Society for Mental Health
27208 Southfield Road
Lathrup Village, Mich. 48075

Minnesota Association for Mental Health
4510 W. 77th St.
Minneapolis, Minn. 55435

Mississippi Association for Mental
  Health
P.O. Box 5041
Jackson, Miss. 39216

Missouri Association for Mental Health
411 Madison St.
Jefferson City, Mo. 65101

Mental Health Association of Montana
201 S. Last Chance Gulch
Helena, Mont. 59601

Nebraska Association for Mental Health
Lincoln Benefit Life Bldg., Suite 320
134 South 13th St.
Lincoln, Nebr. 68508

New Jersey Association for Mental
  Health
60 South Fullerton Ave.
Montclair, N.J. 07042

New York State Association for Mental
  Health
250 West 57th St., Room 1425
New York, N.Y. 10019

North Carolina Mental Health
  Association
3701 National Dr., Suite 222
Raleigh, N.C. 27612

North Dakota Mental Health Association
P.O. Box 160
Bismarck, N.D. 58501

Ohio Association for Mental Health
50 West Broad St., Suite 713
Columbus, Oh. 43215

The Oklahoma Mental Health
  Association
3113 Classen Blvd.
Oklahoma City, Okla. 73118

Mental Health Association of Oregon
718 W. Burnside St., Room 301
Portland, Ore. 97209

Pennsylvania Mental Health Association
1207 Chestnut St.
Philadelphia, Pa. 19107

Rhode Island Association for Mental
  Health
333 Grotto Ave.
Providence, R.I. 02906

South Carolina Mental Health
  Association
1823 Gadsden St.
Columbia, S.C. 29201

South Dakota Mental Health Association
101½ S. Pierre St., Box 355
Pierre, S.D. 57501

Tennessee Mental Health Association
1717 West End Ave., Suite 421
Nashville, Tenn. 37203

The Texas Association for Mental Health
103 Lantern Lane
Austin, Tex. 78731

Utah Association for Mental Health
1370 South West Temple
Salt Lake City, Ut. 84115

Virginia Association for Mental Health
1806 Chantilly St., Suite 203
Richmond, Va. 23230

The West Virginia Association for
  Mental Health
702½ Lee St.
Charleston, W.Va. 25301

Wisconsin Association for Mental Health
P.O. Box 1486
Madison, Wis. 53701

APPENDIX C

Professional Associations

American Academy of Psychoanalysis
40 Gramercy Park North
New York, N.Y. 10010
(212) 477-4250

American Association of Marriage
and Family Counselors
225 Yale Ave.
Claremont, Calif. 91711
(714) 621-4749

American Association for Marriage
and Family Therapy
924 W. Ninth St.
Upland, Calif. 91786
(714) 981-0888

American Association of Sex
Educators, Counselors and Therapists
Suite 304
5010 Wisconsin Ave., N.W.
Washington, D.C. 20016
(202) 686-2523

American Psychiatric Association
1700 18th St., N.W.
Washington, D.C. 20009
(202) 797-4900

American Psychological Association
1200 17th St., N.W.
Washington, D.C. 20036
(202) 833-7600

Association for Advancement of
Behavioral Therapy
420 Lexington Ave.
New York, N.Y. 10017
(212) 682-0065

National Association
of Social Workers
1425 "H" St., N.W.
Washington, D.C. 20013
(202) 628-6200

APPENDIX D

Federal Agency Resources

Aging:

Administration on Aging
330 Independence Ave., S.W.
Washington, D.C. 20201

National Institute on Aging
National Institutes of Health
Bethesda, Md. 20014

Office of Long-Term Care
Public Health Service
5600 Fishers Lane
Rockville, Md. 20857

Alcoholism:

National Institute on Alcohol
  Abuse and Alcoholism
5600 Fishers Lane
Rockville, Md. 20857

Child Abuse:

National Center on Child Abuse
Office of Child Development
P.O. Box 1182
Washington, D.C. 20013

Child Development:

National Institute of Child Health
  and Human Development
National Institutes of Health
Bethesda, Md. 20014

Office for Child Development
P.O. Box 1182
Washington, D.C. 20013

Drug Abuse:

National Institute on Drug Abuse
11400 Rockville Pike
Room 110
Rockville, Md. 20852

Handicapped:

Office for Handicapped Individuals
200 Independence Ave., S.W., Rm. 338D
Washington, D.C. 20201

Learning Disorders:

U.S. Office of Education
400 Maryland Ave., S.W.
Room 4159
Washington, D.C. 20202

Mental Retardation:

President's Committee on Mental
  Retardation
Office of Human Development
200 Independence Ave., S.W.
Room 305F
Washington, D.C. 20201

Neurological Impairment:

National Institute of Neurological and
  Communicative Disorders and Stroke
National Institutes of Health
Bethesda, Md. 20014

APPENDIX E

National Agencies Listed by Special Problem

Aging:

National Council on the Aging
1828 L St., N.W.
Washington, D.C. 20036

Alcoholism:

Alcohol and Drug Problems
    Association of North America
1101 15th St., N.W.
Suite 204
Washington, D.C. 20005

National Council on Alcoholism, Inc.
733 Third Ave.
Suite 1405
New York, N.Y. 10017

Autism:

National Society for Autistic Children
Information and Referral Service
306 31st St.
Huntington, W.Va. 25702

Child Abuse:

National Committee for the
    Prevention of Child Abuse
111 East Wacker Dr.
Room 510
Chicago, Ill. 60601

Child Development:

Day Care and Child Development
    Council of America
622 14th St., N.W.
Washington, D.C. 20005

Drug Abuse:

National Coordinating Council
    on Drug Education, Inc.
1830 Connecticut Ave., N.W.
Washington, D.C. 20009

National Council on Drug Abuse
8 South Michigan
Chicago, Ill. 60603

Epilepsy:

Epilepsy Foundation of America
1828 L St., N.W.
Washington, D.C. 20036

Learning Disorders:

Council for Exceptional Children
1920 Association Dr.
Reston, Va. 22091

Marriage and Family:

American Association of Marriage
    and Family Counselors
225 Yale Ave.
Claremont, Calif. 91711

Mental Retardation:

American Association of Mental
    Deficiency
5201 Connecticut Ave., N.W.
Washington, D.C. 20015

National Association for Retarded
    Citizens
2709 Ave. E. East
Arlington, Tex. 76011

191

APPENDIX F

State Mental Health Authorities

Alabama
State Department of Mental Health
502 Washington Ave.
Montgomery, Ala. 36104
(202) 265-2301

Alaska
Division of Mental Health
Department of Health and Social
  Services
Pouch H-04
Juneau, Alas. 99801
(907) 465-3368

Arizona
Division of Behavioral Health Services
Department of Health Services
2500 E. Van Buren St.
Phoenix, Ariz. 85008
(602) 271-3438

Arkansas
Division of Mental Health Services
Department of Human Services
4313 West Markham St.
Little Rock, Ark. 72201
(501) 664-4500

California
Treatment Services Division
State Department of Health
744 P St.
Sacramento, Calif. 95814
(916) 445-1605

Colorado
Division of Mental Health
Department of Institutions
4150 South Lowell Blvd.
Denver, Colo. 80236
(303) 761-0220 X402

Connecticut
Department of Mental Health
90 Washington St.
Hartford, Conn. 06115
(203) 566-3650

Delaware
Division of Mental Health
Department of Health and Social
  Services
Governor Bacon Health Center
Delaware City, Del. 19706
(302) 834-9201

District of Columbia
Mental Health Administration
Department of Human Resources
1875 Connecticut Ave., N.W.
Washington, D.C. 20009
(202) 629-3447

Florida
Mental Health Program Office
Department of Health and Rehabilitative
  Services
1323 Winewood Blvd.
Tallahassee, Fla. 32301

Georgia
Division of Mental Health and Mental
  Retardation
Department of Human Resources
47 Trinity Ave., S.W.
Room 535, Health Bldg.
Atlanta, Ga. 30334
(404) 656-4908

Hawaii
Mental Health Division
Department of Health
P.O. Box 3378
Honolulu, Hi. 96801
(808) 548-6335

Idaho
Division of Community Rehabilitation
Department of Health and Welfare
700 W. State
STATEHOUSE Mail
Boise, Ida. 83720
(208) 384-3920

Illinois
State Department of Mental Health and
  Developmental Disabilities
160 N. LaSalle St., Room 1500
Chicago, Ill. 60601
(312) 793-2730

Indiana
State Department of Mental Health
5 Indiana Square
Indianapolis, Ind. 46204
(317) 633-7570

Iowa
Division of Mental Health Resources
Department of Social Services
Lucas State Office Bldg.
Des Moines, Ia. 50319
(515) 281-5497

Kansas
Division of Mental Health and
  Retardation Services
State Department of Social and
  Rehabilitation Services
State Office Bldg.
Topeka, Kans. 66612
(913) 296-3774

Kentucky
Bureau for Health Services
Department for Human Resources
275 E. Main St.
Frankfort, Ky. 40601
(502) 564-3970

Louisiana
Division of Mental Health
State Health and Human Resources
  Administration
P.O. Box 44215
Baton Rouge, La. 70804
(504) 389-5791

Maine
Bureau of Mental Health
State Department of Mental Health and
  Corrections
411 State Office Bldg.
Augusta, Me. 04330
(207) 289-3161

Maryland
Mental Hygiene Administration
State Department of Health and Mental
  Hygiene
Herbert R. O'Connor State Office Bldg.
201 West Preston St.
Baltimore, Md. 21201
(301) 383-2695

Massachusetts
State Department of Mental Health
190 Portland St.
Boston, Mass. 02141
(617) 727-5600

Michigan
State Department of Mental Health
Lewis Cass Bldg.
Lansing, Mich. 48926
(517) 373-3500

Minnesota
Mental Health Program Division
Department of Public Welfare
Centennial Office Bldg.
St. Paul, Minn. 55155
(612) 296-2710

Mississippi
State Department of Mental Health
607 Robert E. Lee Office Bldg.
Jackson, Miss. 39201
(601) 354-6132

Missouri
Department of Mental Health
2002 Missouri Blvd.
Jefferson City, Mo. 65101
(314) 751-3070

Montana
Mental Health Field Services Bureau
State Department of Institutions
1539 11th Ave.
Helena, Mont. 59601
(406) 449-3965

Nebraska
Division of Medical Services
Department of Public Institutions
P.O. Box 94728
Lincoln, Nebr. 68509
(402) 471-2851

Nevada
Division of Mental Hygiene and Mental
Retardation
4600 Kietzke Lane, Suite 108
Reno, Nev. 89502
(702) 784-4071

New Hampshire
Division of Mental Health
Department of Health and Welfare
105 Pleasant St.
Concord, N.H. 03301
(603) 271-2366

New Jersey
Divison of Mental Health and Hospitals
State Department of Institutions and
Agencies
135 W. Hanover St.
Trenton, N.J. 08625
(609) 292-4242

New Mexico
Mental Health Division
State Department of Hospitals and
Institutions
113 Washington St.
Santa Fe, N.M. 87501
(505) 988-8951

New York
State Department of Mental Hygiene
44 Holland Ave.
Albany, N.Y. 12229
(518) 474-6576

North Carolina
Division of Mental Health Services
Department of Human Resources
325 N. Salisbury St.
Raleigh, N.C. 27611
(919) 733-7011

North Dakota
Mental Health and Retardation Services
Division of Mental Health and
Retardation
State Department of Health
909 Basin Ave.
Bismarck, N.D. 58505
(701) 224-2766

Ohio
State Department of Mental Health and
Mental Retardation
30 E. Broad St., 12th floor
Columbus, Oh. 43215
(614) 466-2337

Oklahoma
State Department of Mental Health
P.O. Box 53277
Capitol Station
Oklahoma City, Okla. 73105
(405) 521-2811

Oregon
Mental Health Division
Department of Human Resources
2575 Bittern St., N.E.
Salem, Ore. 97310
(503) 378-2671

Pennsylvania
Division of Mental Health
State Department of Public Welfare
Health and Welfare Bldg., Room 308
Harrisburg, Pa. 17120
(717) 787-6443

Rhode Island
Division of Mental Health
Department of Mental Health,
Retardation and Hospitals
The Aime J. Forand Bldg.
600 New London Ave.
Cranston, R.I. 02920
(401) 464-3291

South Carolina
State Department of Mental Health
P.O. Box 485
Columbia, S.C. 29202
(803) 758-7701

South Dakota
Division of Mental Health and Mental
Retardation
State Department of Social Services
State Office Bldg., Third Floor
Illinois St.
Pierre, S.D. 57501
(605) 224-3438

Tennessee
Psychiatric Services Division
State Department of Mental Health and
 Mental Retardation
501 Union Bldg.
Nashville, Tenn. 37219
(615) 741-3348

Texas
State Department of Mental Health and
 Mental Retardation
Capitol Station
P.O. Box 12668
Austin, Tex. 78711
(512) 454-3761

Utah
Division of Mental Health
Department of Social Services
554 South Third East
Salt Lake City, Ut. 84111
(801) 533-5783

Vermont
State Department of Mental Health
Agency of Human Services
79 River St.
Montpelier, Vt. 05602
(802) 828-2481

Virginia
State Department of Mental Health and
 Mental Retardation
P.O. Box 1797
Richmond, Va. 23214
(804) 786-3921

Washington
Bureau of Mental Health
Department of Social and Health
 Services
Mail Stop 422
Olympia, Wash. 98504
(206) 753-5414

West Virginia
State Department of Mental Health
State Capitol Bldg.
Charleston, W.Va. 25305
(304) 348-3211

Wisconsin
Division of Mental Hygiene
State Department of Health and Social
 Services
State Office Bldg., Room 534
1 West Wilson St.
Madison, Wis. 53702
(608) 266-2701

Wyoming
Mental Health and Mental Retardation
 Services
Division of Health and Medical Services
The Hathaway Bldg.
2300 Capitol Ave.
Cheyenne, Wyo. 82002
(307) 777-7351

American Samoa
Mental Health
Department of Medical Services
LBJ Tropical Medical Center
Pago Pago, Tutuila
American Samoa 96799

Guam
Community Mental Health Center
Division of Mental Health
Guam Memorial Hospital
P.O. Box AX
Agana, Guam 96910

Puerto Rico
Division of Mental Health
Department of Health
G.P.O. Box 61
San Juan, P.R. 00936
(809) 767-9303

Trust Territory
Mental Health Division
Department of Health Services
Office of the High Commissioner
Trust Territory of the Pacific Islands
Saipan, Mariana Islands 96950

Virgin Islands
Division of Mental Health
Department of Health
P.O. Box 1442
St. Thomas, V.I. 00801
(809) 773-1992

APPENDIX G

For More Information, Contact Any of the Following

Community Mental Health Centers

Crisis Hotlines

Psychiatric Hospitals or Clinics

Psychiatric or Psychology Departments at Universities and Colleges

Local Branches of state Psychiatric, Social Work, or Psychological Associations

State or Local Chapters of mental health associations, such as The National Alliance of the Mentally Ill and The National Mental Health Association

The National Alliance for the Mentally Ill
2101 Wilison Boulevard, Suite 302
Arlington, VA 22201

National Mental Health Consumers Association
213 Monroe Street
Rockville, MD 20850

National Mental Health Association Information Center
1021 Prince Street
Alexandria, VA 22314

Bibliography

Barbach, L. G. *For Yourself: The Fulfillment of Female Sexuality*. Garden City, New York: Doubleday, 1976.

Berne, E. *Games Alcoholics Play*. New York: Ballantine Books, 1978.

Binder, V. et al. *Modern Therapies*. Englewood Cliffs, New Jersey: Prentice-Hall, 1976.

Bloom, L. Z. et al. *The New Assertive Woman*. *New York: Dell, 1976.*

Bloomfield, H. et al. How to Survive the Loss of a Love. New York: Bantam, 1977.

Calhoun, L. G. *Dealing with Crisis: A Guide to Critical Life Problems*. Englewood Cliffs, New Jersey: Prentice-Hall, 1976.

Driekers, R. and Soltz, V. *Children: The Challenge*. New York: E. P. Dutton, 1964.

Dobson, J. *Straight Talk to Men and Their Wives*. Waco, Texas: Word, Inc., 1980.

————. *What Wives Wish Their Husbands Knew About Women*. Wheaton, Illinois: Tyndale House, 1975.

Fadiman, J. and Kewman, D. *Exploring Madness: Experience, Theory and Research*, 2nd ed. Monterey, California: Brooks/ Cole, 1979.

Hughes, R. and Brewin, B. *The Tranquilizing of America: Pill Popping and the American Way of Life*. New York: Harcourt Brace Jovanovich, 1979.

James, M. and Jongeward, D. *Born to Win*. New York: New American Library, 1978.

Kaplan, H. S. *The New Sex Therapy: Active Treatment of Sexual Dysfunctions*. New York: Bruner/ Mazel, 1974.

Krantzler, M. *Creative Divorce: A New Opportunity for Personal Growth*. New York: M. Evans, 1975.

Kopp, S. B. *If You Meet the Buddha on the Road, Kill Him*. Palo Alto, California: Science & Behavior Books, 1972.

Missildine, W. H. and Galton, L. *Your Inner Child of the Past*. New York: Simon & Schuster, 1974.

Rogers, C. R. *On Becoming a Person*. Boston: Houghton Mifflin, 1970.

Rogers, C. R. and Stevens, B. *Person to Person: The Problem of Being Human*. Moab, Utah: Real People Press, 1967.

Rubin, T. I. *The Angry Book.* New York: Macmillan, 1969.

Satir, V. *Peoplemaking.* Palo Alto, California: Science & Behavior Books, 1972.

Steiner, C. *Scripts People Live.* New York: Bantam, 1975.

Sue, D. W. *Counseling the Culturally Different, Theory and Practice.* Somerset, New Jersey: John Wiley, 1981.

Tennov, D. *Psychotherapy: The Hazaradous Cure.* Garden City, New York: Doubleday, 1976.

Weil, A. *The Natural Mind: A New Way of Looking at Drugs and the Higher Consciousness.* Burlington, Maryland: Houghton Mifflin, 1972.

Wheelis, A. *How People Change.* New York: Harper & Row, 1974.

Whitlock, G. E. *Understanding and Coping With Real-Life Crises.* Monterey, California: Brooks/ Cole, 1978.

Yalom, I. D. & Elkin, G. *Every Day Gets a Little Closer.* New York: Basic Books, 1974.

―――. *Existential Psychotherapy.* New York: Basic Books, 1980.